Five-Mile Spur Line:
A Railroad History of Sycamore, Illinois

By Clint Cargile

ZEA MAYS PUBLISHING, LLC
SYCAMORE, ILLINOIS

ZEA MAYS
PUBLISHING

Edited by Kelly Unger

Cover and interior designed by Steve Anderson
Northern Illinois University, Outreach Communications

Printed by Envision 3

ISBN 978-0-9897167-0-3

Table of Contents

In my mind, the red brick building known as the Sycamore train depot has always been there. I have passed by it thousands of times. It has always been old. It has always "seen better days." But I also knew it played a significance role in Sycamore's past. While not as prominent or as well-known as the DeKalb County Courthouse, I felt the depot was still a part of the city's history that was worth investigating.

On several occasions, former City Manager Bill Nicklas and I discussed the need for improvements to the west end of downtown. These discussions inevitably turned to the Sycamore train depot and its role in the history of DeKalb County. Bill worked with Auto Meter (owner of the depot building at the time), and with the help of the Sycamore City Council, Mayor Ken Mundy, City Manager Brian Gregory, and the future owner of the property—the DeKalb County Community Foundation (DCCF)—the Sycamore train depot was remodeled, repurposed, and redefined.

The stabilization and renovation projects could not have been completed without the help of many people, too many to try to mention. However, the DCCF was instrumental in raising the money to complete the project and Executive Director Dan Templin and project lead Tim Suter should be singled out for appreciation, along with the many contributors to the renovation fund campaign.

The Sycamore train depot again serves the people of DeKalb County, not for local commerce, but for promoting local philanthropy. Freight no longer passes through the depot. Now, ideas pass through there. Charitable needs are defined and developed there. Non-profit agencies request and receive funding there. A freight house that once processed packaged goods, agricultural supplies, industrial equipment, and the U. S. mail, now nurtures the organizations and solutions that will shape the future of DeKalb County. The depot again holds the power to transport us to new and exciting places, to transform our lives.

Just as we restored the depot's structure and secured its future, it seemed only fitting to uncover the building's past. To do that, Clint Cargile was hired to research and write the depot's definitive history. After he uncovered the significance of the Sycamore & Cortland Railroad to Sycamore's past, his research expanded to encompass the city's entire railroad history. Thus, this book.

The story within is not unique, but it is wholly American. In the 19th century, railroads were spreading everywhere, and communities waged vigorous battles to bring them to their front doors. What is special about the Sycamore railroad story is that it is ours. Our ancestors took the initiative to bring a railroad to our town. And it wasn't easy. This is a story of people, places, and events that you might recognize, and others that might be new to you. Most of all, this story is about us, our community, our county, and the city we call home.

Enjoy.

Doug Roberts
June 12, 2013

When I began this project in early 2011, I planned to write a short history of a single building, Sycamore's historic train depot on the corner of Sacramento Street and DeKalb Avenue. With renovations for the 130-year-old depot getting underway, Doug Roberts and Tom Matya reached out to Northern Illinois University's Department of History, seeking a graduate student to research the depot's history. The department chair, Beatrix Hoffman, and the graduate advisor, Anne Hanley, forwarded the request to me, a new student in the program, knowing that I had a background in researching and writing local history.

Tom, Doug, and I first met in their offices on the top floor of the Sycamore Center, also known as the Daniel Pierce Building, built in 1905 and named for Doug's great-great-great-grandfather. I soon learned that every branch of Doug's family had deep roots in Sycamore's history, including its railroad history. Doug's great-grandfather, Frederick B. Townsend, helped bring the electric railroads to Sycamore in the early 20th century (chapter 9). Doug's great-great grandfather, Charles O. Boynton, and his great-great-great grandfather, Stephen Townsend, sat on the first elected board of directors for the Sycamore & Cortland Railroad (chapter 2).

I asked Tom and Doug what, exactly, they wanted me to write: a short newspaper article, a slightly longer magazine article, a scholarly piece for an academic journal? Then Doug said those magic words that historians long to hear: "Go where the research takes you."

Sycamore's last train passed through town in 1984. Since that time, a whole generation of residents either grew up or moved here without a railroad engine rumbling through their streets. I discussed this project with several people, and many of them didn't even know Sycamore had an old depot (if you look carefully, you'll find that Sycamore still has four). When I explained where it was located, I often received the same response: "I thought that was just some old warehouse." And basically it was. The depot had been used as a warehouse for almost half a century.

After some preliminary research on the depot's history, I became fascinated by the local railroad company that built it. I realized I couldn't tell the story of the depot without including the story of the Sycamore & Cortland Railroad. After further research into this company, its directors, and their motivations, I knew I couldn't tell the company's story without spanning the entire history of Sycamore, because the story of the railroad coming to Sycamore is the story of Sycamore itself.

I went where the research took me, from Sycamore's mud-rutted streets to its iron railroads, from a time when locomotives were a necessity to a time when, locally, they became inconvenient and obsolete. My research took me through 175 years of Sycamore's past, to its people, its glory days, its tragedies and triumphs, and I have enjoyed the ride. I hope you do too.

Clint Cargile
June 6, 2013

ACKNOWLEDGMENTS

A book of this scope isn't possible without the assistance and support of a number of people. But before I get to them, I have to acknowledge the one person without whom this book really wouldn't have been possible: Doug Roberts, the driving force behind both my research and the depot restoration.

I am especially grateful to the staff and volunteers at the Joiner History Room, Sycamore History Museum, DeKalb Public Library, DeKalb County Community Foundation, Northern Illinois University Regional History Center, Ellwood House Museum, Chicago & North Western Historical Society, Abraham Lincoln Presidential Library, and the U.S. National Archives. I'd also like to thank all of the organizations that invited me to share my work publicly: the Sycamore History Museum, the Rotary Club of Sycamore, Sycamore Kiwanis, NIU's Lifelong Learning Institute, the Boy Scouts of America—Three Fires Council, Oak Crest Retirement Center, and NB&T Advantage Club.

Special thanks also go to the following: Fellow NIU history graduate students Trevor Neff and John Parr, for helping me sift through old files and documents. Another NIU crony, Rob Glover, for being so enthusiastic about local history and throwing himself headlong into every history mystery I could lob at him. Herb and Sasha Neu, for an infectious love of local history, no matter where you live. Paul Rubeck, for sharing unique stories and an even more unique collection of local memorabilia. Charles Stats, railroad historian, and all the local historians who published work that paved the way for this project. Bob Richards, for the road tour of DeKalb County's railroad history. Betty Hampa, for seeking me out to tell her father's story, and helping to layer this book with so many personal details. Jim Lyons, for forcing me to do actual field research (in an actual field). Lynden Bute, for teaching me a thing or two about art and design. And Lisa Sharp, for designing an awesome building and teaching me a thing or two about architecture.

I also owe a wholehearted thanks to Michelle Donahoe, director of the Sycamore History Museum; Dan Templin, director of the DeKalb County Community Foundation; Joe Pierson, Chairman of the Chicago & North Western Historical Society; Candy Smith, Sycamore City Clerk; all of the folks at NIU's College of Liberal Arts and Sciences External Programming: Anne Petty Johnson, Mark Pietrowski, Julie Konczyk, Lise Schlosser, and Katie Faber; all the NIU professors who helped me with this project, both directly and indirectly: Bradley Bond, Beatrix Hoffman,

ACKNOWLEDGMENTS

Anne Hanley, Stanley Arnold, Aaron Fogleman, Jim Schmidt, Brian Sandberg, Kenton Clymer, and Michael Gonzalez; and a couple guys who taught me that writing about history doesn't have to be boring: Mike Magnuson and Brady Udall.

A special round of thanks goes to DeKalb County Historian and Joiner History Room Director Sue Breese, who located most of the images in this book, answered hundreds of my emails, and knows everything there is to know about Sycamore history. I made it my mission to stump her, and I don't know if I ever did. I also owe a special debt of gratitude to my editor, Kelly Unger, who makes me look better than I am; to Steve Anderson of NIU Outreach Communications, for his amazing graphic design work; and to Tom Matya, who kept me (mostly) on task.

And last but not least, I thank my beautiful and talented wife Gillian King-Cargile, who offered both emotional and editorial support, all the while suffering through endless stories about trains, depots, and early-American transportation. Never fear, my dear, I will bore you with something else now.

A NOTE ABOUT SOURCES

A History [book] cannot go into detail as does a [news]paper published at the time the incidents… happen. The newspaper is the best index of the life of a community.

O. T. Willard, Sycamore historian, 1939

As O. T. Willard's quote suggests, newspapers provide us with first-hand, boots-on-the-ground accounts of events as they unfolded. For that reason, the majority of this book's research comes from newspapers. And the majority of that research comes from one newspaper in particular, the *True Republican*, which published continuously from 1857 to 1968. Most of its issues have been preserved by the Joiner History Room, DeKalb County Archives. In 2010, each issue was scanned and made available online as part of the Illinois Digital Newspaper Collection (IDNC), a project of the History, Philosophy, and Newspaper Library at the University of Illinois at Urbana-Champaign.

H. L. Boies

Much of Sycamore's earliest history comes to us courtesy of Henry Lamson Boies, who settled in Sycamore in 1853, became editor of the *True Republican* in 1863, and published the county's first history book, *A History of DeKalb County, Illinois*, in 1868. Other 19th and early 20th century historians of Sycamore and DeKalb County often copied Boies's work verbatim.
 H. L. Boies ran the *True Republican* until his death in 1887. His son, Edward Irving Boies, took over and ran the newspaper until 1930.

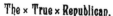

H. L. BOIES & CO., Prop's.
Sycamore, Illinois.

Without the preservation of these newspapers, both physically and digitally, this book never would have been possible. Any time the text contains an unattributed quote, it comes from the *True Republican*. In addition, the *True Republican* went through a few slight name changes over the years. To avoid confusion, I always refer to it as the *True Republican*.

Railroads In and Around Sycamore (c.1910)

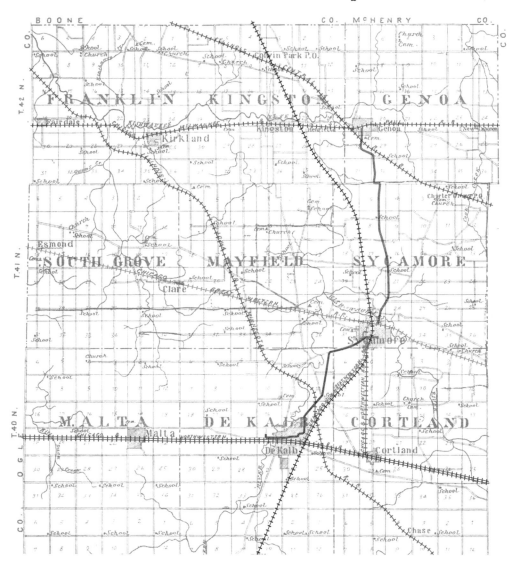

	Railroad	Year Built
++++++	Sycamore & Cortland	1859
++++++	Chicago & North Western	1853
++++++	Chicago & North Western — Northern Illinois line	1885
++++++	Chicago Great Western	1887
++++++	Chicago Great Western — DeKalb & Great Western line	1895
	DeKalb-Sycamore Electric Railway	1902
	Woodstock & Sycamore Traction Company	1910

Sycamore's Railroads and Depots

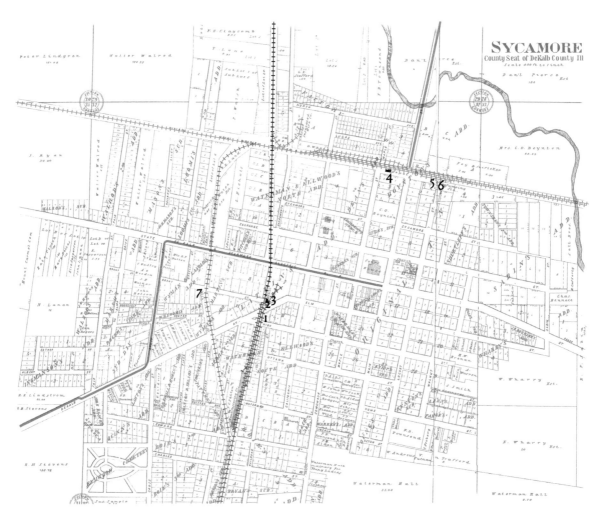

Sycamore's Depots

Constructed by:	Years in Operation
1 Sycamore & Cortland	1859–1865
2 Sycamore & Cortland	1865–1880
3 Sycamore, Cortland & Chicago	1880–1963
(purchased by the Chicago & North Western in 1883)	
4 Minnesota & Northwestern	1887–1951
(consolidated into the Chicago Great Western in 1892)	
5 Chicago Great Western freight depot	1923–1951
6 Chicago Great Western	1951–1978
7 Grant Street Station	1897–1906(?)
(passenger depot for the DeKalb & Great Western)	

Railroad

+++++++ Sycamore & Cortland

+++++++ Chicago & North Western — Northern Illinois line

+++++++ Chicago Great Western

+++++++ Chicago Great Western — DeKalb & Great Western line

▬▬▬▬ DeKalb-Sycamore Electric Railway

▬▬▬▬ Woodstock & Sycamore Traction Company

Introduction

*It is certainly the duty of the present to commemorate the past,
to perpetuate the names of the pioneers, to furnish a record of their settlement,
and to relate the story of their progress.*

Portrait & Biographical Album of DeKalb County, Illinois, 1883

In exploring our local history, we find such a rich mixture of colorful characters and events that it would be impossible to tell the story of Sycamore in a single volume. For this reason, the pages contained in this volume focus on only one aspect of Sycamore's storied past, but it is one aspect that ensured Sycamore's very existence: transportation. Transportation—or more importantly ease of transportation—gave birth to the industrial revolution and facilitated an entire nation's unprecedented growth. And in the 19th century, there was no greater advance in transportation than the railroad.

When the large railway companies bypassed Sycamore in the mid-19th century, Sycamoreans decided to shape their own destiny and build their own railroad. In 1859, the Sycamore & Cortland Railroad Company (S&C) was born. Even though it was the shortest organized railroad in the country, the little five-mile "spur line" connected Sycamore to a major rail line running through Cortland and became an immense source of local pride. It also became the source of many local stories and legends: Sycamore's residents banded together and funded the project themselves (true); they built the railroad with their own blood, sweat, and tears (sort of); the S&C ran a horse-drawn rail car for years until they could afford a real engine (not really); DeKalb, Sycamore's rival to the south, got the railroad first only because of a surveyor's error (false).

Railroad Terminology

"Spur line," "branch road," or "feeder trackage" were names given to shorter railroads—sometimes privately owned—that connected smaller communities to the larger railroads, much in the same way that streams or tributaries feed the country's vast waterways. These terms also referred to the small stretches of track that branched from a main line to accommodate factories, stockyards, lumberyards, or any other business that needed regular access to the railroad. Spurs, branches, and feeders ranged from a few miles in length to only a few yards.

1

This book will tell these stories and more. It will also show how Sycamore's newly built spur line made a moderate-sized village into one of the region's most thriving cities. This mutual, almost symbiotic relationship was facilitated by the multiple depots that provided access to the railroad (see map on page xvi). The newly renovated two-story brick depot that stands presently on the corner of DeKalb Avenue and South Sacramento Street was actually the third depot built by the S&C. The two depots that preceded it were simple board and frame structures of relatively normal size and design for a town of Sycamore's population. The company constructed its third and final depot in 1880, choosing sturdy brick and elegant stone trimmings to make the building stylish and long lasting, and also to protect it from the fires so common to depots of that period.

The handsome brick depot sits on a lot that once housed Livingston and Nancy Walrod, two of Sycamore's earliest white settlers. They arrived in 1836 and originally settled in the old town north of the Kishwaukee River. It is unknown when they removed to the south side of the river and built a home on the lot near the present-day depot. Nancy Walrod's maiden name was Ellwood, and she was the oldest of eleven Ellwood siblings, nine of whom would follow their sister to DeKalb County. Her brothers Reuben and Chauncey became instrumental in bringing new business and enterprise to Sycamore, including the Sycamore & Cortland Railroad. When the depot was completed in 1880, Chauncey Ellwood, the railroad's longtime manager, considered it his crowning achievement.

During the S&C's 24 years of independent operation, the city treated the railroad and its depots like public monuments. Sycamore's five-mile spur line was built in a time of extreme competition among frontier towns. It brought in settlers, businesses, and manufacturing, which in turn brought in more railroads: the Chicago & North Western (C&NW), the Chicago Great Western (CGW), and the electric railroads of the early 20th century. Sycamore owed its prosperity to that original railroad. Without it, the town would have dried up and disappeared in its infancy, passed over by progress and left to decay on the wild northern Illinois prairie.

Today, the stately brick depot is all that remains of the railroad that saved Sycamore. In the building's heyday, it stood as the very soul of the city. Anyone approaching Sycamore—whether by train, wagon, horseback, or on foot—saw the depot's flagpole rising 70 feet over the city. As they moved closer, they saw the finely crafted weathervane in the shape of a train engine that ornamented the depot's steep, truncated roof. Closer still and they could make out the mansard roof's elegant iron cresting and the intricate double cornice brackets under its eaves, indicative of the Italianate style popular with Chicago architects of the time. Below the roof, bright red bricks blazed in the sun. They had been fired in the "Brickville" kilns just north of town. The depot's dressings and foundation consisted of Batavia limestone, the creamy, bluish-white stone commonly used in Sycamore's elegant churches.

Though the depot's architect and builders remain unknown, they successfully blended the styles of the city's sophisticated private homes and the boxier brick structures of its business district. When completed, the depot stood as a testament to the tastes of its owners and to the prosperity and hospitality a person could expect to find upon entering Sycamore.

That Great Arterial System of the Country

To understand just how significant the train depot was to Sycamore, it is essential to understand the role that railroads—and depots—played in shaping the United States. Railroads tell the history of local communities and the story of American expansion. They show how an industrious people conquered the continent through the spread of culture and commerce.

These were the years Mark Twain christened "The Gilded Age," in which a burst of industrial and agricultural growth spread across the northern and western states, bringing fortune to many and unprecedented wealth to an uncommon few. Improved roads and canals enhanced this revolution, but industrialization boomed because of the railroads, which brought raw and manufactured goods to market faster than any other mode of transportation. By the end of the 19th century, the railroad industry employed more workers than any other industry in the United States, and working for the railroad was both a well-paid and well-respected occupation.

Although some scholars argue that the railroads brought wealth only to some, these same scholars agree that the railroads brought mobility to all, which allowed Americans to travel faster, farther, and cheaper than ever before. People could ship their goods off to markets otherwise unreachable. They could ship their children off to schools otherwise inaccessible. When rain, snow, and mud made the roads impassable—a common annoyance before the advent of paved roads—the trains still powered through. In all, railroads injected business into the nation's remote communities and freed a far-flung population from isolation.

A town could receive no better present than the iron horse and steel ribbon connecting it to the outside world. The Sycamore newspaper the *True Republican* reported, "you might as well in these times expect a limb of your body to grow strong while severed from its main artery, as expect a town to flourish, that is disconnected from the railroad, that great arterial system of the country."

The railroad boom in Illinois began in 1836 when the state legislature granted a charter to the Galena & Chicago Union Railroad (G&CU) to build a line from Chicago to the Mississippi River at Galena. The G&CU hoped to capitalize on the lead mines near Galena while gaining access to the Mississippi River, the country's most lucrative shipping lane. From that point on, every railroad company in Chicago saw the Mississippi River as their main objective. They were so eager to get there that they'd lay temporary ties and tracks on raw prairie so engines could still pass until work crews caught up and laid the permanent track. Some rail lines laid 10 or more miles of track per day. By 1860, Chicago supported 10 railroad companies, saw over 100 trains a day pass through its various depots, and had earned its place as the country's leading railroad hub. On May 10, 1869, when the golden spike completed the country's first transcontinental railroad, Chicago became the railroad center of the world.

The Train Depot

Between 1830 and 1950, approximately 140,000 railroad depots were built in the United States. While many of these depots were built to replace previous depots that had been destroyed by fire, fallen into disrepair, or could no longer sustain the local population, this huge number shows the pervasive presence the railroad depot had on American life.

Early depots were simple wood-frame structures that resembled sheds or small barns. They offered shelter from the weather, but little else. To feed the steam engines' constant hunger for fuel and water, railroads built their depots seven to eight miles apart, which is why small towns still dot the northern Illinois landscape at about that same distance.

Later depots, however, were more than simple utilitarian buildings designed to facilitate travel; they were built for public service. They served as the town hub. The whole world came and went by way of the depot, and everyone knew how lucrative proximity to a depot could be. If your store or hotel sat across from the depot, then your store or hotel was the first to be frequented by the weary traveler. But this kind of economic power could also prove divisive, pitting neighbor against neighbor over which side of town the depot would

A typical 19th-century scene outside of a small-town depot.
(Library of Congress)

be located. In some cities, developers purposefully located the depot on or outside the edge of town to promote growth, knowing that the town would inevitably spread in the depot's direction. This is the most likely reason that the S&C's directors built their depot southwest of Sycamore's business center (and because several of them already had sizable land investments in that area).

Those towns fortunate enough to secure railroad service knew they had to impress the passing public with the quality of their depot. The larger railroads kept several standard depot designs on file so they could build quickly and cheaply. These standard depots became common in the 1870s, when several communities, like Sycamore, had outgrown their earlier structures. Around this same time, however, several companies began incorporating popular architectural styles into

their depots, which often reflected the tastes of the companies' directors. A depot could also reflect what the directors thought of themselves and their town. There are two schools of thought on this idea: a large and elegant depot could represent a sense of prosperity and confidence; it could also represent an overblown sense of self-worth. Many companies employed famous architects to bring prestige to their depots. A depot was, after all, the first building newly arriving passengers encountered when they stepped off the train. As such, depots had to be clean, friendly, and comfortable. They also had to be intelligently designed, because they were constantly busy and had to accommodate railroad workers, freight, and an eclectic mix of passengers, all at the same time. If they failed to make a good first impression, then they failed the entire community.

Depots also served as convenient landmarks. If you were a traveler looking for someone in a new town, the depot agent most likely knew him or her. The depot was also a good location for a rendezvous because it was easy to find and usually not far from the heart of town. If you couldn't see the depot outright, you just followed the train tracks or the sound of the whistle. Or you could ask someone, "Where's the depot?" There wouldn't be a soul in town who couldn't answer. In Sycamore, merchants often used the depot as a point of reference in their advertising. "By the depot," "North of the depot," "Just down from the depot," ran at the bottom of several advertisements.

In the early 1880s, when some Sycamoreans complained about local youths gathering outside the new depot, the *True Republican* jumped to the youths' defense, arguing that it was impossible for them not to gather there. The depot was the most exciting place in town! Almost everyone and everything that came into Sycamore came by way of the depot. Newspapers and mail came on early morning trains. Additional news, personal messages, and weather reports came by way of the telegraph office inside the depot. Almost every item sold in local stores arrived at the depot first. The latest technological wonder—be it a revolutionary new steam engine or the simple recreational velocipede (i.e., a bicycle)—could be glimpsed on the depot platform before its owner whisked it away to a factory, farm, or store. Young women might catch a peek at the latest fashions and patterns before the popular local drayman, Harry Little, loaded the crates onto his cart and delivered them around town. Courthouse visitors or special guests for Sycamore's numerous festivals arrived at or departed from the depot before they could move on to their next destination. Married couples departed and returned from their honeymoons by way of the depot. Politicians pulled into town amid great fanfare and the blaring of the local brass band. Special trains conveyed families to and from funerals. If a family member passed away in a distant town, the casket was unloaded and stored at the depot until relatives arrived to retrieve it. In times of war, great crowds swarmed the depot to see their men off to the front lines. Sycamore's depot saw off the brave young volunteers in every major conflict from the Civil War to World War II.

It is no wonder that Sycamore's youth found the depot such a popular hangout. For them, that one building symbolized wealth, opportunity, freedom, and escape. It was a gateway to the rest of the world.

The Depot Remembered

Even though the depot has been out of service for over forty years, several DeKalb County residents have fond memories of the place. Sycamore firefighter Paul Rubeck remembers how the freight cars were always lined up outside the depot, with workers always loading and unloading. "No matter what time of day, there were always people there," he said. "It was always busy."

Clifford Danielson, long-time president of the National Bank and Trust Company of Sycamore and first recipient of the Chamber of Commerce's Outstanding Citizenship Award (which still bears his name), loved to tell the story of his arrival in Sycamore. It was 1926, and when he first stepped off the train, the first building he saw was the depot. Lawyer Ron Klein paid his way through law school at the University of Illinois by working long summer hours at the canning factory just south of the depot. He remembers having to go up to the depot to unload freight for the factory.

The depot played a significant role in the family history of DeKalb resident Gerald Willey. When he was a boy, whenever his mother rode past the building, she would tell him, "That's where your grandparents used to meet." In 1914, Willey's grandmother, Winifred Alling, a schoolteacher, stayed on a farm near Sycamore during the school week. Each weekend, a young farmhand named Ora Shull took her by horse and buggy to the Sycamore depot so she could take the train home to Lombard, Illinois. Each time she returned to Sycamore, Shull was waiting at the depot to take her back to the farm. Two years later, they married.

Betty Hampa of Genoa has a strong personal connection to Sycamore's depot, and she delights in sharing her stories. Betty's father, Martin Hampa, worked in the railroad business for over 40 years. He also has the distinction of being the last depot agent to work at the depot before the C&NW sold it in 1963. When Betty was a teenager, she helped her father with clerical work in the depot office, filling in shipping forms on an LC Smith billing typewriter. She fondly recalls how the men from

the nearby fire station and grain elevator would walk over on their lunch break, sit down on a freight crate, and swap stories while enjoying a few rounds of cards. Sometimes Betty joined in the games, and sometimes she won.

Betty still remembers the distinct train-engine smell that once permeated that whole part of town. She claims that every time she drives down DeKalb Avenue, she still has the urge to stop outside the old depot and look both ways to see if the train is coming.

An antique lock featuring the logo for the Sycamore & Cortland Railroad (courtesy of Paul Rubeck)

Dawn of a New Era

America's railroad industry conquered the continent, created some of the most powerful corporations in the world, and ushered in a new age of American prosperity. But in the 1920s, the railroad's golden age came to an inglorious end, brought low by a simple contrivance: the rubber tire. Cars, buses, and trucks dominated the transportation industry, depleting the passenger and freight profits that had built and sustained the railroads for nearly a century. Despite a brief resurgence during World War II, the railroad industry never recovered. Many railroads were abandoned, their depots left to rot.

Since the 1970s, preservationists have saved hundreds of depots across the country, reappropriating them for a wide variety of uses. Restored and remodeled depots have been converted into banks, restaurants, schools, stores, museums, and visitor, cultural, and community centers. For the past half-century, Sycamore's historic depot has functioned as little more than a warehouse and storage facility. As this volume will show, it is so much more than that. Today, the depot embodies the enthusiasm and principles of the people who built it. It serves as a window into the past and a link to the legacies of Sycamore's founders. Most importantly, it forever ties the city to the Sycamore & Cortland Railroad, the five-mile-spur line that spurred 125 years of rich railroad history.

Sycamore Rises from the Prairie, 1835-1857

In the 1830s, waves of American pioneers waggoned west, ready to punch their plows into the rich black soil of the Midwest's fertile prairies. Speculators and merchants soon followed, eager to sell their wares and services to the settlers who had already done the plowing. DeKalb County saw its fair share of these sturdy pioneers. At the time, the region was "undisturbed, unbroken, unsettled wilderness." Though isolated from major water routes, it had been blessed with arable acreage, an abundance of timber in its island groves, and a good source of water in the Kishwaukee River. Blackberries, raspberries, and gooseberries grew wild. Walnuts, butternuts, and hickory nuts dropped from the trees. Besides the agricultural potential, the region provided plentiful amounts of deer, chickens, quail, ducks, geese, partridges, and squirrels. The Kishwaukee's clear waters also provided a generous supply of catfish, bass, suckers, and pickerel. According to early DeKalb County historian H. L. Boies, the first settlers found the land along the Kishwaukee "as fertile and beautiful a region of country as they could desire."

Within a few short years, small towns cropped up across "Kishwaukee country." These towns were named for their founders, like Coltonville,

Charter Grove, Johnson's Grove, and Kirkland. The first pioneers credited with settling within Sycamore's present-day city limits were Lysander Darling and Carlos Lattin. In 1835, they arrived separately at the Kishwaukee River and decided to stake their claims on the fertile ground they found there. Darling built his cabin in the lowlands north of the river. Lattin built his on the highlands south of the river, on what is now Sycamore's State Street. His cabin stood eight logs high, sixteen feet wide, and twenty-four feet long. Several prominent pioneers soon followed, including Marshall Stark, Elihu Wright, Peter Lamois, Jesse Kellogg, Erasmus Walrod, John Hamlin, Jesse Rose, Edward White, Zacharia Wood, Captain Eli Barnes, and the Waterman brothers: John, James, Robert, and Charles. Most of these men joined Darling and staked their claims north of the Kishwaukee River, leaving the site of present-day Sycamore largely unsettled.

The first year proved difficult for all the settlers. A harsh winter sent many of them back East. Those who stayed suffered under heavy spring rains that destroyed most of their crops. The few who saw success still had no good way to reach distant markets to sell their goods or to restock desperately needed supplies. A trip to Chicago could take several days, which few farmers could afford to spend away from their fields. Even if they could manage the journey, the farmers would not have encountered the bustling transportation hub that Chicago would become by mid-century. Boies described Chicago as nothing more than a "wretched little hamlet of mud and misery." Still, Chicago was the closest market available.

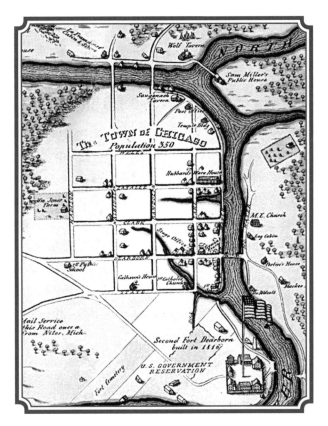

Chicago c. 1835

After each spring deluge, swelled rivers filled the lowlands with water, which would stand stagnant for days or even weeks, creating ripe breeding grounds for disease-carrying mosquitoes. Due to poor drainage, roads became impassable to wagon teams. If travelers tried to avoid the roads, they had to contend with the thick grass, flowers, shrubs, and weeds that dominated the unbroken prairie. The livestock they carried in tow had to endure the prickly cockle burrs and burdock that clung to everything. Boies summed up life in Sycamore in 1836: "Poverty, rags, a scanty diet and the shakes were the fashion of the times."

The First Railroad Boom

A promise of better days came in 1836 when the Galena & Chicago Union Railroad (G&CU) received its charter to build a line from Chicago to the Mississippi River at Galena. Soon, other railroad companies arrived, securing charters and guaranteeing great wealth to towns along their paths. Back East, scores of individual investors and companies snapped up vast tracts of land. According to Boies, they hoped to see a railroad move into their "embryo towns," which "would stimulate an almost magical growth" and send land values soaring. One such company, C. Sharrer & Co. of New York, purchased two square miles of land below the Kishwaukee River that encompassed most of present-day Sycamore. It sent out surveyors who dammed the river and built a fence around its investment.

In 1837, with the land rush in full swing, a 16-year-old boy from New York arrived in Sycamore, little-realizing that he and his brothers would someday shape the future of DeKalb County. Reuben Ellwood saw the untamed West as a land of opportunity that could free him from the unrewarding life of labor he faced back home. The second of seven brothers, he had struck out west with all the other land speculators who had dreams of future railroad dollars. When he arrived in Sycamore, he staked a claim to 160 acres. His older brother Chauncey, a lawyer, soon joined him. Together they set about building a farm while Chauncey worked to secure his legal license for the state of Illinois.

By year's end, several nervous investors realized that the railroads weren't going to arrive as fast as everyone had thought. The land bubble burst, values plummeted, and thousands of investors were left holding the bag. C. Sharrer & Co. abandoned its claim. Reuben Ellwood,

Reuben Ellwood

however, dutifully worked his land for another four years. He then returned to New York, where he attended school and worked various public service and manufacturing jobs. He did not return to Sycamore until 1857, determined as ever to see a railroad come through that town.

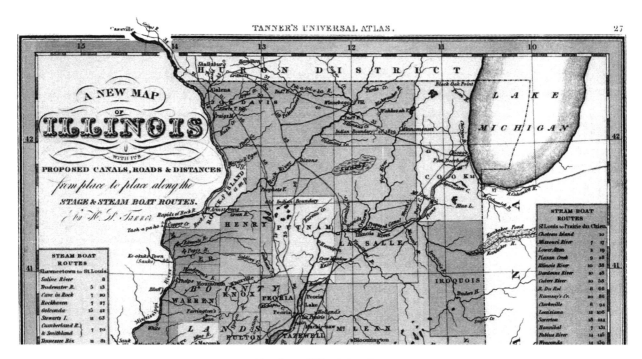

Northern Illinois in 1833

Fight for the County Seat

In the early days, Illinois was divided into only a few counties, some of them stretching for hundreds of miles. As a result, settlers had to travel for days over muddy and treacherous roads to reach their county seat. To solve this problem, in 1836 the state legislature went into the business of creating new counties. More counties meant more county seats, and several seed towns knew that securing a seat of justice would ensure their survival for years to come. DeKalb County started off as part of LaSalle County, which encompassed the whole northwestern portion of the state. When that county was divided, DeKalb became part of Kane County. In March 1837, legislators carved a 36-mile-long and 18-mile-wide rectangular chunk out of Kane County to create present-day DeKalb County. In October of that year, state-appointed commissioners met to determine the location of the county seat. They spent three days canvassing the region before deciding on "a lonely, windy, grassy, desolate spot" south of the Kishwaukee River.

"What's In a Name?"

No one is quite sure of the origin of the name "Sycamore," though there are several theories. Most early histories of Sycamore claim that the name is a translation of the Native American word "Kishwaukee." Another common translation for "Kishwaukee," however, is "swift water." But there is an ongoing debate among scholars about the meaning of the word "waukee," which appears in several place names (Milwaukee, Waukegan, for example). A common translation is "land" or "earth," but this doesn't account for how early explorers originally recorded the names. White explorers transcribed Native American words phonetically, which means that one Native American's "waukee" might not be the same as another Native American's "waukee."

Another origin theory is that sycamore trees once grew in abundance along the Kishwaukee River, but early accounts from the region's first settlers do not mention sycamore trees in the area. In 1894, former resident I.R.B. Arnold commented, "During my thirty-five years residence in and near Sycamore, I never saw a sycamore tree within a hundred miles of that city." In those days, the hard maple dominated the landscape, providing the shade so often extolled by early settlers as one of the chief benefits of living in Sycamore.

At the time, Sycamore existed in name only—there was not yet a physical town—but its selection as the county seat made practical sense; it was a prime location on heavily timbered, fertile, high ground alongside a favorable river. But there was another reason the commissioners chose Sycamore: transportation. In 1837, the Illinois' capital was located in Vandalia, in the southern part of the state, and legislators believed a state road would one day stretch from Vandalia all to way to Lake Superior. Sycamore would lie directly on that road. Likewise, a proposed road from Chicago to the Mississippi River could also run through Sycamore. With two such major roads intersecting within the county, Sycamore made the ideal location for the county seat, though several parties argued otherwise.

In 1838, Sycamore faced the first of many fights for its right to the county seat (years later these fights came to be known as "county seat delirium"). The town of Coltonville, which stood west of Sycamore and was already populated by several homes and businesses, contrived to take the county seat for itself. Men from both towns rode day and night to knock on doors and drum up support for their respective towns. Despite Coltonville's strenuous efforts, Sycamore prevailed at the polls. In 1839, a bit of shady political trickery sent the county seat "officially" to Coltonville, though this move was contested by several angry Sycamoreans. In August 1840, another county-wide vote and a legislative act confirmed Sycamore as the permanent seat of justice for DeKalb County. Within a few years, Coltonville dried up and disappeared; its only legacy is the road just west of Sycamore that still bears its name.

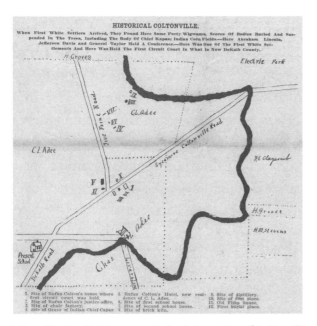

Coltonville stood at the present-day intersection of Coltonville Road and North First Street. When the county seat went to Sycamore in 1837, many of Coltonville's residents relocated to that city. Coltonville soon faded into history. This map appeared in a 1912 issue of the *True Republican*. It was pieced together based on the recollections of Hosea W. Willard, one of Sycamore's earliest pioneers.

For two years, the only indication that Sycamore stood as the county seat was a colored flag streaming atop a tall, solitary pole in the middle of an empty prairie. But in 1839, Captain Eli Barnes and James S. Waterman surveyed and laid out the town and its two principal streets. State Street ran east and west, intersecting with Main Street, which ran north and south. According to some accounts, Barnes and Waterman designed the wide streets to allow wagons to make a full U-turn at any point. The city auctioned off lots to finance construction of its first courthouse, which was built on the south side of State Street, opposite the present courthouse's location. James Ellwood remembered the building as "a little old hovel of a courthouse." The 20-by-30-foot, two-story wooden structure had a single courtroom located on the second floor. County commissioners held their first court session in the new building before it had windows and doors. On Sundays, the courtroom was used for worship services. The services alternated denominations week-by-week, and this practice continued until, one-by-one, each denomination built its own church.

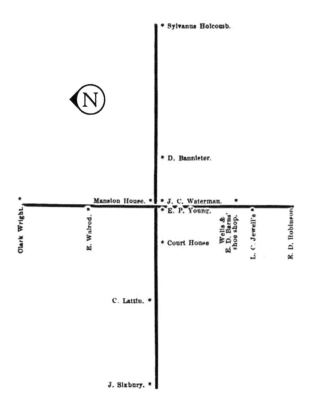

Sycamore in 1840

This simple map of State and Main streets in Sycamore originally appeared in H. L. Boies's *History of DeKalb County, Illinois* (1868).

With the county seat secure, Sycamore's residents grew confident that their town would play a major role in DeKalb County's future. Captain Barnes built the "Mansion House," a large and extravagant tavern and boarding house on the northeast corner of State and Main, where the public library now stands. Many of Sycamore's newly arrived settlers spent their first few days in town boarding in this tavern while they looked for land or waited to build a cabin on land already purchased. In one corner of the tavern, John and Charles Waterman opened Sycamore's first store, which turned a tidy profit off all the men boarding at the Mansion House.

By 1841, Sycamore had grown to twelve homes, two stores, two hotels, a mill, a blacksmith shop, and one well. The population stood at about 70. By 1850, the population had grown to nearly 400. These were flush times across the United States, and Sycamore used the country's prosperity to full advantage. Sycamore's farmers, however, ran up against the same age-old problem: how to get their goods to market. Transportation was so slow and treacherous that any goods sold at market would rarely cover the cost of the trip. While Sycamoreans enjoyed the blessings of good health and "bountiful crops," their city could never truly prosper without improved roads.

Battling the Unfathomable Mire

By the mid-1840s, northern Illinois roads were busier than ever. Constant streams of grain-laden teams flowed in and out of Chicago, but the roads were often wet, muddy, miserable, and impassable. When Sycamore's first permanent lawyer, Andrew Brown, moved from Chicago to Sycamore in 1840, his trip by coach lasted two wretched days, thanks, in part, to the coach falling into a slough "from which it was extricated with great difficulty." One of the earliest settlers in DeKalb County, Charles Marsh, who later founded the Marsh Harvester Works in Sycamore with his brother William, wrote in his memoir of his own difficulty with those early roads:

Muddy roads plagued Sycamore's early pioneers, making travel both difficult and dangerous.

Many a time have I been stuck in the mud of a main road or in the sloughs that had to be crossed when following the devious wagon tracks across the wild prairie. In such cases we had to lift out and tote to shore—whether of slough or of mud—more or less of the load, and then we might have to use a rail, which, when the conditions justified we usually carried along, to pry up the wheels so as to lessen the resistance of the mud or sod; and sometimes we had to lead the horses forward onto firmer ground and hitch them by a chain to the end of the wagon pole.

Marsh related a frightening incident that took place in the dead of winter during his youth. He and his brother were driving a wagon down "the narrow canal of liquid mud used as road" when one wheel dropped into a hole. Marsh spilled over the side and landed directly in front of a wheel, "which advanced sufficiently to force my head completely under the mud." Fortunately for Marsh—and for the future of Sycamore—he managed to free himself unharmed, but he still had to travel another 12 miles in the freezing winter winds while fully soaked and covered in mud.

To combat the county's transportation problems, some towns built plank roads, which they made by lining up thousands of hardwood planks to cover the desolate miles between neighboring towns. One such road, built by public subscription, operated as a toll road between Sycamore and St. Charles. Its benefits were short lived, however, because the hardwood planks quickly warped under the unrelenting exposure to winter's bitter cold and summer's harsh heat. The road soon "became as rough as corduroy," and no one wanted to risk the wear-and-tear such a clamorous trek could have on their wagons, their horses, and their backsides. The road's operators soon abandoned it and nearby settlers "confiscated" the hardwood planks.

The Great Failure

In late 1845, word spread that the Galena & Chicago Union Railroad Company would make another attempt to build its line from Chicago to Galena. Sycamoreans knew that if they gained this transportation advantage, people throughout the county would flock to their town. On January 7, 1846, James S. Waterman traveled to Rockford as a representative of DeKalb County to meet with the G&CU's directors. He lobbied the directors to include Sycamore on their route. Waterman's efforts fell short, however, because many Sycamoreans still survived on slender means and the town had little money to subscribe to the railroad. The G&CU built its line north of DeKalb County, where it passed through Belvidere and Rockford before ending at Freeport (it never reached Galena).

Waterman tried again in 1851 when he entered into talks with the Chicago, St. Charles & Mississippi Air Line Railroad (CStC&M), who proposed to run a line from Chicago to St. Charles and then to Sycamore. From there it would run through South Grove and Oregon before continuing on to the Mississippi River at Savannah. Sycamoreans invested $20,000 in stock in the new company, a move that alarmed the G&CU, who had another line projected to connect Chicago and the Mississippi River, also by way of St. Charles. Agents from the G&CU approached Sycamore's residents and tried to convince them to go with their railroad instead. Otherwise, the agents claimed, they would bypass Sycamore to the south and run their line through the tiny, almost non-existent villages of Buena Vista (present-day DeKalb) and Pampas (present-day Cortland).

The first settlers arrived in Buena Vista and Pampas in 1835, but in the ensuing two decades the villages saw little growth. At the time the G&CU threatened to build its railroad through both villages, they still resembled Sycamore in its earliest days. They each had a tavern, some dry-goods stores, and a small cluster of cabins. They had populations of less than a hundred and functioned primarily as way stations for farmers transporting their goods to and from Chicago.

To the railroad companies, both Buena Vista and Sycamore would have been logical locations to build a new line, because both had an abundance of the two natural resources steam engines needed to operate: water and wood. Both towns were located on the Kishwaukee River, and both had an ample supply of timber. But at that period, any railroad would have preferred Sycamore to Buena Vista. Besides being the county seat and the larger and more developed of the two cities, Sycamore had grown into a prosperous business center. The only card Buena Vista had up its sleeve was the G&CU's desire to beat the CStC&M to the Mississippi, a card the G&CU would play only if it couldn't convince Sycamore to sign with them.

But work was already underway on the CStC&M, including preliminary bridge work and several miles of grading. The G&CU, finding that it could not change the minds of the confident Sycamoreans, saw no other option but to follow through on its threats and run its railroad straight through the middle of the county, crossing through Pampas and Buena Vista to Sycamore's south. In an effort to beat its rivals, the G&CU pushed its construction forward at full steam, finishing the line in only a few months. Buena Vista changed its name to DeKalb and freight service started in May of 1853. Passenger service began that fall and the line became famous throughout the region as the Dixon Air Line.

According to H. L. Boies, the railroad's impact on DeKalb was noticeable almost immediately:

Houses sprang up as by magic. The neighboring farmers who visited one month would hardly recognize the place when they visited it the next…. Stores, shops, warehouses, hotels, and dwellings filled up the village plat, and the evidences of taste and refinement were to be seen in its streets and dwellings.

Despite the G&CU's speedy construction and DeKalb's remarkable progress, Sycamoreans weren't worried. They would soon have a first-class railroad of their own. But shock and panic suddenly rippled through the town when word spread that the CStC&M's financing had fallen through. Almost overnight, construction came to a halt and the company abandoned the project. To add insult to injury, it sold off the bulk of its property in Chicago to the G&CU for a tidy profit. Decades later, the *True Republican* reported that "for many years, the embankments and bridge pilings [of the CStC&M] could be seen as a monument to the great failure."

Boies noted that if the people of Sycamore had taken up the G&CU's offer to build through their city, "the villages of Cortland or DeKalb would never have had an existence, and Sycamore would probably have become one of the largest towns in northern Illinois."

So it was that a petty Chicago railroad rivalry created DeKalb and Cortland, two of the county's most flourishing towns of the 19th century, while leaving Sycamore almost "dead on the vine."

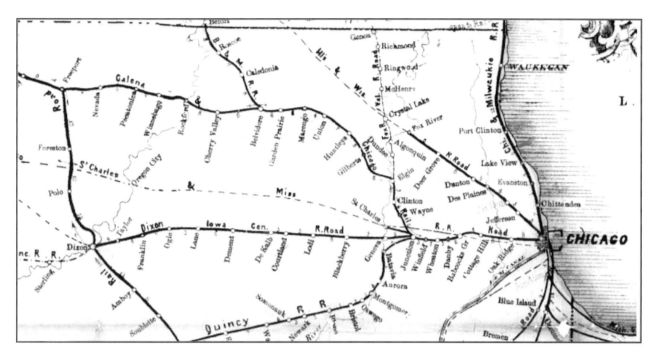

This 1855 railroad map shows the G&CU's Dixon Air Line (here called the Dixon Iowa Central), which was the making of several towns along its route, including DeKalb and Cortland. To the north, the dotted line shows the proposed route for the failed Chicago, St. Charles & Mississippi Air Line, which would have passed through Sycamore. (Library of Congress)

Flush Times

Times were so good in DeKalb that people there began to question why the county seat wasn't located in their city. DeKalb was growing rapidly (its population had jumped from less than a hundred to over 1,500 in two years); it was more centrally located in the county; and most important of all, it had a railroad to provide easy access to a courthouse. Fortunately for Sycamore, times were good in that city also. Despite the tragic loss of the railroad to its southern neighbors, Sycamore reaped the benefits of a nationwide agricultural boom in the mid-1850s.

By 1856, railroads stretched across almost every county of northern Illinois, opening up new avenues of trade for prairie towns across the region. As long as the enterprising farmers of Sycamore could reach a railroad depot, whether by plank road or primitive prairie trail, they could get their goods to Chicago, and from there to markets across the nation.

Improved transportation wasn't the only factor behind the surging economy. The Crimean War consumed Europe, disrupting the entire continent's supply chain, which sent the demand for grain soaring. Several European countries had to import grain from the United States, which caused the price of a bushel of wheat to jump from 30 cents to $1.50. The increased demand for food stimulated the farming market, and the farmers, in turn, stimulated innovation in their efforts to produce more food faster. Because the Midwest's largely unsettled prairie land could be purchased cheaply, pioneers flooded into the region, snapped up the readily available acreage, and plowed the fertile fields into huge profits. Many towns swelled under this entrepreneurial spirit, and many farmers, merchants, and prospectors went into debt building new houses, warehouses, barns, and businesses. They borrowed from local banks to purchase large tracts of land, and they bought on credit from local merchants to purchase supplies and equipment. Charles Marsh described the economic explosion in his memoir, noting that everyone was "buying more land, buying machinery, carriages, sewing machines, melodeons, and fine furniture, and generally running into debt; merchants gave credit to anyone who would buy, and manufacturers had expanded to meet the inflated demand."

In Sycamore, this system of borrowing and credit allowed local merchants to share in the prosperity of the city's booming agricultural economy. New shops cropped up all along State Street, ready to supply the incoming settlers. If a farmer couldn't pay his debt on time, merchants happily extended his credit, secure in the knowledge that he would pay it back once he'd reaped the next harvest. By the summer of 1856, Sycamoreans held more debt than at any other time in the town's history, but the crops proved plentiful and the future looked bright. According to the *True Republican*, "it was flush and easy times everywhere."

Then the bottom fell out.

In February 1856, the Crimean War came to an end, European markets stabilized, and the United States was left holding a huge surplus of grain. The price of wheat plunged from $1.50 a bushel to 40 cents. Farmers who had calculated their ability to pay their debts on the higher price now found themselves unable to satisfy their creditors. The resulting depression hit northern Illinois hard. Throughout the prairie land, farmers abandoned their fields, merchants closed their shops, and banks went under. The problem was more widespread than just northern Illinois. The "flush and easy times" really had been everywhere, and the entire country had fallen into the same debt trap as Sycamore. Nationwide, banks that had over-extended credit failed by the hundreds, and the entire country plunged into a depression.

Sycamore, once so promising and enterprising, faced its greatest challenge. *The DeKalb County Republican Sentinel,* rival newspaper to the *True Republican,* reported on the economic nightmare:

> These are indeed, hard times. Our citizens are badly in debt; there is scarcely one-fourth of a crop to be sent to market to raise money; money is very scarce, so that it is difficult to get loans to any considerable amount with the best of securities, and the time for the collector to be round after the taxes, which are enormously high, is fast approaching; and we beg leave to ask in all sincerity, what are the people to do? We confess our inability to answer the question. It seems to us that the prospect is gloomy enough.

For once, the *True Republican* seemed to agree with its rival:

> All across the country, the tempest of troublous times is raging—towns are being depopulated, farms sold under the sheriff's hammer, business prospects and plans wrecked and crushed, and other results proceeding from the Hard Times manifesting themselves.

The *True Republican,* however, remained more optimistic than the *Sentinel*. While its coverage of the crisis described "the general derangement and stagnation of commerce" and the "dark night of embarrassment and distress" that had settled over the city, it called on the city to regain its confidence in the face of adversity and push forward to return the "old-accustomed smile" to the "care-worn features of our merchants and

other business men." The depression was certainly felt in everyone's pocketbooks, but that didn't mean it had to be felt in their minds.

A Brilliant Future Before Her

Even without the financial crisis, the winter of 1857 to 1858 would have been a hard one. Bitter cold winds and never-ending snow blanketed the region. Arrests for firewood theft were on the rise. A visitor to Sycamore described a snowstorm during his stay at Paine's Hotel on the southeast corner of State and California streets:

> The wind blows a perfect hurricane, accompanied with driving snow that blinds and suffocates—you draw your cloak about you, button up your overcoat and boldly rush into the storm, but with one blast from the East you right about and beat [back] into Paine's.

Despite the hard times, the social life of Sycamore soldiered on. James' Hall hosted Christmas and New Year's balls featuring Sycamore's celebrated brass band. The same venue also served as a popular place for the young people to enjoy a "hop," where they could dance to the dulcimer and violin of Wolcott's Quadrille Band or any other popular band making its way around the midwestern circuit. Sycamore still maintained its role as the county seat and the monthly "Court Week" was always a thrilling occasion when it rolled around. "If any Sycamorean desires to 'see and be seen," the *True Republican* suggested, let him not be absent from town during court week." If someone didn't have any business at court that week, then the newspaper offered the following solution: "Kill your neighbor's dog, sell him a spavined horse, or neglect to put up his fence when you go through it, and let him sue you, and then hire a lawyer."[1]

If Sycamore's residents needed to escape the confines of their daily lives and take a little diversionary excursion out of town, they were not completely without railroad options. They could hop on the Sycamore & Cortland Express, "a new, convenient, and comfortable carriage" that ferried travelers to and from the Cortland depot for only 37½ cents. Of course, according to the local paper, the Cortland depot wasn't much of a depot at all, but an "old hulk of a building which has been obtruding its unsightly shape too long upon the view of the public." The paper suggested "it be dragged away and demolished as soon as possible." The town of Cortland did just that in late 1857, when the G&CU erected a new 94-by-40-foot structure, solidifying Cortland's status as a "railroad town."

Travel between Sycamore and Cortland remained dangerous, however. In winter, the wagon wheel ruts would freeze into solid ridges that made for a bumpy and uncomfortable ride. A summer visitor sarcastically described the trip as showcasing "a beautiful specimen of Western roads," meaning that it was a good example of the treacherous, muddy sloughs that crisscrossed most of the country's unsettled territories.

This ad for the Sycamore & Cortland Express appeared in the March 19, 1857 issue of the *DeKalb County Republican Sentinel*. (Author's collection)

---

[1] It should be noted that the *True Republican* always supported Court Week because the number of visitors it brought into town created a financial boon for local businesses. *The DeKalb County Republican Sentinel*, however, viewed Court Week as a burden on the local taxpayer and claimed that it provided "pecuniary advantage" to a select few only (i.e. the business owners).

In a 1906 issue of the *Sycamore Tribune*, James Ellwood recounted the story of his arrival in Sycamore during the harsh winter of 1855. When he arrived in Cortland by train, he disembarked at the village's tiny depot, which he described as little more than a freight car. Then he joined several other men atop a crowded carriage destined for Sycamore. The inside of the carriage was full of women and children. Along the "lumbering" journey, the carriage carefully maneuvered around snow drifts "six to eight feet in height." At times, men climbed down from the top of the carriage to steady it as it passed over treacherous ground. That night it rained, and when Ellwood awoke the next morning, his first in Sycamore, he found that "most thoroughfares were impassable."

For four years the farmers and merchants of Sycamore had shipped and received their goods by this same inconvenient route, but in 1858, winter's heavy snowmelt saturated the road, making it nearly impassable. On the worst days, carriage and freight services suspended operations. On the best days, those who braved the trip still found themselves mired in an inescapable muck. The *True Republican* described Sycamore's residents having to survive that spring "with mud and slosh prevailing underfoot." The depression had already wiped out several merchants and farmers, and now muddy roads afflicted the rest. Shipments were delayed. Mail delivery was erratic. Profits were lost.

"The road from Sycamore to Cortland is the 'Jordan' of the Sycamoreans," the *True Republican* reported, "and a 'hard road to travel' it is, to be sure, especially in muddy weather." The paper then endorsed the brave carriage operator who performed his job as best he could "under the circumstances," and it offered a solution to everyone's problems: "Some of these days we shall have a railroad across this Jordan of ours, when the proprietor of the present excellent accommodation line may exclaim (in no regretful mood, we trust): 'Othello's occupation's gone.'" [2]

Throughout the financial crisis and inclement weather, the *True Republican* retained its obstinate optimism, predicting a busy trade season in the summer:

> Unusual attention is being directed to Sycamore as a point for establishing business. We know that Sycamore enjoys a business reputation in Chicago, which will compare favorably with that of any other village in the west; and we believe that notwithstanding the seeming disadvantages under which she labors, a brilliant future is before her.

---

[2] A line from Shakespeare's play, which, in this instance carries a double meaning. Othello laments the loss of his occupation as a general, just as the carriage driver will be put out of business by the railroad (though the carriage driver will not regret this). Another interpretation is that Othello is lamenting the end of war itself, just as the people of Sycamore, once they have their railroad, will never have to battle that insufferable, muddy-muck-of-a-road ever again.

The paper called for confidence, for Sycamoreans to believe in their own abilities, and if anyone doubted such abilities, the paper called on them to look at what they had already accomplished "in spite of the deprivation of railroad advantages."

This brilliant future, *True Republican* editors believed, would materialize if Sycamore grew out of its untamed pioneering ways and entered the civilized world. One idea: remove the wild animals that roamed the streets. Such animals were "an emblem of inaction and supineness, which our citizens know nothing of" and "altogether too suggestive of the farm and the sheepfold to harmonize with the progressive ideas of our people." Another idea was to improve the streets and plant shade trees throughout the city to enhance its appearance. And a third idea, the most ambitious of all, came about in 1857, when Sycamore saw the return of Reuben Ellwood, who had been gone from those parts nearly 15 years. Ellwood returned to the region with five of his brothers, all of whom brought with them an entrepreneurial spirit that would forever reshape the county. The Ellwoods were not the type of men to sit around and wait for things to come their way. So when Reuben and several other leading businessmen put their heads together, they decided they would no longer wait for a big railroad company to approach Sycamore. Sycamore would build its own railroad.

The Waterman Brothers

John C. Waterman
(b. September 9, 1814; d. October 19, 1883)

James S. Waterman
(b. May 20, 1820; d. July 19, 1883)

Robert W. Waterman
(b. December 15, 1826; d. April 12, 1891)

Not Pictured: Charles Waterman (b. November 4, 1817; d. May 3, 1897)

Before Sycamore was Sycamore, the Waterman brothers pioneered their way into unknown and unsettled territory and helped build a town from an empty prairie. They worked tirelessly to establish Sycamore as DeKalb County's center of commerce, law, education, manufacturing, and finance. Their efforts created Sycamore's first financial institution, brought numerous industries into the city, and secured the county seat.[1]

The Waterman brothers were born into a prosperous New England family that was soon brought low by the father's sudden death. At a young age, John Waterman had to take over his father's responsibilities. Charles Waterman left the family's New York home in 1836 and struck out for Illinois. In 1838, John and James joined him. When the three brothers arrived at the original Sycamore settlement north of the

---

[1] The village of Waterman in south DeKalb County is not named after the Sycamore Watermans. It is named for Daniel B. Waterman (no relation) who helped bring the Chicago & Iowa railroad through that area in the early 1870s. The village then grew up around the railroad.

Kishwaukee River, John and Charles set up Sycamore's first business, a dry goods store in a 16-by-18-foot cabin.

At the age of 18, James Waterman became the county surveyor. Several towns in DeKalb County owe their present arrangement to his designs. He also laid out the streets and lots for Sycamore's new location south of the Kishwaukee River. According to county historian Lewis M. Gross, "The inhabitants of [Sycamore] for all future time, may thank Captain Eli Barnes and James S. Waterman for the broad streets that now add so much to the beauty of the village."

When the town shifted south, John and Charles relocated their store with it. They set up in one corner of Eli Barnes' Mansion House, the city's first hotel. Sycamore became the county seat and Charles took advantage of the traffic influx by operating a four-horse stagecoach between St. Charles and Sycamore. In 1840, 13-year-old Robert Waterman joined his brothers and worked as a clerk in their store.

Charles Waterman was the first member of his family to depart Sycamore. In the 1840s, he relocated to Freeport, where he ran a successful farm and mercantile business. His land became known as Waterman's Mills.

Robert Waterman led a storied life that took him all the way to the highest office in California. After leaving his brothers' store, he worked as a clerk and postmaster in Geneva. He followed the gold rush to California in 1850, but soon returned to Illinois and entered politics. He attended the first Republican National Convention, accompanied by Abraham Lincoln. In 1873, he returned to California, where he established a number of lucrative silver mines. The people of California elected him as their Lieutenant Governor in 1886. When Governor Washington Bartlett died the following year, Robert succeeded him as the state's 17th governor, holding that office until January 1891.

John Waterman served as DeKalb County's first treasurer. In conjunction with his numerous civic duties, he continued to operate his mercantile business, which he kept open for 40 years. At the time of his retirement, he had the longest-running business in town.

James Waterman led a life as interesting as his brother Robert. In Sycamore's early days, he took part in a bloody gun battle against "The Resurrectionists," a gang of grave robbers working for a St. Charles medical school. When James surveyed Sycamore in 1839, he snapped up vast tracts of land in the southern part of the city. When the town eventually spread in that direction, he made a considerable return on his investment.

James built the Waterman Block of downtown offices and partnered in several businesses therein. He later expanded these businesses into Genoa, Cortland, and DeKalb. His land speculations throughout northern Illinois, Iowa, and Wisconsin proved to be immensely profitable. His investments in Robert's California silver mines were even more so. In 1855, he co-founded Sycamore's first bank, and in 1869, he played a major role in bringing the Marsh Harvester Works to Sycamore, which pushed the city into a new era of industry and manufacturing.

James donated land and funds to build several of Sycamore's buildings. At the time of his death, he was the wealthiest man in DeKalb County. He left no heirs to his estate. When his widow, Abbie Waterman, passed away in 1887, most of his property and fortune were divided among Sycamore's churches and schools. His residence on Somonauk Street and 500 acres adjoining were left for the creation of Waterman Hall, a school for girls.

As early as the 1840s, John and James Waterman lobbied to bring railroad service to Sycamore. It took them nearly 20 years, but in 1858, they played an instrumental role in creating the Sycamore & Cortland Railroad Company. John sat on the original board of directors and held several officers' positions, including vice president. James served as the company president for over a decade. When the Watermans' railroad dream finally paid off, it transformed the city in ways never imagined and made the brothers into two of Sycamore's wealthiest and most well-regarded residents.

As stipulated in Abbie Waterman's will, land and money from her husband's fortune were set aside to build Waterman Hall, a school for girls (pictured here c. 1895). The school opened in 1889 and operated for 30 years before changing over to a boys' school. It continued as a boys' school until it closed during the Great Depression.

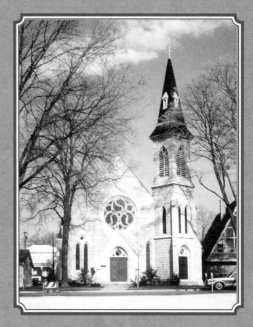

James and Abbie Waterman helped found the St. Peter's Episcopal parish in 1855. In 1877, James assisted Chicago architect George O. Garnsey in designing the interior and exterior of the elegant new church and had it erected entirely at his own expense.

Let Every Man Do His Best, 1858-1859

On Friday evening, July 30, 1858, a harsh easterly wind swept through Sycamore, damaging several buildings and injuring much of the local wheat crop. Despite the danger, a large and lively crowd packed the courthouse to hear a presentation from the board of directors of the newly formed Sycamore & Cortland Railroad Company (S&C). Reuben Ellwood, Judge Edward L. Mayo, and Daniel B. James—three of the company's thirteen directors—presented the townspeople with a plan to fund and build Sycamore's very own branch railroad.[1] The 4.6-mile "spur line" would run directly south out of Sycamore and connect with the Galena & Chicago Union (G&CU) depot at Cortland. From there, passengers could transfer over to the G&CU cars, which ran directly into Chicago. The directors gave Sycamore's residents every confidence that the railroad should and would be built. The new line would place the city "in the first rank among the inland towns of the Prairie State." Sycamore would no longer be "a world within itself."

For Sycamore to achieve this dream, the S&C's directors needed to raise $25,000, which they

Edward L. Mayo   **Daniel B. James**

planned to do through the sale of company stock. They knew that money was tight and that residents were skeptical about the plan, but they did have some collateral to ease everyone's fears. The G&CU saw the financial benefit this spur line could bring to its own business, and it had already promised to donate all of the rails and rolling stock—the engine along with freight and passenger cars—if the endeavor ever got off the ground. The S&C's directors used the strength of this promise to convince the cash-strapped community to get behind the project. As further incentive, they promised to award all contracts to local labor, and they offered to swap company stock in exchange for contract work.

[1] According to papers filed with the Illinois State Legislature, the Sycamore & Cortland Railroad Company officially organized on June 29, 1858. The *True Republican* did not mention the company until it reported on the July 30 public meeting. The Illinois State Legislature officially granted the S&C its charter on February 19, 1859. See Appendix A for the original legislation. For a list of the S&C's founding directors and all subsequent directors, see Appendix B.

Sycamoreans "heartily applauded" the company's plans, and the *True Republican* threw its full support behind the project. The paper reported that "our citizens are fairly awake to the importance of this road," and it encouraged all the residents of Sycamore to do their part in purchasing stock: "Let every man do his best!" The following week, the newspaper ran a long editorial outlining the benefit the railroad would bring to Sycamore:

Shall We Have a Railroad?

Every consideration of financial prosperity, of commercial necessity, and of actual comfort and convenience, should prompt our citizens to enlist earnestly in the work of building the Sycamore and Cortland Railroad. There would not have been such a spontaneous effort at this juncture… if the truth had not come home to every reflecting man in our midst that this railroad was a necessity which we could no longer live without…. This railroad is to benefit no other town, no other community, no other men, than Sycamore, its business community, and its citizens…. [Any] man that should contend that it would not raise the price of real estate ten per cent, would be by ninety-nine out of every hundred men voted a proper candidate for the lunatic asylum…. The truth is, there is no man who will say that we do not need the road, there is no one who will say that it will [not] pay, and there ought to be none who will say that we cannot build it.

No one could accuse the *True Republican* of acting without bias, however. In fact, it operated as the S&C's personal publicity machine. In March 1858, founder and publisher Charles Waite sold the paper to three local investors, one of whom was S&C co-director Daniel B. James, who also owned the James Block, the building where the newspaper was headquartered on the second floor. Another of the paper's owners, Caleb M. "Jersey" Brown, later secured the contract to grade the roadbed for the S&C's tracks. The newspaper's third owner, James H. Beveridge, became an S&C shareholder and was elected to the board of directors in April 1859. Furthermore, the S&C directors located their temporary office directly above the Roger, Wild & Smith dry goods store, which placed it on the second floor of the James Block and made it a cozy neighbor to the *True Republican*.

While the S&C's board of directors tirelessly canvassed the town to raise the necessary subscriptions, the "Our Village" section of the *True Republican* ran regular updates under the heading "Our Railroad." It reported on the "commendable energy" the directors expended on their new enterprise, and it never missed an opportunity to call on those who had not yet purchased stock to buy up whatever they could afford.

For all the pride the *True Republican* took in the project, the railroad was not without its detractors. Some members of the community opposed a plan that called for heavy spending during a deep financial crisis, and they urged their fellow residents to remain frugal and consider their finances carefully before deciding whether to invest in the new railroad. This coalition of railroad skeptics included poor farmers and merchants struggling through the depression, as well as wealthy businessmen who could easily afford the investment. They contended that the railroad would never prove profitable and would plunge the city deeper into debt. Some also argued that the entire enterprise was designed to line the pockets of a select few—the railroad's board of directors—while everyone else bore the brunt of the financial burden.

Much of the antagonism toward the railroad came from the *DeKalb County Republican Sentinel*. Its editors did what many newspaper editors of that period did when confronted with a contentious local issue: they either ignored it entirely or attacked it indirectly. The paper never criticized the railroad project outright, but it often spoke against the wasteful spending and reckless speculation that put the country in a crisis in the first place. Above all, the *Sentinel* lectured on the futility of throwing money at a financial crisis. While the *True Republican* featured regular updates on the railroad's progress and never missed an opportunity to sing its praises, the *Sentinel* barely said a word. In one article

that was unusually optimistic for the *Sentinel*, it reported on Sycamore's recent progress and future potential; however, the railroad project—well under way—was never mentioned. In the year that spanned the railroad's inception and completion, the *Sentinel* reported on the project two times, and only then to provide mundane details, such as the dimensions of the new depot.

In response to the *Sentinel* and other "cynics," the *True Republican* claimed that all their doubts would be put to rest by "ocular demonstration" when the engine finally rolled into town. But when subscriptions for the railroad stock fell short of expectation, the *True Republican's* efforts began to carry underlying threats to anyone who refused to invest: "We should be sorry to hear that there was a single man among our large property-holders who refused to subscribe…. There can be no excuse for men of means not subscribing liberally." A few weeks into the fundraising effort, the paper shifted its tone, blatantly attacking all men of means who had not yet purchased stock, declaring them "sharks or bloodsuckers, fastening themselves upon our community, sucking out the life-blood of the country, gorging themselves with the fruits of the severe toil of our hard-working citizens, and hoarding up their stores, doing good to nobody." The paper went on to call such a man "a curse to any community… Let him be acknowledged to have no public spirit." The *True*

Republican then went so far as to declare that any man of means who did not invest in the railroad was *"Anathema Maranatha,"* an expression used by the biblical Paul in his first letter to the Corinthians to indicate that any man who did not serve the Lord was doomed to destruction. In effect, the paper had declared that the railroad project was sacred, and not supporting it not only insulted the community, but God Himself.

A Sure Thing

Thanks to the "commendable efforts" of the railroad's board of directors—and, no doubt, the relentless threats from the city's largest newspaper—in just over a month the S&C raised the necessary funds to begin work on the railroad. On September 7, 1858, the *True Republican* ran the following headline: "OUT OF THE WOODS!—OUR RAILROAD A SURE THING!" The article noted that "this is an assurance that will infuse into our community new life, and energy, and hope.... In the present hard times, the raising of the stock of the Railroad Company is an evidence of the strong determination that prevails among our citizens to fulfill for Sycamore such a destiny." It also proposed the question, "If she has thus progressed *without* a railroad, what may she not do *with* a railroad?"

With the funding secured, the S&C's directors wasted no time in getting construction underway. They immediately advertised for contractors to provide the ties and to begin grading the bed for the railroad. They then secured the services of an experienced topographical engineer, F. L. Hildebrand, to survey the new route and oversee its construction. As mentioned, the contract for grading and laying the ties went to *True Republican* co-owner "Jersey" Brown and his partner, a man with the last name Ames from Chicago.

TO RAIL ROAD CONTRACTORS

SEALED proposals will be received until September 18 for the construction of the Sycamore and Cortland Railroad. Said Road is about 4 1/2 miles in length, and is required to be built during the coming autumn. Bids will be received for furnishing ties and completing the entire work of the Road ready for ballasting, or separate bids for the whole grading or for sections of 1/2 mile each, with culverts, also separate bids for ties, and also separate bids for laying ties and track.

Profiles and specifications can be seen at the Banking office of J.S. Waterman and after September 11, 1858

Address J.C. Waterman, Pres. Or H. L. Boies, Sec.Sycamore, September 4th, 1858

The *True Republican's* ad for contractors

On September 29, 1858, the S&C broke ground on its new line. The laboring party consisted of 40 to 50 local men working in two teams, one in Sycamore and one in Cortland, with each team pushing toward the other so they could meet somewhere in the middle. Several of these men were undoubtedly relieved to find work during those hard times.

Progress proved slow, however, due to three weeks of unrelenting rain that turned all of Sycamore into a seeping mud-pit. To add to the difficulty, the rain let up only long enough to usher in several days of severe snow. The snow piled precariously atop "the villainous pinnacles and promontories of congealed mud," which made travel or construction of any kind nearly impossible. Despite the "extreme unfavorableness of the weather," the contractors soldiered on. By mid-November, they had completed over a mile in each direction. By January 1859, working under extreme cold and snow, they had nearly completed the grading and began hauling the 5,500 wood ties onto the railroad bed.

In April, the *True Republican* spurred the workers: "Push it along, gentlemen. Strain every nerve; put forth every exertion; leave no stone unturned. Every interest of our village cries out for an early consummation of the enterprise." And the contractors did push on, part of the time working under the glow of a comet hovering in the night sky, which was widely reported in several national newspapers.

The railroad faced further delays when spring started late that year, keeping the farmers busy in their fields and depriving the project of its labor force. Everyone put in extra work in their own fields under the expectation that by late summer or early fall they would be sending their grain and produce out on the train, distributing it to the wider market. The railroad's completion had to be postponed while the contractors rounded up enough men to continue construction. The *True Republican* ran the following: "Labor, both of men and teams, will find ready employment upon the Railroad and elsewhere."

The biggest threat to the entire enterprise came in midsummer when the railroad bed was completed, the ties laid, and all that remained was for the G&CU to deliver the promised iron rails. The company had the iron rails ready to ship to Cortland, but then it elected a new board of directors who decided they weren't going to give the S&C its promised rails or the rolling stock. Instead, the directors decided to sell everything to the company for fair market value. In a panic, the S&C directors called an emergency meeting with the people of Sycamore to explain the predicament. With the track fully graded, the ties mostly laid, and thousands of dollars of the public's money already spent, the railroad's failure at this juncture would have been a complete disaster for Sycamore. The S&C directors hastily outlined a plan to raise the funds through an additional stock sale, but that would take time, and they needed the rails immediately. So seven of the S&C's directors stepped forward—James H. Beveridge, James and John Waterman, Reuben Ellwood, Charles Kellum, H. L. Boies, and William J. Hunt—and put up the money themselves, with the understanding that the company would pay them back at some future date. These funds procured the rails and saved the project. While the contractors rushed to install the new rails, the S&C began selling additional shares to raise money for the rolling stock. Within only a few days, Sycamoreans stepped up to the challenge and snapped up the new shares. Now the company had the rails and enough money to purchase its own locomotive and rolling stock. It was back on track to finish the railroad by the fall.

To explain away the railroad's repeated delays, the *True Republican* offered the simple excuse that "this fall was as soon as it was really desired by the country." The paper also eased stockholders fears by declaring: "the engine bell will sound in our streets before sleigh-bells are heard again."

The First Depot

The S&C located its depot in the southwest corner of town, on the northeast corner of the intersection at Sacramento Avenue and High Street. Some community members quibbled over this location, arguing that it put the depot too far from the courthouse and the city's business center. Others defended the location, arguing that it prevented the train from screaming right through the middle of town, inconveniently—and dangerously—cutting Sycamore in half like the railroad in DeKalb had done to that city (and still does today). The location also forced anyone traveling to the courthouse to walk past just about every business in town, thus creating a boon to the local economy. There were also more personal reasons at play. If the railroad extended all the way to the courthouse, then the tracks would have crossed Somonauk Street, which housed several of Sycamore's wealthiest citizens, including several of the S&C's board of directors. It is doubtful that any of them wanted a railroad chugging through their backyards. Moreover, several of the railroad's directors owned land near the depot site. In August 1858, less than two months after the S&C officially organized, James S. Waterman and Reuben Ellwood purchased 200 acres of land in the southwest corner of town. They had it surveyed and laid out into village lots. When the depot site was confirmed, they sold many of these lots for a considerable profit. The rest of the land they kept as an investment.

In early 1859, news of the railroad attracted Chicago and Eastern investors who soon began arriving in town to speculate on land and business prospects. By summer, the neighborhood surrounding the new depot grounds buzzed with activity. Piles of brick and stone stood amongst the yellow stacks of fresh lumber that covered the whole area. Within weeks, the skeletal framework of new stores, shops, and private dwellings filled the landscape.

The *True Republican* reported that 30 new dwellings were under construction at one time, many of which were intended as rentals for the new residents the railroad would undoubtedly bring to town. Multiple warehouses, grain elevators, lumberyards, and stockyards made their appearance near the depot. New churches and a new school also sprang up. By summer's end, the city could boast that every hotel, boarding house, and rental home was full, with hardly a "For Rent" sign to be found. To accommodate all of these new arrivals—and to spare them from the mud that so often plagued the city—the city council made plans to build new sidewalks and regrade the streets.

By early fall of 1859, Sycamore's numerous improvements gave it the appearance of a brand new city. In a time when towns throughout the country saw real estate values cut in half, landowners in Sycamore saw their real estate values increase substantially.

According to an 1898 issue of the *True Republican*, the man responsible for building Sycamore's first railroad depot was Russell B. Tewksbury, a local contractor who went on to serve with the 105th Illinois Infantry in the Civil War before relocating to Chicago. Tewksbury's simple wood-frame depot measured 20-by-60 feet and stood two stories high. A covered porch extended seven feet from the building and wrapped around all four sides. Tewksbury and his men completed the building and a nearby 25-foot well by early September, just a few short weeks before the locomotive's much-anticipated arrival.

With the railroad depot complete and only a few iron rails remaining to be laid, the *True Republican* captured the general mood around town: "Our citizens begin to feel as though they could see their way out of the woods, and they are getting 'good and ready' to give a glorious shout."

In Cortland, the S&C tracks ran straight south until they reached what is now North Spruce Street and made a sharp turn east toward the depot on West North Avenue.

The Engine Is Coming!

At 4 p.m. on Saturday, October 8, 1859, a shrill whistle split the air, signaling that Sycamore's "promise of greater prosperity" had finally arrived. The cry went out: "The engine is coming!" and Sycamoreans of all ages filled the streets. They stared at the distant plumes of white smoke belching up in the sky, listened as the faint *chuffa-chuffa-chuffa* grew louder, felt an unfamiliar rumbling beneath their feet, and then rushed *en masse* to the depot to herald the arrival of Sycamore's first iron horse.

The wood-burning locomotive—miniscule by today's standards—would have seemed colossal as it pulled up alongside the new depot. A festive atmosphere surrounded the building as everyone swarmed the rumbling locomotive, clamoring to get a look at the machine they had all helped bring to town through hard work and sacrifice. The S&C had purchased the eight-to-ten-year-old locomotive second hand for $6,000, which was all the company could afford. John Waterman had travelled east to pick it up from another railroad. He had spent an additional $500 to get it in working order. None of that mattered to Sycamore's proud residents, however, as they stood outside the depot and listened to the guttural sound of the engine's strange mechanical breathing, watched the steam erupt from its towering haystack boiler, and marveled at the massive size of this remarkable piece of technology. Sycamore's first engineer, George Chilson, greeted the crowd with another ear-splitting blast of the locomotive's steam whistle and everyone breathed in the sickly sweet smell of oil and metal, an odor that would permeate Sycamore's streets for the next 125 years.

The only known photograph of Sycamore's first engine, taken c. 1865. The author has found conflicting information as to the identity of the two men. Local historian O. T. Willard identified them as (L-R) Ed Rose, conductor, and William Ayre, engineer. Other sources have identified the man on the right as engineer John Tucker. In those days, locomotives went by a single name; numbering and coding did not come about until many years later. The S&C aptly named its first locomotive *Sycamore*.

The *True Republican* summarized the significance of the occasion: "It was the event that signalizes our actual connection with the great railroad world—the event that cancels forever the by-word that 'Sycamore is an out-of-the-way place.' We are now a town among towns, a point among points." Even the *Sentinel* begrudgingly marked the occasion: "We are now able to speak positively concerning the S&CRR… and who will not concede to Sycamore a commendable degree of enterprise for having, in these hard times, built a railroad."

On the following Monday, the S&C's directors celebrated the engine's long-awaited arrival with a free round-trip excursion to Cortland. They did not have a passenger car yet, so they laid boards across flatbed freight cars for seating. Over 100 Sycamoreans took up the offer and a merry mood accompanied the almost 10-mile round trip. During this inaugural run, however, local lawyer A. C. Allen experienced an unfortunate mishap, which the *Sentinel* no doubt delighted in reporting:

> Squire Allen was standing just behind a board, used as a seat, which projected several feet on each side of the car. As the train was moving with tolerable speed, one end of the board struck a fence post, and the squire, who was composedly enjoying the beauties of the surrounding scenery, was very unceremoniously called upon to change ends, which he proceeded to do with a degree of speed quite uncommon to the man. Quick as a flash the Squire's head was where his feet ought to be, and his heels were cutting a series of flourishes in the space above, quite amusing to beholders. Not satisfied with his position, the Squire inverted himself as soon as possible thereafter, minus a watch christal, a few inches of shin bark, and plus an Assault and Battery bump on top of his cranium. The Squire thinks the railroad is an institution, but he is enthusiastically advocating the expediency of procuring a class of cars with immovable seats.[2]

The next day, the S&C began its regular schedule with two runs to Cortland, the first at 10:30 a.m. and the second at 7:00 p.m., returning at 12:00 p.m. and 8:00 p.m. The engineer would blow the whistle 20 minutes before each departure to give passengers plenty of time to get to the depot. The engine ran at an average speed of 15 miles per hour and each run took approximately 20 minutes. Including the transfer at Cortland, and depending on the time of the connection, a one-way trip to Chicago took approximately three-and-a-half hours.

Within the first few days of operation, shipments of wheat began piling up inside local warehouses and storage elevators, deposited there by area farmers eager to get their goods to market. Over the next few weeks, fresh goods and capital flowed into the town. "Every fair day witnesses our streets filled up with carriages from the country," the *True Republican* reported, "bringing in all sorts of produce which is exchanged for cash, groceries, dry goods, etc."

---

[2]The *True Republican* made no mention of this incident.

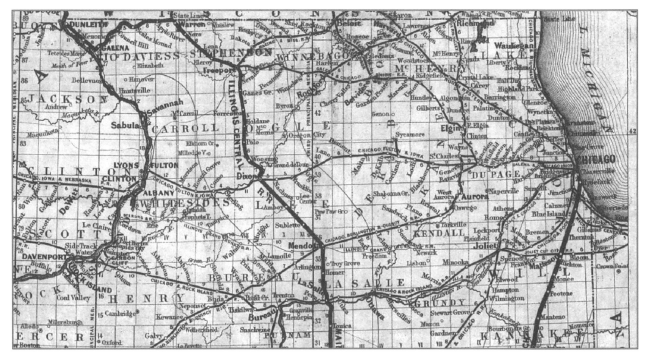

This 1862 Illinois railroad map shows the G&CU's Chicago, Fulton & Iowa line (formerly known as the Dixon Air Line) connecting Chicago to the Mississippi River by way of Cortland and DeKalb. The S&C line is included on the map, though not mentioned by name. (Library of Congress)

While the branch railroad ran only the 4.6 miles between Sycamore and Cortland and seemed miniscule compared to the larger railroads that stretched across the Midwest, it became the most important outlet to the city's commerce. It spread Sycamore's influence across a much wider territory, gave new life to the city's struggling merchants and businessmen, and ushered in a new era of prosperity.

SYCAMORE & CORTLAND RAILWAY.

A train leaves Sycamore at 11 15 A. M., arriving at Cortland (5 miles) 11 35 A. M., in time for the train to Chicago on the Fulton Branch of Galena & Chicago Union Railway.

Returning—Leave Cortland at 3 00 P. M., on the arrival of the train from Chicago.

JOHN C. WATERMAN, Pres., Sycamore, Ill.

The above timetable is from an 1867 issue of *Appleton's Railway Guide*. The S&C's directors knew that having a railroad would get Sycamore listed in national railway guides, which would bring more exposure to the city. (Author's collection)

In 1947, almost 90 years after the railroad's completion, local historian O. T. Willard characterized the arrival of Sycamore's first locomotive as "the one outstanding event that figured in the future prosperity of early Sycamore."

DeKalb c. 1860

If Sycamore had not built the spur line, the small but fast-growing city of DeKalb would have overtaken its neighbor to the north and secured the county seat.

Based on newspaper coverage of the railroad's construction, it may have seemed like the S&C directors, in their mad rush to completion, were competing in some sort of race. What the directors didn't know at the time was that they actually *were* in a race, but not against another town or railroad. A year after the S&C began operations, a divided nation teetered on the brink of civil war. Iron was redirected to the war effort, which made prices soar. Larger railroads had to stop new construction. Smaller railroads that had not yet completed their tracks had to cease operations altogether. If the S&C had delayed its work for one year, the cost of new rails and rolling stock would have grown beyond the company's reach. Sycamore's little spur line never would have existed, new businesses never would have appeared, and the "hard times" would have consumed the town. Without the prosperous growth Sycamore needed to prove its worth to the region, it would have been stripped of the county seat by the more prosperous DeKalb. To say that Sycamore's five-mile spur line merely offered convenience to the town is a gross understatement. The Sycamore & Cortland Railroad saved the town from oblivion and allowed Sycamore to continue growing to meet the demands of the competitive frontier market.[3]

---

[3] Sycamore's success, however, had an adverse effect on Cortland. Farmers in and around Sycamore and in the northern part of the county had relied on Cortland to ship their goods. The S&C took most of that market. Cortland's brief brush with prosperity came to an end and it never again enjoyed the growth it had experienced in the 1850s.

The Ellwood Brothers

The name of Ellwood is as closely interwoven in the history of DeKalb County and its development and prosperity as that of any family that ever lived within the limits of its rich territory.

U. S. Congressman Albert J. Hopkins, 1886

Ellwood Family c. 1895

Back Row (L–R) – unidentified boy, Abram (Reuben's eldest son), and Isaac.
Front Row (L–R) – Chauncey, Alonzo, Hiram, and James. (Ellwood House Museum)

No family had a larger impact on DeKalb County than the Ellwoods. Their numerous businesses, factories, and civic efforts transformed the entire region. According to the *True Republican*, the brothers "were blessed with a sturdy physique, indomitable energy, and natural business acumen."

Abraham and Sarah Ellwood with daughters

Abraham and Sarah De Long Ellwood had 11 children, all born in Montgomery County, New York. At the urging of their son Reuben, Abraham and Sarah moved to Sycamore in 1855. They are pictured here with their daughters (L–R) Alida Young, Malinda Sixbury, and Eliza Bowman.

Abraham Ellwood and Sarah Delong of Montgomery County, New York, had eleven children: four girls and seven boys. Of those eleven children, nine would eventually settle in DeKalb County. The first Ellwood to arrive was not one of the well-known brothers, but Nancy Ellwood, the oldest sibling. She and her husband Livingston Walrod moved to Sycamore in 1836. Their son, James Walrod, was the first white settler born in Sycamore.

Nancy's brother and sister, Reuben and Malinda, followed a year later, along with Malinda's husband, Joseph Sixbury.

Reuben Ellwood was only 16 when he made the journey by covered wagon to Sycamore. He quickly acquired 160 acres of land. His older brother, Chauncey, joined him in 1838. The brothers took up farming while Chauncey also

practiced law. They weren't terribly successful, and after a few years of toil, they headed back east, but they kept the land they owned in Sycamore. Reuben worked in a broom manufacturing business with his brothers James and Hiram. He later tried his hand at politics and was elected to the New York Legislature in 1851.

In 1855, Reuben encouraged his family to move to the land he owned in Sycamore. His parents relocated there, along with four of his brothers. Alonzo opened a hardware store and James took up farming. Two of the brothers began operations in DeKalb: a grocery and drug store for Hiram and a hardware store for Isaac. When farming didn't work out for James, he entered the mercantile business with Chauncey and ran it successfully for many years.

Reuben joined his brothers in 1857 and became a partner in Alonzo's hardware store. Chauncy followed a year later and opened a mercantile business. Alonzo later ran a flaxseed mill with Chauncey and a separate hardware store with James Waterman. After Reuben and Chauncey helped found the Sycamore & Cortland Railroad, Reuben made a large amount of money selling real estate he had purchased around the depot site. In 1875, he organized the Reuben Ellwood Manufacturing Company, which built agricultural implements in a large factory near the depot. Several of his brothers became shareholders and worked for the company.

Isaac, the youngest Ellwood brother, achieved the most success. In 1874, he entered into a partnership with Joseph Glidden to manufacture Glidden's revolutionary new product: barbed wire. Isaac commenced building a barbed wire empire that made him one of the wealthiest men in Illinois and forever changed the course of the county. Isaac's success allowed him to play a key role in bringing the Northern Illinois State Normal School (later Northern Illinois University) to DeKalb in 1895.

While the brothers achieved success in the private sector, they proved their worth in the public sector as well. Hiram was elected county treasurer in 1859. In DeKalb, he served as a board of trustees member, the city school director, city supervisor, postmaster, and eventually Mayor. When Sycamore officially incorporated as a city in 1869, Reuben Ellwood was elected its first mayor. In 1882, he was elected as a representative to the U.S. Congress. Alonzo served as county assessor, chairman of Sycamore's board of trustees, and city alderman. James became Sycamore's postmaster in 1898.

While founding and furthering the business and civic interests of DeKalb County, the Ellwood brothers remained loyal not only to their fellow citizens, but to each other. They regularly partnered with, invested in, and supported one another's business enterprises. Every year on New Year's Day, the whole family gathered for a reunion at Chauncey's house on Somonauk Street.

Chauncey was not the wealthiest or most successful Ellwood brother, but he had a reputation as the most easygoing and approachable. Of all the brothers, he was most deserving of the title "Jack-of-all trades." While still a young man in New York, Chauncey taught classes on mathematics, philosophy, and Latin. He studied law, immersed himself in politics, and served as a postmaster and superintendent of schools. In Sycamore, he was appointed postmaster in 1861. He also served as president of Sycamore's board of education and from 1866 to 1870 he served as secretary of the Illinois state senate. For several years, he was the vice president and general manager of the Sycamore & Cortland Railroad and oversaw the construction of the large brick and stone depot that still stands today. He was also president and manager of Elmwood Cemetery, stockholder and director of both the Reuben Ellwood Manufacturing Company and the Marsh Harvester Manufacturing Company. In addition to these other duties, he owned and operated his own boot and shoe store.

At an 1877 ceremony honoring Chauncey's service to the city, Mayor Nathan Lattin said this about the eldest Ellwood brother: "When years have passed away, and with them he and ourselves, then his name will shine bright on the roll of honor among those who stood faithful and true to the interests, welfare, growth and prosperity of this, the most beautiful little city in the world."

Ellwood Family Tree

10. Isaac
b. August 3, 1833;
d. August 15, 1910
Moved to DeKalb in 1855

11. Alida Young
b. 1838; d. 1889
Lived in DeKalb

7. Livingston*
b. 1825; d. unknown
Lived in Schenectady New York

8. Hiram
b. September 19, 1828;
d. 1898
Moved to DeKalb in 1856

9. James
b. April 26, 1831;
d. September 5, 1907
Moved to Sycamore in 1855

4. Eliza Bowman*
b. 1819; d. 1894
Lived in Cherry Valley, New York

5. Reuben
b. February 17, 1821;
d. July 1, 1886
Moved to Sycamore in
1837–1842; returned in 1857

6. Alonzo
b. June 17, 1823;
d. August 26, 1899
Moved to Sycamore in 1855

1. Nancy Walrod
b.1813; d. 1842
Moved to Sycamore in 1836

2. Malinda Sixbury
b. 1815; d. 1888
Moved to Sycamore in 1837

3. Chauncey
b. December 24, 1816;
d. May 6, 1897
Moved to Sycamore in
1838–1842; returned in 1858

Abraham Ellwood
b. November 7, 1792
d. August 24, 1872

Sarah De Long (Ellwood)
b. February 23, 1795
d. January 17, 1879

Eliza and Livingston were the only Ellwood
siblings who did not move west.

43

Sycamore in the War Years, 1860-1869

The Rail Road has made Sycamore the center of a much larger extent of territory than it was ever able to command before.

True Republican, Nov. 23, 1859

The dawn of a new decade saw the United States facing a divisive war that would nearly destroy the nation. Despite this looming threat, Sycamore's streets flourished with new houses, new businesses, and new faces. The population swelled to 2,280, and the newspapers filled their local columns with updates on who was building what and where. The railroad had brought a "reviving impulse" to a "decaying town." Capital flowed in and new businesses followed. Hotels overflowed with permanent residents as new housing became scarce and rentals quickly filled. The *True Republican* reported: "This little railroad has been the foundation of all that steady and healthy growth and increase with which we have since been favored."

Although Sycamore's railroad brought prosperity to the town, it also brought added attention to the poor state of Sycamore's streets. Sycamoreans believed the railroad would "permit us to turn up our noses" at the muddy roads that had forever impeded the city's progress. The railroad, however, made the problem much worse. The increased traffic from residents trying to reach the depot made the recently graded roads muddier than ever before. The site around the depot was purported to be the worst offender of all. Local newspapers complained that following any heavy rain, visitors fresh off the train found themselves instantly mired "knee deep and upward." And when they reached State Street, they were greeted with a most peculiar sight: several of Sycamore's finest citizens perched along rail fences, performing an embarrassing and precarious sort of shuffle to avoid stepping into the muddy street. Such a sight would have brought only temporary amusement, until the visitors realized that they would have to do the same in order to preserve the state of their dress. Harmon Paine, the proprietor of Paine's Hotel, located northeast of the depot on the corner of State and California streets, helped build a new sidewalk between the two locations so visitors could avoid Sycamore's muddy roads, at least until they arrived at his establishment.

While Sycamore set about improving its roads for its influx of visitors, the new railroad performed a different, more heroic deed in Cortland. When a house in Cortland caught fire and the flames spread rapidly, the only person who saw them was George Chilson, the Sycamore & Cortland (S&C) engineer, who had been sitting in his locomotive at the Cortland depot waiting for the Galena & Chicago Union (G&CU) train to arrive from Chicago. The quick-thinking engineer forced the engine to vent such a harsh and grating noise that Cortland's residents rushed into the streets, saw the blaze, and quickly extinguished it before it spread to the rest of the town.

The railroad's early days were not without difficulty. During its first winter of operation, the engine proved to be no match for the heavy snows. When it became stuck in the drifts, the engineer had to shut it down or it would quickly burn up its supply of wood and water. When the train shut down, passengers and freight had to be rescued by sleds equipped with straw, quilts, and robes for warmth. In addition, the well dug near the depot failed soon after completion. The steam engine couldn't operate without water, so at a considerable expense, the railroad temporarily hired men to haul water in buckets from the Kishwaukee River to the depot. On some occasions, due to a lack of water, the railroad had to cancel runs altogether, which lost the company considerable revenue. The railroad was in operation for over a year before a work crew successfully reached a water vein by sinking a 60-foot well outside the depot.

By 1862, the company had incurred $10,000 in debt to the G&CU. It had borrowed money for materials during the initial construction, and later for repairs to the rails and to the engine. The S&C's directors and shareholders could not pay the debt, so they offered to sell $10,000 in stock (a quarter of the company) to the town of Sycamore. Sycamore held an election to vote on the proposal and it passed 2 to 1. Sycamore's citizens now owned a quarter of the S&C, making the company literally a public institution. From that moment on, the annual appointment of a new board of directors had to be put to a public vote.[1]

The little branch line also suffered from scheduling conflicts. Passengers who arrived in Cortland on a late-night train either had to wait until the next day to catch the S&C or hire a late-night stage to transport them to Sycamore. In 1863, the railroad bought one of Cortland's stage businesses, outfitted a horse-drawn streetcar with flanged wheels so it could be pulled on the rails, and hired Harry Little to run it. The *True Republican* reported that "the easy, elegant, well warmed, well lighted little coach now makes the journey from Cortland the most social and pleasant part of the trip from Chicago instead of being, as it once was, a terror."

---

[1] Newspaper reports indicated that these elections usually saw a low turnout. Voting was based on shares (1 share = 1 vote). So the public vote accounted for only a quarter of the total vote. In addition, elections were always held the first week of January, which would have been a difficult time for Sycamoreans to travel to vote in an election in which they had little influence.

Myth of the Horse-Drawn Railcar

In *Past and Present of DeKalb County, Illinois, vol. 1* (1907), Lewis M. Gross stated that the Sycamore & Cortland Railroad was built in 1859, but due to a lack of funds, the company could not afford an engine. As a result, "for many years the goods were placed on cars and hauled from Cortland to Sycamore by horses." Gross's book contains the earliest version of this horse-drawn-railcar story, and it has persisted ever since, appearing in newspapers and other local history books.

Because both the *True Republican* and the *Sentinel* reported on the exciting events surrounding the arrival of the engine in 1859—with the railroad tracks barely complete—we know that the horse-drawn-railcar story is a myth. The S&C had a fully functional engine on the day the railroad opened for business.

The myth may have grown out of stories of a horse-drawn railcar that ran on a St. Charles railroad for an indeterminate amount of time in the early 1850s. It also may have been influenced by the independent operators who outfitted their horse-drawn wagons and carriages to run on the tracks between Sycamore and Cortland. In the S&C's early days, irregular timetables often left passengers stranded, sometimes for hours, awaiting their connection. If a passenger arrived at Cortland on the night train, he or she had to wait until morning to catch the next S&C run to Sycamore. Independent operators took advantage of these irregular schedules and used the tracks to carry passengers and packages between cities after the last trains had run for the day. When the railroad began adding more daily runs in the mid-1860s, there was no longer a need for this mode of transportation and it soon disappeared.

The 1860 Presidential Race

In 1860, Sycamore's newspapers devoted the bulk of their columns to politics and the impending presidential election. The *True Republican*, of course, backed Abraham Lincoln, and it wasted no space in rallying Sycamoreans to Old Abe's side, claiming they were fighting against "Fraud, Fusion, Cotton, Disunion and Treason." Sycamore held regular Republican rallies, which filled the streets and meeting halls with hundreds of ardent Lincoln supporters. As the election grew near, guest speakers came to town nearly every evening—usually by way of the S&C—and packed Sycamore's halls with large crowds. Many of these meetings ended with jubilant, torch-lit parades through the streets.

After a report on one well-attended rally, the *True Republican* sacrificed a little column space to a corresponding rally held by the Democrats: "P.S. The Domocrats [sic] held a meeting at the court house on the same evening. About 40 persons were present, and the enthusiasm was quite as great as could be expected in the rank of those engaged in the work of digging their own graves." As the election grew near, the editorial battle between local newspapers grew heated. At one point, the editor of the *True Republican*—an ardent Lincolnite—attacked his Democratic counterpart at the *Sentinel* with this fiery insult: "Beelzebub and chief lieutenant devil must yield the palm to the graceless liar, the cowardly slanderer, the low, filthy, blackguard that now conducts the *Sentinel*."

The new railroad had arrived just in time to facilitate Sycamore's political activities. With easy access to the main line through Cortland, people from all over the region could travel to Sycamore to attend the rallies. Likewise, Sycamoreans could attend rallies all over the state. The S&C even provided discounted tickets to those traveling to political conventions in Chicago. In August 1860, the *True Republican* ran the following tongue-in-cheek piece:

> Shipped in good condition, from the depot, in this place as our due proportion to the immense gathering at Springfield tomorrow... fifty real, live, wide-awake, rail-splitting Republicans. Success to the boys and the cause in which they are engaged. We hope that they will renew their political strength, get a peep at "Old Abe" at his home, return in safety, with their "lamps trimmed and burning" lighting the path to victory in November.

The Conflict Begins

After the firing on Fort Sumter in April 1861, Sycamore felt the fever of civil war the same as every other town in the region, and it quickly threw itself into the war effort. The newspapers called on the young men of Sycamore to rush through their farm work so they could enlist at a moment's

notice. Sycamore's women set to work sewing garments and banners for the volunteer soldiers. Citizens pooled money to support poor families who had sent off their men to fight. The county fair gave away cash prizes in a marksmanship contest where the participants shot at a figure of Jefferson Davis. Sycamore held a "war meeting" at the courthouse, in which the people passed a tax to raise a $50 bounty to any recruit from DeKalb County. Similar meetings were held throughout the war and usually involved a wounded soldier paraded onstage to tell his tales of heroism and sacrifice. The new taxes always passed.

A curious sight on Sycamore's muddy streets would have been the daily drilling of the city's stalwart volunteers, who, accompanied by fife and drum, marched around town armed with broom handles that a local hardware store had donated until the young men could get real guns. Many of the boys grew impatient while awaiting orders from Springfield. When the orders finally came, the whole town turned out at the depot to see off the young soldiers. The *True Republican* reported on the emotional event: "Never before have we seen tears flowing from so many eyes at once. Even strong men bowed their heads and wept at the scene." When the train whistle blew, the volunteers yelled their goodbyes and the cheering but somber crowd waved their handkerchiefs until the cars were out of sight. At Cortland, the soldiers boarded a westbound G&CU train and headed to camp at Dixon. From there, they trekked down muddy roads, survived off quarter rations, and camped in sheep pens and cattle sheds on their way to the battle fields that would test their mettle.

Several prominent Sycamoreans answered the call to duty. The editors of both the *True Republican* and the *Sentinel* enlisted, as did the S&C's depot agent and conductor, Edward M. Knapp.[2] A local doctor was appointed to the army's board of medical examiners. A local businessman procured horses to pull Union artillery. Even the Sycamore Brass Band played its part, accompanying several regiments to Missouri, where it entertained the troops with music that "cannot be surpassed in any village east or west." In all, 307 Sycamore men served the cause.[3]

Sycamore Soldiers On

The railroad had provided a brief relief from the hard times, but the war brought those prosperous days to an abrupt end. Due to inflation and the scarcity of men and materials,

While he was away at war, Lt. Colonel Everell F. Dutton corresponded with his wife several times a week. In August 1864, while stationed near Atlanta, Dutton had not received a letter in quite some time, so he wrote to his wife, asking, "Why the dickens don't I get a letter from my darling[?]" He then sarcastically asked if it was because the S&C's railroad had been cut and torn up by the enemy (the fate of most Southern railroads caught in the war zone).

---

[2] Edward M. Knapp was killed at the battle of Shiloh/Pittsburg Landing (April 6-7, 1862).

[3] Author's note: The focus of this book prevents me from elaborating on Sycamore's significant contributions to the Civil War, which deserve far more attention than they receive here. For further reading on the subject, see *History of DeKalb County, Illinois* by H. L. Boies. Boies dedicated nearly half of his book's 530 pages to the Civil War, calling it "the most interesting, most honorable and most eventful portion of the history of the County of DeKalb."

few new businesses and buildings went up and real estate sales slowed to a crawl. Sycamore's farmers and the railroad, however, did benefit from the sudden demand for grain brought on by the war.

While the male population made its way south, Sycamoreans still found some time for celebrations and city improvements. They continued the annual Fourth of July celebrations, and they kept planting new shade trees all around the city to improve its appearance and cool the streets and homesteads on those warm summer days. Late in the war, however, Sycamore's beautiful shade trees, which were considered one of the city's "chief attractions," were attacked by borer insects and most of them eventually died. Without the money to replace them, Sycamoreans suffered these dead, decaying, skeletal trees for several years until they could be removed and replaced with hardier maples and elms. The stately maples came to dominate Sycamore's streets throughout the rest of the century.

Sycamore still had no telegraph, so any news from the battlefront came in by way of the railroad: from newly arrived passengers, returning soldiers, or the increasingly erratic mail shipments. Each arriving train brought a throng

From an 1870's humor magazine:

Teacher: Children, when the war broke out and all the able-bodied men enlisted in the army, what motives took them to the front?

Brightest Boy (triumphantly): Locomotives!

of residents down to the depot, all eager to hear news of friends or loved ones. The depot grew busy with a never-ending stream of returning and injured soldiers, many of whom, the newspaper reported, quickly grew restless and longed for "the excitement of the tented field." Throughout the war, veteran soldiers and raw recruits filled the streets, making Sycamore a lively place until the inevitable day when the soldiers gathered at the depot and returned to active duty.

Despite the absence of the city's young men, records show that Sycamore's leaders remained focused on familiar local problems, such as muddy streets, inadequate sidewalks, and cows running loose in the city and stealing hay from the wagons of unsuspecting farmers (a quickly passed city ordinance put an end to this last transgression).

The Chicago & North Western Arrives

During the war years, the most significant event to affect Sycamore's railroad history took place on June 20, 1864, when the G&CU merged with the Chicago & North Western Railway (C&NW).

The C&NW could trace its origins back to June 2, 1859, when investors chartered the company to buy the defunct Chicago, St. Paul & Fond du Lac Railroad (which had bought up and absorbed a few railroads in its own time). Several C&NW investors had strong business interests in Chicago, and they wanted to see that city grow into the region's most important transportation hub. So with Chicago as the company's base of operations, they began branching their railroads across Illinois and into Wisconsin, Minnesota, and Michigan's Upper Peninsula. But by 1864, the C&NW controlled just 315 miles of track, which paled in comparison to its rival, the G&CU, which operated 545 miles of track.

By this time, railroad companies had been consolidating for years—merging with and absorbing smaller railroads to stay competitive—but it came as a great shock when the C&NW and the G&CU suddenly announced their plan to merge in 1864. These were two of the biggest, wealthiest, most competitive railroad conglomerates in the nation, and people just didn't think a merger between them was possible. It came as an even greater shock when, on June 20, 1864, stockholders for both companies voted in favor of the plan.

At the time, the C&NW-G&CU deal was one of the biggest mergers in railroad history. The new company's combined 860 miles of track made it the nation's longest railroad carrier. Newspapers across the country called the merger "The Great Consolidation."

Because the Galena & Chicago Union Railroad was a misnomer—the company had never actually built its tracks to Galena—the new board of directors dropped the name. From that point on, when the S&C ran its little locomotive down to Cortland, it no longer met up with the G&CU. It met up with the Chicago & North Western Railway.

Sycamore Recovers from the War

The close of the war brought another building boom to Sycamore. Despite exorbitant inflation and a deficiency of supplies, returning soldiers went straight back to their trades. Confidence in the economy returned with them. New buildings and businesses soon sprang up all over town, including the Wilkins Block (at the site of the present-day Sycamore Center), the first substantial building erected since before the war.

In the vicinity of the depot, enterprising Sycamoreans built a new grain elevator, a hay press, a steam sorghum factory, a machine shop, a cooper's shop, several lumberyards, and an iron foundry. Sycamore also hired Chicago architect Gurdon P. Randall to design a new schoolhouse to replace one that had recently burned down. The schoolhouse, the most elegant seen in the county at that time, was featured in several architectural journals. In October 1865, several patriotic citizens pitched in and raised almost $4,000 to build a monument in front of the courthouse to honor Sycamore's fallen soldiers. Even though money remained tight, there was a general sense that Sycamore's better days were ahead.

For many years this drawing of Sycamore's schoolhouse by Gurdon P. Randall became representative of Sycamore. It was featured in several local history books and travel guides. It is reprinted in a book of architectural designs that Randall published in 1868, showcasing his best work. H. L. Boies featured it before the title page of his *History of DeKalb County, Illinois.*

Struggle for the County Seat

In early 1865, DeKalb lawyer I. V. Randall went before the state legislature at Springfield and presented a bill to remove the county seat from Sycamore and relocate it to DeKalb. By now, Sycamore had built up a large population of merchants and businessmen who had a vested interest in the future of their town. A delegation of angry Sycamoreans descended on Springfield with petitions in hand and invective speeches at the ready. They saw to it that the bill was quickly defeated. H. L. Boies noted that the petitions presented by both sides carried more signatures than people living in the county, including several signatures from people long deceased.

To prevent future takeover attempts—by DeKalb or anyone else—Sycamoreans knew they had to be enterprising and vigilant. They needed more manufacturing. They needed to extend the railroad or secure a second one. As for the S&C, its directors thought a good start might be the construction of a new depot.

New Growth and a New Depot

As early as 1863, the S&C's directors discussed plans to build a "small but elegant" new depot and then convert the old depot to accommodate freight. The *True Republican* hailed the plan, stressing the "unsightly" condition of the original depot and its tendency to be "surrounded by mud of uncommon depth and dire adhesiveness." Due to the war, however, the project became mired in delays and construction of the second depot did not begin until late summer of 1865. The new depot stood on approximately the same spot as the present-day depot, but a little southwest, partially blocking Sacramento Street. To accommodate the new depot, the S&C had to extend its tracks across Coltonville Road (now DeKalb Avenue). When the S&C completed the depot in December of that year, the *True Republican* noted its "beautiful style" and called it "a much needed improvement."

The first depot was moved directly west across the tracks, onto the "triangle lot" on the southwest corner of Sacramento Street and Coltonville Road (DeKalb Avenue) now known as Johnson's Junction. After a few alterations and additions, it was converted into the Lattin coal shed, which stood on this site until May 1905, when it was removed to make room for John L. Murphy's grain elevator. Even though the original building only functioned as a depot for six years, it still served the city of Sycamore for an additional forty.

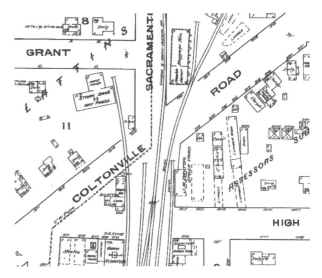

This 1885 Sanborn map shows the Lattin coal shed—formerly the S&C's first depot—on the "triangle lot" on the southwest corner of Sacramento Street and Coltonville Road (now DeKalb Avenue).

The "triangle lot" is now known as "Johnson's Junction," named for Sycamore's longtime mayor Harold "Red" Johnson, who served from 1957 to 1991.

Despite having a new depot, growth proved elusive to Sycamore, because in August of 1866 a massive hailstorm swept across the county, wiping out crops, killing livestock, and destroying property. Sycamore's total damages were estimated at $250,000. On top of this disaster, the Sycamore Bank failed only a few months later. Sycamore depositors lost nearly $50,000, including the funds raised to build the Civil War monument. The city would not erect the monument for another 30 years.

Sycamore's farmers who struggled through that tough year were rewarded the next when crops flourished and prices stabilized. New businesses arrived in town: a flax factory, a cheese factory, and a new foundry. The city finally received a telegraph line, allowing improved railroad communication and more frequent contact with the outside world. The S&C pulled in over $11,000, more than doubling what it earned in each of its first years of operation. It added a new grain elevator to its ever-expanding inventory, giving local farmers easier and more stable access to storage. The railroad averaged 50 passengers a day, which prompted the company to begin making four daily runs—sometimes more when businesses needed to ship extra freight—and to purchase a "more convenient" and "better-looking" combination passenger and baggage car. This car replaced the shoddy second-hand one the company had been using for seven years. The old car was unceremoniously burned and the scrap iron salvaged.

The S&C did run into difficulties while maintaining its success. The branch line needed constant—and expensive—improvements. The grading could quickly become uneven and bumpy for long stretches. These rough track conditions contributed to several engine breakdowns. The S&C did not have the means to repair its own engine, so the Sycamore had to be run to the G&CU—and later the C&NW—repair shop in Chicago. These companies supplied replacement engines during the repairs, but the cost of repairs and renting replacement engines put the company deeply in debt. Between 1864 and 1870, the S&C ran up $9,000 in charges and paid back only $4,000. The railroad's president, James S. Waterman, argued the S&C's case to its creditors and asked for forgiveness of its debts. He claimed that the little railroad greatly benefitted the C&NW and would remain invaluable in the future. The C&NW eventually forgave more than half of the remaining debt.

Moving Forward

In 1869, Sycamoreans decided it was finally time to form a civil government. The town had already served as the county seat for over 30 years. For the past decade it had existed as an

A Political Rally in Sycamore

The following article appeared in the *Chicago Tribune* on October 2, 1866. It provides a glimpse of a typical 19th-century political rally in Sycamore, as well as the role the railroad played in such events:

Senators Trumbull and Wilson at Sycamore
--Sycamore, Ill., September 23, 1866

> Yesterday was a great day in DeKalb County. Senator Trumbull [and Senator Wilson] had been advertised to speak.... At ten o'clock a.m., a special train with the Committee of Arrangements and leading citizens and the Sycamore brass band, was run up to Courtland to meet the distinguished speakers. On returning to Sycamore, a procession was formed at the depot, headed by a fine cavalcade of the returned soldiers, under charge of General Daniel Dustin, Chief Marshall, assisted by General Waite, General Dutton, Major Sullivan, Captain Norris and others.
>
> Then followed two brass bands, the distinguished speakers, President of the day, Committee of Arrangement, and invited guests, in carriages followed by a long procession of carriages through the principal streets of the town around the Public Square, and brought them to the hotel of H. Paine, where a half hour was spent in introducing our citizens to the Senators, after which the dinner was held to the satisfaction of all.

A parade led the group back to the courthouse square, where Chauncey Ellwood introduced the honored guests, who each spoke for several hours to a gathered crowd of between 5,000 and 7,000.

incorporated village that operated under a town government made up of elected trustees. It was not until March 4, 1869, that Sycamore officially organized its first civil government, making it a city. The people then elected Reuben Ellwood as the first mayor.

That same year, Sycamore's railroad facilities attracted the city's first significant manufacturing business. Charles and William Marsh had been looking for a place to manufacture their state-of-the-art harvesters. They located their factory, the Marsh Harvester Works, along the railroad tracks just south of the depot. From there, the company could easily load its harvesters directly onto the S&C's freight cars and ship them all over the country (and later, the world). The Marsh factory grew into Sycamore's biggest employer. For over 30 years, Sycamore had operated as a mostly agricultural community, but the Marsh Harvester Works ushered in a new age of manufacturing that would characterize the city for decades to come.

Charles Marsh

William Marsh

CHAPTER THREE

THE SYCAMORE MARSH HARVESTER MANUFACTURING COMPANY
Marsh Harvesters, Cheese Boxes and Agricultural Implements. Sycamore, Ills.

Marsh Harvester Works in Sycamore

This drawing of the Marsh Harvester Works appeared in the *Combination Atlas Map of DeKalb County, Illinois*, published in 1871. The factory stood on the west side of the railroad tracks south of the depot. Note the S&C train passing in front of the building.

The Marsh Harvester

Throughout the 1860s, a struggling economy, multiple crop failures, and the Civil War had worked in unison to check Sycamore's prosperity, but Sycamore persevered. The city did not undergo a great expansion, but through its enterprising actions, it saw huge improvements. Old wooden structures were removed and replaced with fine brick buildings. New stores opened, offering higher-quality goods. New churches, schools, and factories decorated the landscape. The S&C

carried the materials that built and stocked these endeavors, all the while improving its own railroad and equipment.

And despite the ongoing animosity that existed between Sycamore and DeKalb over the county seat issue (the *True Republican* did once insinuate that if Sycamoreans bought property in DeKalb, they would bring some "character and dignity" to the place), the two cities still—on occasion— worked together to facilitate each other's growth. In January 1871, a DeKalb newspaper had this to say about its northern neighbor:

> Sycamore has enterprise, hospitality, sociability. Enterprise, because when anything is to be done, Sycamoreans take hold with a united will and do it…. Hospitality, because when strangers come there, every door is thrown open… hence, strangers are attracted to reside, and when once there, find it too pleasant a place to leave…. [Sociability, because] nowhere in the county is there a city whose social qualities are so apparent and so well known abroad as those of Sycamore.

The *Pioneer* in Sycamore

In 1948, to celebrate the 100th Anniversary of railroad service out of Chicago, the C&NW sent the *Pioneer* on an 8-week, 7-state, 58-city tour aboard the *Centennial Train*.

The *Pioneer* has the distinction of being the first railroad locomotive to operate in the West. The Utica & Schenectady Railroad built the engine in 1837 and operated it for nine years before selling it to the Michigan Central Railroad. After two years, the Michigan Central sold it to the Galena & Chicago Union Railroad. The G&CU ran it on the first line west out of Chicago. The *Pioneer* made its maiden western voyage on October 24, 1848. When the aging engine could no longer compete with newer models, the C&NW—who had taken over the G&CU—demoted it to short work runs around Chicago. It was retired from service around 1874.

For a time, the C&NW used the *Pioneer* as a "loaner" engine. In the 1860s, the little locomotive ran on the Sycamore & Cortland line when the *Sycamore* had to go into Chicago for repairs. On at least a few occasions, it was operated by S&C engineer John Tucker and his young fireman, Silas Othello Pike.

S. O. Pike was born in a log cabin on State Street in 1849. In the late 1860s or early 1870s, he worked as a machinist at the Marsh Harvester Works and as a fireman for the S&C Railroad, where he was responsible for maintaining the steam engine's boiler fire. He later served as Sycamore's chief of police, worked as the superintendent of Sycamore's water works, and led the local band, "The Fantastic Aramaguzelums." For many years, he was responsible for setting off Sycamore's Fourth of July fireworks.

In 1930, at the age of 81, Pike paid a visit to the *Pioneer*, which was then on display at a railroad station in Chicago. For several years, it had been left to rust at Turner Junction (now West Chicago) before the C&NW recognized its significance, restored it, and put it on display. Pike shared stories of his days firing the *Pioneer* on the S&C line and even climbed into the cab to look it over. The *True Republican* reported on the event under the headline "Two Pioneers Meet After Sixty Years."

S. O. Pike (right) and the *Pioneer* in 1930

The *Pioneer* today, on permanent display at the Chicago History Museum

Into the Gilded Age: 1870-1879

The Industrious mechanic… is worth far more to a town than a wealthy retired gentleman who lives upon the interest of his funds and produces nothing.

True Republican, December 14, 1872

After the Civil War, New York's railroad tycoons raced to connect their vast empires to the Chicago market. They bought and consolidated smaller railroads that operated anywhere between the two cities, which created vast and powerful conglomerates unlike anything the nation had ever known. Competition became especially fierce between Cornelius Vanderbilt, who controlled the New York Central Railroad, and Jay Gould, who controlled the Erie Railroad. The two men had a strong interest in moving into the Chicago market, and an even stronger interest in outmaneuvering each other. Their bitter rivalry became fodder for newspaper headlines nation-wide, and brought a new awareness to how the whims of a few powerful men could affect the lives of millions.

The *True Republican* began to criticize the rapidly expanding railroad corporations for becoming far-reaching and increasingly powerful while their directors had few, if any,

While railroad companies merged and consolidated during the 1870s, they began marketing themselves with trademarked, easily recognizable logos, such as these logos for the Chicago & North Western, which span several decades. (Author's collection)

local interests. Such companies, the paper argued, would never look out for the interests of small-town people. It focused its editorial energies on "the great tribulations of the tax-paying." The paper's increasing attacks on corporations and big business spread to local businessmen as well. The quote at the beginning of this chapter was directed at the wealthy businessmen who originally built Sycamore, including the Ellwoods and Watermans and other founders of the Sycamore & Cortland (S&C) Railroad.

The feud between the *True Republican* and Sycamore's business elite heated up during the 1870 state elections when Chauncey Ellwood sought the Republican nomination for state senate. Chauncey had never been far from politics. In his native New York, he had represented the newly formed Republican Party at several state conventions. When he came to DeKalb County with his brothers in the 1850s, he had continued working for the party's interests. From 1867 to 1869, he served as Secretary of the Illinois State Senate, but he became plagued with accusations of scandal, bribery, and supporting only railroad interests. During his campaign for the senate nomination, he was accused of colluding with a corrupt railroad ring in the Illinois Legislature that sought to enrich the railroads at the expense of the people. While these allegations were never proven, Chauncey's political rivals pounced on the idea that the Chicago & North Western Railroad (C&NW) had paid to put him in the Secretary position and now the company was actively campaigning to get him elected as a senator. Charles Marsh, who'd had a falling out with the Ellwoods over a bad business deal, ran against Chauncey on the grounds that DeKalb County had to escape from the Ellwoods' "big breeches pocket." The *True Republican* threw its full support behind Marsh and he eventually secured the nomination.

Chauncey Ellwood

The *True Republican* had another reason to go on the offensive against Chauncey Ellwood and a few other local businessmen. In the 1868 presidential election, General Ulysses S. Grant rode his military prestige into the White House, but corruption and scandal in his administration plagued his first term. Several staunch Republicans disagreed with the president's policies and the direction of the Republican Party. Before the 1872 presidential election, they split from the party and started the Liberal Republican Party. The new party sided with the Democrats and put forth Horace Greeley as its candidate against Grant. In Sycamore, Chauncey Ellwood became the chairman of the Liberal Republican County Commission. When he organized a joint convention with DeKalb's Democratic County Commission, the *True Republican* called it an "unholy alliance" and vowed to expose the "cloven hoof" of this new coalition. The paper called Chauncey a "liberal sorehead" who had "repented of his Republicanism." In response, Chauncey became a supporter of Sycamore's new Democratic newspaper, the *City Weekly*, even providing it with the occasional editorial.

Greeley lost the election and the Liberal Republican Party dissolved, but in the ensuing years, many of its supporters—including several of Sycamore's prominent businessmen—shifted their allegiance over to the Democratic Party or the short-lived Greenback Party. The *True Republican* saw these men as self-serving profiteers and continued attacking them as such.[1]

Cornelius Vanderbilt

Cornelius Vanderbilt (1794-1877). Upon the news of the Commodore's demise in January 1877, the *City Weekly* made the following tongue-in-cheek boast about one of Sycamore's own railroad "tycoons": "In railway management, Chance [Chauncey] Ellwood has no rival since the death of Commodore Vanderbilt."

A Second Railroad?

As railroads continued consolidating into powerful monopolies, freight fees began to rise, pinching the pocketbooks of merchants and farmers throughout northern Illinois. Because the S&C connected only with the C&NW, all of Sycamore was at the mercy of the C&NW's rates. The *True Republican* declared that the C&NW "takes from you four times what it ought for freights and fares, grinding you down to the dust with excessive charges." To fight back against these exorbitant fees, which many saw as a form of extortion, farmers and merchants began shipping their goods to and from Chicago the old-fashioned way, by horse and wagon. A Sycamorean would cart his goods into the city and bring back a wagonload of fresh supplies to sell in Sycamore.

While these boycotts created a minor disruption in railroad profits, nothing could restore railroad fees faster than free-market competition. Two railroads in any one town always resulted in a price war, with each railroad battling for the loyalty of local business. If Sycamore truly wanted to battle the C&NW's fees, it needed more than its little spur line to Cortland; it needed a second railroad.

---

[1] Author's note: H. L. Boies, owner and editor of the *True Republican*, was a founding director of the S&C and sat on the board of directors for two decades. It is possible that Boies used the *True Republican* to attack other S&C directors over personal or business disagreements rather than the usual political differences, but I have not found evidence to support that theory (see footnote 7).

For several years, the *True Republican* had been reporting on the advantages of a two-railroad town. It used Rochelle as a prime example, noting that the competition between the C&NW and the Chicago & Iowa (C&I) railroads in that city allowed products to be bought or sold at more advantageous prices. In May 1870, Sycamore buzzed with the possibility of a new rail line coming through town. The Pennsylvania Railroad (PRR) showed an interest in expanding its lines into Minnesota, and Sycamore lay directly on one proposed path. The *True Republican* threw its full support behind the project. "The advantages coming from Railroads everybody understands," the paper reported. "They always open up and benefit the country through which they pass.... We have the liveliest, busiest city in Northern Illinois and the place would have been no place at all at this time without [our railroad]."

At a packed public meeting, one of the PRR's directors, Lewis Steward, gave an impassioned speech to the animated crowd:

> This country is ground down to the earth by the extortionate demands of grasping Railroad Monopolies. Wherever competition between two or more routes exists... freights are reduced to about one-half what they are where there is no competition... The monopolies have got the upper hand of the people and they must be broken down. There is no way to break them down but by competition.

When several Sycamoreans criticized the new taxes that would be necessary to build a second railroad, the *True Republican* responded, "No town was ever yet killed by taxation. The dead towns are those where light taxes are paid, and if a man wants to avoid taxation he must go out among the Indians." Those in favor of the railroad claimed that it would boost real estate values, and the railroad revenue itself would cover the majority of any new taxes. The S&C's directors pointed out that their railroad operated relatively cheap considering that it returned "ten times its cost" through the benefits it provided the city.

If the railroad was built elsewhere, the *True Republican* warned, then Sycamore would become a dead town, and everyone's sons and daughters would leave them for the town where "there is life and growth and animation."

The prospect of a second railroad increased a month later when the C&I expressed interest in running its Rockford branch through Sycamore. New York native Francis Edward Hinckley, founder and president of the C&I, came to a public meeting in Sycamore to explain his plans and to answer any questions or concerns. He carefully laid out how the railroad would benefit Sycamore—or DeKalb, if Sycamore chose not to invest in it—and explained that the railroad could be completed with new trains running through the city in as little as four months. The *True Republican* noted that Hinckley charmed the crowd with his "pleasant manners" and his "upright, honest, cheerful, sanguine ways." As part of the deal, however, the S&C would have to be absorbed by the C&I. This merger concerned many Sycamoreans, who believed that the S&C's stockholders stood to gain more than anyone from this deal. Reuben Ellwood spoke at the meeting, then, offering to sell his shares at one quarter of their value to show that he was not pursuing this deal for money, but for the future of Sycamore. If the railroad bypassed Sycamore, he argued, then "the balance of the population will be changed, and inaccessible as we shall be to so many, we shall lose the County Seat." He also noted that the S&C track, equipment, cars, and engine all needed repairs or replacement, and the cost of that alone would be almost half the cost of subscribing to the C&I's offer.

The plan, however, met extreme opposition from a populace who worried about the massive debt it would incur in subscribing to this new railroad. The growing mistrust of the railroad monopolies also made many residents reluctant to throw in with an outside entity that had no ties or loyalty to Sycamore or its people. What would keep this railroad from merging with another and destroying the free-market competition that made a second railroad so desirable in the first place? All of these hopes and apprehensions came to naught, however, when the *True Republican* looked into Hinckley's finances and determined that he "wasn't worth his board bill." The whole deal quickly fell apart and Hinckley took his railroad schemes elsewhere.[2]

Throughout the 1870s, rumors concerning a new railroad in Sycamore continued to crop up, but none ever panned out, including the aforementioned PRR. This may have eased the minds of those in favor of their own little railroad. For the time being, they could continue putting their trust in a local business run by local directors, even if that business operated under the thumb of the C&NW.

A Tragic Boon

In the early 1870s, two major disasters indirectly benefited Sycamore and brought a boost to the railroad economy of the entire region. The first disaster took place from October 8-10, 1871. "The Great Chicago Fire" still stands as the largest disaster the city of Chicago has ever known, but it could have been much worse if it hadn't been for Chicago's extensive railway system, which allowed masses of displaced citizens to escape the ruined city and relocate elsewhere in

---

[2] Hinckley eventually found success by running his railroad through southern DeKalb County. The C&I line brought new growth to that area, especially to the township of Squaw Grove, which honored the railroad's founder by naming the village of Hinckley after him.

northern Illinois. In addition, out of Chicago's ashes rose a huge demand for labor and building materials, which poured into the city on these same railroads. Contractors from across northern Illinois—including several from Sycamore—referred to Chicago as "New El Dorado" and flocked to the city to find employment and good wages. While Chicago's misfortune created opportunity for the railroad and for many Sycamoreans, it also stunted Sycamore's development. Due to the redirection of materials and labor to Chicago, Sycamore's growth, which had been steady since the Civil War, saw very little expansion in the months following the great fire.

The ruins of Chicago's Union Depot after the Great Chicago Fire. (Library of Congress)

The second tragedy to boost the railroad industry's business and reputation was "The Great Epizootic of 1872," an epidemic of equine influenza that swept through the nation's horse population in only two months. It started in New England and quickly spread south and west. Infected animals were too weak to work, and owners refused to take out their healthy horses for fear of contagion. Overnight, horses, wagons, and carts disappeared from city streets and business ground to a halt. Thousands of livery stable, freight car, and streetcar operators found themselves out of work. Merchants could not send or receive deliveries. Milk and produce shipments spoiled. Luggage piled up at railroad depots and outside hotels because there was no way to transport it. Newspapers carried daily updates of the disease's impact, but it soon became so widespread that Sycamore's *City Weekly* declared that it was useless to report on the epidemic. Several Chicago businesses sent notices to their clients informing them of shipping delays. One such notice ran in the November 7, 1872 issue of the *City Weekly*:

> Sir: You are probably well aware that the dreaded horse epidemic is fast spreading over the country. It has already reached Chicago, and scarcely a horse can be seen on the streets.... We are now obliged to deliver all of our goods at the trains... and shall strive to be as prompt as usual in our shipments..

THE HORSE PLAGUE—SKETCHES ABOUT TOWN DURING THE EPIDEMIC.—By Theo. R. Davis.—[See Page 896.]

This drawing from a November 1872 *Harper's Weekly* depicts an urban scene during the horse epidemic. (Author's collection)

Steady Growth

The S&C remained popular and profitable through the first half of the 1870s. Over 80 passengers a day passed through Sycamore's depot. On busier days, passengers packed the coach to capacity and the overflow had to pile into a freight car. By the end of 1872, the railroad earned $1,200 a month on passenger tickets alone. The company launched a series of improvements, beginning with turntables built at each end of the line.[3] In 1873, the railroad replaced the entire track with new iron rails.[4] As for freight, Sycamore's elevators overflowed with fresh grain that the train couldn't ship fast enough. On some days, farmers had to wait five hours to have their grain unloaded.

Workers at the grain elevator often stayed well into the night to sort the grain for the next day's shipments. By 1874, the freight coming out of Sycamore averaged 32,000 tons per year and the rail line averaged 22,000 passengers. The company used its profits to regularly rebuild and refurbish its equipment. By the railroad's 15th year, there was hardly a rail or tie that hadn't been upgraded.

The epidemic, however, provided an unforeseen benefit: it forced people to use the railroad system, many of them for the first time. Even though railroads had revolutionized transportation in the latter half of the 19th century, there were still those who relied on horse-drawn transportation either out of mistrust or fear of this relatively new, potentially dangerous technology. The epidemic forced these holdouts to switch to the railroad, and when the epidemic finally passed, many of them didn't switch back.

---

[3]Until that time, without the ability to turn, the S&C engine had always travelled one direction facing forward and returned in reverse.

[4]The new rails turned out to be of a poor quality. They began to warp after only a few years, which caused the cars to rock and weave along, pitching passengers from side to side, forcing them to grip their seats, parcels, and each other for the trip's duration. To the delight of many, the S&C replaced the inferior rails in 1877.

While these improvements benefited the town and made for a more profitable business, they also angered several stockholders, who felt the profits should be paid out as dividends. The railroad did not pay out a single dividend until 1874.

Downtown Sycamore c. 1875

A southwest view of State Street between Somonauk and California streets. The large building at the end of the street is Paine's Hotel, which later became the property of Levi Winn, who tore it down soon after this picture was taken and replaced it with a much grander hotel (see opposite page). The rooftop in the upper left corner belonged to the S&C's second depot (though hardly visible, this is the only known image of that building). In the foreground, wooden planks cross the muddy slough in the middle of State Street. The construction materials piled up to the right were used to build Central Block (see page 83).

That year proved to be a significant one for DeKalb County. The younger brother of Reuben and Chauncey Ellwood, Isaac Leonard Ellwood, who resided in DeKalb, partnered with barbed wire inventor Joseph Glidden to manufacture and sell Glidden's revolutionary invention through the I. L. Ellwood Manufacturing Company. Within a few short years, Isaac Ellwood's company had sold millions of pounds of barbed wire across the country, which made him one of the richest men in Illinois. For DeKalb County, the barbed wire industry was a game changer. Companies like Marsh Harvester in Sycamore had started DeKalb County's conversion from agriculture to manufacturing, but the barbed wire industry ultimately drove the industrialization of DeKalb County. Barbed wire also made the city of DeKalb more of a threat to Sycamore. Both towns ramped up their competition, and they did so through manufacturing.

Sycamore experienced a building revival it had not seen since the founding of the railroad. In 1875 Reuben Ellwood founded the Reuben Ellwood Manufacturing Company. It specialized in agricultural implements and began churning out hundreds of Ellwood Riding Cultivators from its new factory on the east side of the railroad tracks, south of the depot. While the cultivators made the company famous, it also manufactured everyday hardware goods,

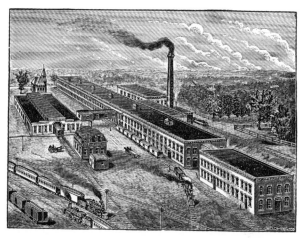

I. L. Ellwood Manufacturing Company in DeKalb

Isaac L. Ellwood

The Reuben Ellwood Manufacturing Company

including rakes, plows, barrel cases, and door hinges. Despite the competition, the Marsh Harvester factory could barely keep up with its record number of orders. In one month alone, the company shipped 250 freight cars of harvesters. State Street saw the construction of the new Universalist Church and Winn's Hotel, the finest hotel in the city. Winn's stood on the corner of State and California and replaced the popular Paine's Hotel. It was designed by Chicago architect John Ackermann, who had also designed houses

Winn's Hotel

for George P. Wild and Chauncey Ellwood. The three-story hotel contained a bar and billiards parlor and could accommodate 150 guests. It also had the distinction of being the closest hotel to the S&C depot, a fact that it highlighted in all of its advertising.

Sycamore owed much of its increased success to an improved national economy. Goods from Sycamore—both agricultural and manufactured—now found their way to all parts of the country. When the C&NW introduced refrigerated cars on its line passing through Cortland and DeKalb, Sycamore's farmers could ship butter, cheese, and eggs all the way to Boston or California. Twenty years before, these men would have been hard-pressed to get their goods down the muddy road to DeKalb.

Sycamore II

A major event in the history of the S&C took place on Tuesday, May 11, 1875, when the company finally replaced its antique, wood-burning engine with a brand new coal burner: *Sycamore II*. The new engine—a 4-4-0 type Baldwin locomotive with 15-by-24-inch cylinders and 62-inch diameter drivers—weighed in at 28 tons and was capable of carrying 200 pounds of steam. The engine cost the S&C $9,000. It was manufactured by Burnham, Parry, Williams & Co., at the Baldwin Locomotive Works in Philadelphia. William Baldwin, manager of the Philadelphia works, accompanied the engine to Sycamore and remained in town to get it in "perfect working order." The *True Republican* called it "a fine and powerful looking piece of machinery."

On Saturday, May 15, Chauncey Ellwood celebrated the company's biggest achievement since its founding by organizing a free ride to Cortland for 500 residents.[5] Everyone "stowed in and around four cars" and departed from the depot at 4 p.m. Upon arrival at Cortland, the S&C's directors passed out cigars specially made for the occasion. The excited crowd spent a half hour enjoying their cigars and admiring the new engine before returning to Sycamore. According to the *True Republican*, "John Tucker, our old engineer, will desert his old love, 'Sycamore No. 1,' and hereafter tread the footboards of 'Sycamore No. 2.'" If Tucker pushed the new engine to its limits, he could make the run to Cortland in five minutes (the most common run time was 12 to 15 minutes).

---

[5] The *True Republican* reported that the free ride was announced "from the lips of our corpulent friend" Chauncey Ellwood.

The *Sycamore II*

The engine house (pictured left c. 1880 and right c. 1920) provided the *Sycamore II* with steam and water from the Marsh Harvester Works. The factory's heat also kept the engine warm in winter. The S&C eventually built a turntable outside the engine house doors.

To store the new engine and protect it from the elements, the S&C built a 25-by-70-foot brick engine house south of the depot, attached to the north end of the Marsh Harvester Works. Having no more need for the *Sycamore I*, the railroad sold the engine, most likely for scrap. Its fate remains unknown. The following February, the S&C acquired an elegant new passenger car—"larger, more roomy and easier than any the company ever before have had"—to complement the fine new engine.

Chauncey Gets "Caned"

On Saturday evening, September 22, 1877, the entire city turned out to celebrate Chauncey Ellwood's service as the S&C's vice president and general manager. The city-wide celebration began with a parade that included the Sycamore Brass Band and Sycamore's military and fire companies in full dress. The parade carried the crowd to Wilkins Hall, where Sycamore's most prominent citizens put aside their political differences and spoke in honor of Chauncey and his work. Sycamore's mayor, Nathan Lattin, began the evening:

> The war club and the tomahawk are, for the time being, buried deep out of sight, and all meet to show respect to and good will toward one of our active, enterprising and public-spirited fellow townsmen, one whose interests have been largely identified with the interests and prosperity of Sycamore for the past twenty years.

The mayor went on to outline Sycamore's history during the time Chauncey had lived there, from its days as a small village of wooden structures with very little business or enterprise, to the present, in which large brick businesses, busy factories, and handsome residences lined the city's streets. Chauncey's most important accomplishment, Lattin noted, was in managing the railroad:

> Today our little railroad commands the respect of not only individuals, but also of other railroad corporations, and by it Sycamore is made one of the principal railroad points of Illinois and its importance is appreciated by all the commercial centers east and west. It is but justice to say that to Chauncey Ellwood belongs the credit largely of our enviable position.

Mayor Lattin then presented Ellwood with an elegant cane, its handle capped in gold and appropriately engraved with the image of a locomotive, tender, and passenger coach.[6] Several other prominent community members rose and gave speeches praising the man who "has been identified with many and perhaps most of the leading business enterprises of the town for years." Chauncey himself arose and gave an emotional response, thanking the city that he believed was "unsurpassed by any city in the State for the high moral standing of her business men." He claimed that he could not take credit for the S&C's successes, giving that honor instead to the "cordial cooperation" of the company's president—James Waterman—and the board of directors. He also praised the C&NW, noting that it was "due much of the success which our road has obtained," and that he had never asked it for a favor that "has not been readily and cheerfully granted." He concluded by thanking all the people of Sycamore for giving him "one of the happiest events of my life."

---

[6] Gold-headed canes were a common gift of the time, given to individuals in recognition of lifelong service to a business or community. It was a precursor to the custom of giving a gold watch.

Rebranding the S&C

Despite the celebration surrounding Chauncey's service and the company's improvements, the latter half of the 1870s were not "flush times" for the little railroad. In 1875, the Chicago, Milwaukee & St. Paul Railroad built a line through the northern part of DeKalb County. It brought new life to Genoa, a city that, at the time, had slipped to the brink of ruin. It also created several new towns in the county, including Kirkland and Kingston. However, the new line's popularity pulled passengers, freight, and thousands of dollars in business away from Sycamore.

After steady gains almost every year since its founding, the S&C lost 26% of its value between 1874 and 1879. At a time when railroad stock values could double or triple in a matter of months, the S&C's value continued to drop. According to an 1879 financial report released by the Railroad and Warehouse Commission of Illinois, the average operating expenses of Illinois railroads were 57% of earnings. For the C&NW, they were just under 48%. The S&C, however, reported operating expenses at 113% of earnings, the worst percentage of the state's 50-plus railroads. The S&C was the only railroad in the state operating at a loss.

With railroad revenue declining, Sycamore had three options to ensure its success as a competitive business center. One or all of them could greatly benefit the city:

1. Secure a north-south line to connect the city to the rich coal fields of southern Illinois and vast timberlands of Wisconsin and Minnesota.

2. Secure a second railroad that could compete with the C&NW and drive down costs.

3. Sell the S&C to a larger railroad company that had more financial resources at its disposal

From the June 22, 1877 issue of the *True Republican*:

The general manager of our S&CRR [Chauncey Ellwood] attended one of the Quaker meetings, last week, and was scared out of some nights' sleep by the eloquent Quakeress's glowing description of the future doom of the lost. A few days after, he was applied to for a pass for them. He filled out the usual blank as follows:

Pass: Brother and Sister Frame.

Where to: out of town, for the Lord's sake.

On account of what: her vivid description of God's creation of Hell.

As early as 1877, rumors began to spread that the S&C's directors wanted to sell their railroad to one of the larger railroad conglomerates. The directors supposedly offered it to the C&NW for $60,000, but the C&NW turned them down. There were a number of reasons the directors would have wanted to unload the railroad, most of them financial, but another reason had to do with the age of the directors and shareholders. Although the board of directors changed a little each year, essentially the same men had operated the railroad for two decades. Most of them were in their 60s, 70s, or 80s and had already operated successful businesses outside of the railroad. If a large company took over the railroad, these men could cash out their shares and retire.

Their company, however, was a hard sell. The S&C owned fewer than five miles of track. It did not own any rolling stock other than the locomotive and tender, one passenger car, and a small handcar. It had no caboose. Any baggage, freight, or livestock cars that ran on the line belonged to the C&NW. So if the directors were serious about attracting a buyer, they needed to boost the company's image.

They took the first step by changing the company's name from the Sycamore & Cortland Railroad to the Sycamore, Cortland & Chicago Railroad (SC&C). There is no surviving record indicating that the company intended to extend the railroad to Chicago, so this move was most likely a marketing strategy designed to draw more attention to the railroad and to dispel its identity as a small, local spur line.

An 1882 freight billing form bears the company's rebranded name: Sycamore, Cortland & Chicago Railroad Company.

A fancy new name, however, could not hide the fact that the company had little to offer in the way of a depot. While no description of the second depot survives—other than it had a wood-frame structure—the absence of information suggests that the building couldn't have been much to speak of. So the second step toward a new image was to build a new depot.

The company's directors had been discussing the possibility of constructing another depot for several years. They wanted to build something grand and elegant, something made of stone and brick. Their motivations may have been more than aesthetic. In 1878, the hay press just east of the depot had burned to the ground. The all-wood depot narrowly escaped, but the fire's proximity probably had some influence on the directors' decision to replace the old building. The city's recent shortcomings may have been another reason the SC&C directors opted for a new depot. In the late 1870s, Sycamore suffered from the economic downturn that afflicted the whole country. At the same time, DeKalb experienced a boon in both business and population growth. A fancy new depot would show that Sycamore could still compete with DeKalb (an "our depot is bigger than your depot" kind of move).

The *True Republican*, whose waning support for the railroad and its directors is evident in its lack of reporting on either, weighed in on the depot issue with this simple response: "We need it." The company did need it, so its directors planned for a depot that would rival many of the depots in Chicago.[7]

April Fool.—Yesterday afternoon as the express train was on its way from Cortland to Sycamore, a fierce whistle caused a rush to the brakes. Some poor fellow to all appearances was lying on the track and ere the train could be stopped he was torn in pieces by the wheels. Parties ran back to gather up the remains, which were found to be those of a "dummy" placed on the track by some wag. The train men looked decidedly sold.

April Fools article from the April 3, 1877 issue of the *City Weekly*

Shifting Allegiances

By the end of the 1870s, the *True Republican* could boast of its role shaping Sycamore into "the most thriving, flourishing, prosperous and attractive little city in the Northwest." The newspaper had, after all, encouraged manufacturing, supported the city's taste for architecture and landscaping, pushed for an efficient waterworks system to battle fires, and sought a public library as a substitute to amoral saloons and billiard parlors. Because of this prosperity, Sycamore could boast of eight churches and six newspapers (five weekly and one bi-weekly). But the *True Republican* had one more battle to fight. It had to erase "one conspicuous

---

[7]Because the *True Republican* regularly defended local interests over big railroad interests, it can be surmised that H. L. Boies was against the idea of selling the railroad, which would explain the newspaper's lack of coverage on railroad matters in the late 1870s and into the 1880s. This type of "media blackout," common to 19th-century newspapers, was the same tactic used by the *True Republican's* old rival, the *DeKalb County Republican Sentinel*, when it opposed the S&C's construction in the late 1850s.

shame and disgrace" upon the city: the "two feet of the vilest mud in America" that stretched across State Street. Residents began referring to it as "the city frog pond." City officials became irate when a blacksmith erected a sign beside the massive mud puddle that read: No Fishing. The *True Republican* encouraged a campaign against this unceasing mud problem that had plagued Sycamore since its inception. It called the condition of State Street "shameful," "a disgrace," and, "a foul blot on… the prettiest and most enterprising little city of Illinois." It claimed that Sycamore was now losing thousands of dollars a year in trade to cities that took care of their roads. "Our soil is black muck," the paper declared. "What shall we do about it?"

Despite the paper's war on mud, the 1870s brought a major shift in the *True Republican's* attitude toward business, manufacturing, and city improvements. While the paper boasted of its role in the city's many advances, it took on a more conservative tone by suggesting that Sycamore already had everything it needed. A prime example of this new view could be seen in a piece published in July 1879, reporting on a new church built a block from the depot. The *True Republican* praised the congregation's hard work, but asked, "Now with nine churches in a population of 4000, and an average attendance of 700, isn't it time for Sycamore to quit building churches[?]"

The idea of not building a church, or anything, for that matter, went against everything the *True Republican* stood for in the previous decades.

By the end of the 1870s, the *True Republican* shifted its editorial focus from public improvements and began attacking the city's numerous high taxes (many of which had been passed to pay for the public improvements, including the never-ending battle against the city's muddy roads). The paper also attacked corporate interests and the businessmen who, it claimed, sought profit over public good, including local businessmen—like the Ellwoods and Watermans—whom the paper had previously supported. As a result of this shift, the paper also began to view the SC&C more as a private business enterprise than a public monument and source of civic pride. The editors seemed to feel that more of the railroad's responsibilities should have been funded by the C&NW, which, by this time, had grown into one of the richest companies in the world and profited greatly from Sycamore's little branch line.[8]

Operating under a new name and a new agenda, the SC&C continued chugging right along into the next decade, but its ambitions and changing priorities could no longer count on the support of its longtime champion, the *True Republican*.

---

[8]In 1878, when the C&NW built a reading room for its employees, the *True Republican* reported the story under the headline "Corporations Have Souls."

Riding the Rails

The railroad and depot were such a common part of everyday life in Sycamore that letters, journals, and diaries rarely mention them. Sycamoreans who wrote about their journeys far from home often began from the time they departed Chicago, never mentioning the trip from Sycamore to Chicago, which would have been as routine as a walk to the dry goods store. As a result, we have few accounts of what travel was actually like for Sycamore's early railroad passengers.

In the railroad's early days, engineers made a custom of blasting the locomotive whistle 20 minutes before departure to warn passengers to hurry down to the depot. At departure time, the engineer blasted the whistle another three times. In the March 21, 1925 issue of the *True Republican*, an anonymous contributor described railroad travel between Sycamore and Chicago in the 1860s or 1870s:[1]

A trip to Chicago was a great event. When the engineer sounded the whistle [we] would hurry down to the little unpainted wooden station and board the Sycamore & Cortland "jerk-water" train, which consisted of a few freight cars followed by a car half of which was for passengers and the remainder for express. [We] would change cars at Cortland. About half a mile before the next station was reached, the brakemen would announce the station—Lodi, Blackberry or Turner Junction—and then go out, letting in a blast of cold air, to the platform, which was without a vestibule, and he would begin winding up the hand-brakes. After a couple of brakes had been tightened, he would pass through the car, repeat the name of the station, and wind up the brakes at the other end of the car. Only the brave passed from car to car while the train was in motion, for there was an open space of some 18 inches between cars and a firm grip was necessary to keep from falling between. When the train started again, as the loose links were taken up, each car started separately and when you heard the starting up in front, and as your car started, you braced yourself to withstand the jerk you knew was coming. If nothing unusual happened you arrived at Chicago in about three and a half hours.

---

[1] The exact time period of this account is unknown, but it refers to Sycamore's wooden depot, so the trip took place before the S&C built its brick and stone depot in 1880.

In the 1860s and 1870s the *Sycamore I* and *Sycamore II* locomotives were not always confined to the five-mile spur line. The S&C regularly organized runs to nearby towns for special events, most often political rallies, educational lectures, or church revivals. The engine would switch over to the C&NW's main line at Cortland and carry groups to events in Batavia, DeKalb, Malta, or any other town on the line. Local organizations could charter the engine for special trips. The Freemasons and Odd Fellows used it to attend meetings, receptions, and funerals.

People in Sycamore loved the latest railroad advances. Because Sycamore did not sit on a main railroad line, its citizens had to travel to nearby towns to examine—or even just glimpse—the latest in railroad technology. Fortunately for Sycamoreans, many of these technological wonders passed through Cortland on the C&NW line. The S&C organized special runs so that the curious could watch experimental cars and engines pass by the Cortland depot.

For some passengers, riding in new and experimental trains could be a thrilling adventure. On November 7, 1872, the *City Weekly* published an anonymous contributor's account of several Sycamore boys riding on the C&NW's new faster trains between Cortland and DeKalb:

> In due time the boys arrived in Cortland. Getting aboard the cars on the other [rail]road, away the train dashed, taking them down to DeKalb, a distance of three miles in the unprecedented time of four minutes. The boys, unaccustomed to that rate of speed, were being wrought up to a fearful state of excitement, some of them indulging in audible prayer, while others made an occasional effort to reach the door, seriously contemplating a jump off. Even the intrepid leaders turned pale and came to the conclusion that a safer rate of speed must be adopted. Just as one of them had clutched the conductor by the coat-tail and was making a heart-rending appeal to that official to stop the train, the whistle sounded and DeKalb was gained.

A Conspicuous Ornament to the City, 1879-1882

They have got a new clock to put in the depot. Good! Now hadn't we better have a new depot to put the clock in?

True Republican, February 16, 1878

Plans to replace the city's second depot grew out of the Sycamore, Cortland, & Chicago (SC&C) directors' desire to attract attention to their city and draw interest from other railroads. If they wanted their city to stand out against other cities in the region—especially DeKalb—they needed to improve the company's railroad facilities. If they wanted to attract buyer interest from a larger railroad—which they had been trying to do for years—they needed to appear more marketable. They had to show the world that Sycamore was strong, steadfast, and sophisticated. To do all of these things, they had to start by getting rid of the old "shed" that served as the city's depot.

The plans for the new depot called for a two-story structure, 108 feet long and 36 feet wide. The architect designed the building to be a combination depot, meaning it accommodated both freight and passengers. The one-story north end would serve as a freight house, while the two-story south end—the head house—would accommodate the passengers. "In every respect [the depot] will be one of the best in the smaller cities of the State," the *True Republican* claimed, "and will be a credit to the place." In a later issue, however, the paper noted "had its location been a little nearer central, a fine hall would have been built over it."

In August 1879, the SC&C advertised for 100,000 bricks to construct the new depot. The contract went to Truman W. Van Galder, who operated the largest brickyard in the county in the area north of town unofficially known as "Brickville." To run a brickyard, a brickmaker needed a good water source, large clay deposits, and plenty of wood for fueling his kilns. Brickville provided all three. At the time the SC&C signed its contract with Van Galder, a brick shortage had caused prices to double, so Van Galder wasted no time in firing up his kilns.

Truman W. Van Galder

Truman W. Van Galder (1822–1882) was born in Niagara County, New York, and came to Sycamore in 1858. He operated the largest brickyard in the "Brickville" area north of Sycamore and was the first brickmaker in the county to ship his bricks to Chicago. Soon after delivering the bricks for the SC&C depot, he supplied the 250,000 bricks needed to build I. L. Ellwood's new barbed wire factory in DeKalb. Truman's son, Frank O. Van Galder, worked for several Sycamore and DeKalb newspapers before landing at the *True Republican*. After the death of the paper's owner, H. L. Boies, in 1887, Frank Van Galder co-edited the paper with Boies's son Edward, a partnership that lasted until 1895.

In September, the city extended Sacramento Street from the depot all the way up to the Brickville area. The northern section of this street, which is today called Brickville Road, benefitted the area's brick and tile businesses and made transporting their products to the depot easier. The new road also made it easier for Van Galder to transport his bricks to the new depot construction site.

That same month, the SC&C began negotiations to purchase the lot east of the old depot, which was occupied by the ruins of the hay press and planing mill that burned in 1878. The company planned to build the new depot northeast of the old one, closer to the middle of the lot. This location would have provided more open space around the new depot while allowing the old depot to remain open during construction.

In February 1880, months of negotiations fell apart when the SC&C's directors and the landowners could not agree on a price for the lot. By this time, the stone that would serve as the new building's foundation walls had already arrived and sat stacked in piles outside the old depot. The stone was Batavia limestone, which Sycamore had been importing in large amounts since 1870. Batavia limestone proved popular because of its creamy blue-white color—though it yellowed with age—and because it made a durable support for pressed brick.

The Sycamore Northern Pacific

In January 1880, the names Gould and Vanderbilt returned to the *True Republican* when word arrived that Jay Gould had purchased the SC&C with the intention of expanding it northwest into Minnesota (by way of Wisconsin) and southeast into Indiana (by way of Aurora and Joliet). The story ran in the *Chicago Times*, the *Chicago Tribune*, the *New York Times*, the *Commercial & Financial Chronicle*, and in most railway trade journals, including the *Railway Times*, published out of London. According to each of these papers, Gould had absorbed the SC&C into his vast Wabash, St. Louis & Pacific Railroad empire (commonly known as "The Pacific").

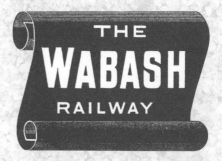

Wabash Railway logo c. 1885

There was just one problem with the story: it wasn't true. The SC&C's directors were just as surprised by the news as anyone else. Several newspapers speculated that Gould had spread the rumor himself to outmaneuver his rival, William Vanderbilt, who had recently become a major shareholder in the Chicago & North Western. Even after Gould's ruse became known, the C&NW's conductors jokingly referred to the SC&C as "The Northern Pacific."

Batavia began mining its famous limestone in the 1830s. The railroad made exporting the limestone easier, and by the 1850s ten limestone quarries operated in and around the city. In the 1870s, Chicago builders used Batavia limestone extensively to rebuild the city after the Great Chicago Fire. The stone was used to construct several buildings in Sycamore, including the William Marsh house in 1872 (top), the former Congregational Church in 1885 (above), and St. Peter's Church in 1878 (see page 27).

The directors mulled over their choices for a few weeks, and finally decided to build the new depot on the same site as the old depot. This presented another challenge: what to do with the old depot while the new one was under construction.

On April 15, 1880, Chauncey Ellwood petitioned Sycamore's city council to allow the SC&C to move the old depot into Sacramento Street during construction of the new depot. Because the old depot already stood partly in the street, the company would have to move the depot over the tracks so that it temporarily operated on the west side of Sacramento Street, mostly blocking that popular thoroughfare. Blocking the street, however, far outweighed the inconvenience of a whole city going without a functioning depot while the new depot was under construction. The city council sided with Chauncey and passed a resolution that granted the SC&C the right to move the depot, "on condition that [the building] shall not obstruct an open drive way of 12 feet on [the] west side of said Sacramento Street."

By July, all of the materials for the new depot had arrived. The lumber, pressed brick, and cut Batavia limestone sat in neatly stacked piles around the lot. The company finally moved the old depot out of the way in late July or early August.

To celebrate the new depot's impending construction, Chauncey Ellwood organized a ceremony to commemorate the laying of the cornerstone. He called on his fellow Sycamoreans to donate items for a copper time capsule that would be sealed and buried beneath the cornerstone. He asked the *True Republican* to provide a written sketch of the town, including "its manners and customs." Because the 130-year-old time capsule remains sealed beneath the depot's cornerstone, we do not know if the *True Republican's* editors provided the requested sketch, but we do know how they responded in the next issue of their paper. On the front page of the August 18, 1880 issue, they ran a long editorial titled "Sycamore Under the Corner Stone." It was an unprecedented attack on the city and its people, and a far cry from the optimistic encouragement the paper showed when the railroad was built 20 years before. Although written in the satirical, Twain-esque style of the times, it is clear that the *True Republican* used this opportunity to unleash its criticisms on the problems it had seen growing in Sycamore for the past decade. It satirized the banks, the wealthy, and the lazy, impersonal businessmen who supposedly cared little for the town in which they operated. Much of the criticism was a veiled attack on the directors of the SC&C, who, after 21 years in business, had become the wealthiest, most powerful men in town.[1]

---

[1] See Appendix B for the article's full text.

In spite of this editorial lashing, the railroad held its cornerstone ceremony on Friday, August 20, 1880. Sycamoreans filled the copper capsule with historical memoranda, coins, newspapers, postage stamps, and other items that captured the life of their town. The time capsule was soldered shut, placed in the ground, and sealed beneath the cornerstone. Despite the *True Republican's* harsh criticism of some of the railroad's directors, the paper's publisher and editor, H. L. Boies, spoke at the ceremony. Speeches were also given by Chauncey Ellwood; Nathan Lattin, the mayor; John L. Pratt, a local attorney; Lewis Curts, a local pastor; and John Syme, a prominent businessman. The railroad company treated all attendees to a barrel of iced lemonade.

The depot's cornerstone sits on the building's southeast corner. It appears to have once held a plaque, which most likely listed the names of the men responsible for constructing the building.

This is the earliest known image of the depot. The windmill was added in 1886 and this image was taken soon after.

Depot Architecture

Railroads kept a ready stock of standard depot designs so they could replace or build a new depot at a moment's notice, an unfortunate necessity due to the high number of fires sparked by passing trains. The SC&C directors, however, wanted their depot to be more than just a simple, functional, yet unoriginal building. It had to have an elegant design while still exemplifying strength and durability. It needed to be handsome, identifiable, and stand out as one of the finest depots in Illinois. To achieve these objectives, the directors hired their own architect to design this unique building. While the architect remains unknown, (see Side Track on page 92) he chose to compose the building of bright red brick and rusticated limestone, and he opted for an Italianate design that blended with the architectural style of many other buildings and homes throughout Sycamore. Large Italianate buildings were popular among Chicago's architects between the Civil War and 1880, but few railroad depots were constructed in this particular style, which made Sycamore's depot stand out among Midwestern depots.

Italianate design in Sycamore

Several Sycamore homes and businesses featured strong Italianate characteristics similar to those found on the depot.

Parke Home

DeGraff Home

Stevens Home

Central Block on State Street
(see also Winn's Hotel, page 67)

Strong characteristics of the Italianate style showed through with the keystones in the depot's arched windows and the tall frieze below the eaves, which was capped by decorative double cornice brackets. Other Italianate elements included the tall, narrow windows, hipped roof, brick pilasters, brick dentils below the cornice, wide space between the upper windows and the eaves, and an overall boxy design.

Decorative cornice brackets could be found on houses and buildings all over Sycamore. The ornamental designs between the depot's double brackets were made of pressed tin.

Irregularly sized blocks of Batavia limestone formed the building's foundation walls, which stood 15 feet tall and 13 inches thick. Nine feet of the wall extended below ground. The blocks above ground were capped with a six-inch limestone slab to separate the foundation wall from the flat, smooth, pressed brick that made up the rest of the building. The pressed brick was laid three bricks thick, and the entire façade was ornamented with stone dressings. Limestone arches with keystones hooded the head house windows and doors.

Segmented brick arches with limestone keystones topped the freight house windows. Brick pilasters rose off a limestone base and stretched the full height of the head house edifice, where they were topped with limestone capitals. A limestone string course separated the head house's two floors.

The head house had dimensions of 34 by 36 feet. Station signs emblazoned with "Sycamore" hung on the south and west sides. Over the head house, the eaves stood 36 feet off the ground and had an overhang of 18 inches. The steep, truncated, pyramidal roof rose another 14 feet into the air, making the building a total of 50 feet tall at its highest point. The roof was tiled in slate, which, although cut thin, required a reinforced frame to support the extra weight. The roof's 8-by-10-foot flat top was covered in tin and surrounded by an ornamental iron crest rail. An interior access ladder ran from this summit down into one of the second-floor offices so that employees could raise and lower the American flag each day (hooks alongside the ladder provided a place to hang a lantern in the otherwise unlit attic). Counting the building's tall flagstaff, the entire structure reached 70 feet into the air, making it Sycamore's most visible landmark.

An elevated platform surrounded the entire structure. At its widest, the platform extended 14 feet from the depot (the property's abnormal shape required an equally abnormal platform). Eventually, the platform extended well north

A slate roof tile found inside the depot during the 2012 renovation. Slate tiles were both expensive and fragile, but common to depots of the time because they protected the roof from hazardous sparks launched from passing trains. Wood shingles were lighter and cheaper, but presented a considerable fire risk. Special paints and other fire-resistant compounds were often added to wood shingles, but these compounds were expensive, required regular application, and were by no means as protective as slate.

The train order signal could be switched by a lever/pulley system from inside the depot. In the above photo, a ladder goes up to the signal so that a depot employee could manually switch the signal from the outside. The ladder was also necessary to keep the kerosene lamp filled, lit, and free of bugs. The depot did not need a train order signal until the C&NW built its north-south line through Sycamore in 1885.

of the depot on both its east and west sides, reaching the large water tank and windmill that were constructed on the property in 1885 to 1886.

Inside the depot, almost the entire framework was constructed with rough-cut pine, including the large structural beams under the first floor. The floors themselves were built with wide slats of hard maple. Strategically placed pulleys ran between floors to relay messages and to allow the depot agent to switch signals on the train order signal mounted just outside a second-floor window.

The basement level of the depot, built entirely of Batavia limestone, stood six feet above ground to allow light through the lower-level windows. The passenger and freight offices were located on the building's first floor. The long freight house had dimensions of 72 by 33 feet. The 17-by-30-foot freight office stood at the south end. The depot's 10-by-8-foot freight scale was located outside the freight office and just inside one of the freight house doors.

Employees could reach the second floor by an interior flight of stairs attached to the freight house's eastern wall. A large window in the south wall provided natural light for a narrow corridor that divided the floor's rooms. The SC&C located its principal office on this floor. The second floor offices were intended to make the depot a multi-use building. Planners hoped that local companies that did a lot of business with the SC&C would rent office space right inside the depot. Few companies actually took advantage of this offer and the rooms were often unoccupied or used for storage. The company's forward-thinking directors might have planned the extra rooms as a selling point; if a much larger railroad took over the SC&C, then these rooms would have allowed plenty of space for expansion.

According to financial documents that the SC&C filed with the Illinois Railroad and Warehouse Commission, the new depot cost $7,998.04.

Within Sycamore, two schools of thought emerged concerning the depot's elegant—or extravagant—design. One side believed it showed that the town was wealthy, prosperous, and full of opportunity. The other side believed it showed the arrogance and pretentiousness of a town too small to maintain such an unnecessarily large structure. The railroad's directors hoped for the former; the *True Republican* seemed to believe the latter.

While the depot's construction was still in full swing, the *True Republican* admitted that with its "massive walls" looming loftily over the street, the building would make "a conspicuous ornament to the city."

A Grand Opening?

The exact date the depot opened remains unknown. It most likely began serving passengers in late 1880 while still under construction. The SC&C moved its office into the new building on Monday, November 8, 1880, before the upper rooms were complete. These rooms were still incomplete a month and a half later when the *True Republican* asked whether the owners would throw a grand opening ceremony around New Year's, complete with supper, dance, reception, "and all the embellishments." Then the newspaper asked, "If not, why not?"

It is also unknown if the SC&C actually held its grand opening, as no record of one exists and the newspaper did not report on it. Given the history of the men involved, and their penchant for celebrating nearly every personal achievement, it can be assumed that some sort of celebration marked the occasion.[2]

---

[2]Although several newspapers were published in Sycamore and DeKalb at this time, only issues of the *True Republican* still exist. As established in chapter 4, the *True Republican* chose to provide minimal coverage of the SC&C and its new depot.

The Depot's Missing Awning

Soon after the depot's completion, several residents complained about its lack of a public horse-watering trough, which had been available at the previous depot. The building also lacked another key feature from the previous depot and almost every other train depot: a trackside awning or canopy to protect passengers from inclement weather. Awnings did more than shield passengers from the rain; they provided shade for passengers, freight, and the building itself. In the summer, they cooled the building, and in the winter, they prevented snow from piling up and kept ice from falling on patrons' heads.

A close examination of the freight house reveals evidence that some type of awning or overhang once existed there. Between the freight house windows and doors on both sides of the depot, support stones jut from the brick walls. Above each stone, bolts remain in the bricks, extending through to the interior walls. These bolts, along with the support stones, most likely supported the brackets for an awning that extended the full length of the freight house. Faded brick on the depot's west side also shows evidence that an awning was once attached to the wall, its top resting on the window keystones. Based on the rest of the depot's design, this cantilevered overhang was probably supported by decorative timber or metal brackets. It would have flared out several feet from the wall.

The white blocks jutting from the
freight house wall supported the awning's brackets.

This artist's rendition shows how the awning might
have looked on the depot's freight house.

So why was this overhang removed? There are several possibilities. It could have been damaged in a storm. It could have caught fire from the sparks of a passing train. It's also possible that the awning did not provide enough clearance for newer, larger trains. When the C&NW ran its Northern Illinois line past the depot in 1885, it used larger engines and cars than the SC&C had used. If these trains couldn't clear the awning—or simply came too close for comfort—then the C&NW would have removed it. Whatever the answer, the C&NW never replaced the awning, creating a major inconvenience to its passengers.

The Illinois Central depot in Galena, Illinois, is another example of a depot built in the Italianate style. It also features an awning that may have been similar to the one attached to the Sycamore depot's freight house. (Author's collection)

If Sycamore's combative and often divisive newspapers could agree on one thing, it was that Chauncey Ellwood was the man responsible for bringing Sycamore's new depot to town. Chauncey didn't design it, and he didn't build it, but as the railroad's general manager, he was the driving force behind the project and oversaw the construction from beginning to end. It was the last of several ambitious improvements he brought to the railroad during his tenure. The town recognized his earlier accomplishments with the grand party they threw for him in 1877, and that celebration may have stirred him to even greater ambitions. To the end of his days, he claimed that the Sycamore train depot was his crowning achievement, his monument to the city he loved so much.

A New Engine

By the close of 1880, Sycamore's population had increased by 50% in 10 years and both the wealth and health of the city showed significant improvement. The *True Republican* remarked that very few residents had died in the city in the past year, leading the editor to conclude that "the practice of dying is not much indulged in at Sycamore." A review of the city's shrinking list of delinquent taxpayers shows that the local economy had recovered from the previous year's misfortunes, including the massive heat wave and drought that destroyed the wheat crop and the pig cholera that wiped out much of the town's livestock. Regardless of what the *True Republican* thought of the railroad or the new depot, at the end of 1880 it had to admit, "Good times prevail and the trade is everywhere large beyond precedent."

Over the next year, the *True Republican* gave only two direct mentions of the depot: one to call attention to how the stockyards near the depot brought a terrible stench to that part of town, and the other to announce the depot's installation of a new rooftop weathervane.

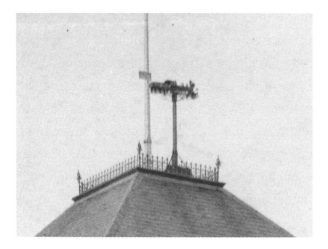

The SC&C's "second engine"

The SC&C commissioned the weathervane in April 1881. Chris Ohlmacher, a local tinsmith and plumber who would later serve as a city alderman and as Sycamore's first superintendent of Water Works, constructed the three-foot-long tin weathervane in the shape of a locomotive. The *True Republican*, in its typical fiscal fashion, gave only a three-word description of the new weathervane: "large and costly." A few months later, when an Elgin newspaper mentioned that the SC&C ran only one engine on its line, the *True Republican* jumped to the railroad's defense, claiming that the

SC&C had, in fact, two engines. It just kept one on top of the depot "in case of emergency."

A Freak Storm and Odd Fellows

The SC&C completed its new depot just in time to face one of the harshest winters in Sycamore's history. In January 1881, the city saw temperatures reach -10°F, and in February and March several feet of snow blanketed the region. One snowstorm in March produced 12-foot drifts. Volunteers tried clearing the track to Cortland, but the snow re-covered the track faster than the men could shovel. Snow drifts concealed doors and windows, and the owner of an outdoor hay scale noted that his scales held 1900 pounds of snow after the storm. The trains did not run for five days, which meant no mail or freight was sent or delivered. Those who braved the open air had to travel to Cortland or DeKalb by sled. They found themselves gliding above the barbed wire fences and past the tops of telegraph poles that barely breached the snow.

It took 127 volunteers several days to finally clear the tracks. The railroad offered free rides to Cortland, and many residents took the unique opportunity to travel through a "snow canal," which rose higher than the passenger cars in several places. Another storm hit only a few days later, and 50 volunteers labored all day and into the night to keep the track clear.

After the devastating 1881 snowstorm, State Street stood buried under several feet of snow (top) and C&NW section workers spent days digging out their tracks (bottom).

By early 1882, local businesses began connecting their stores and offices to the depot by telephone. Elry Hall, the depot agent, ran a phone line from the depot to his house on Grant Street, so he could be on call at all hours of the day.

In April 1882, the northwest Illinois branch of the International Order of Odd Fellows held its 63rd anniversary celebration in Sycamore. It chose Sycamore through the influence of Alonzo Ellwood, the association's grand master. To better facilitate the event, and to accommodate the committee members who would be traveling to and from Sycamore, the anniversary planning association set up its headquarters on the depot's second floor.

On the day of the big event, trains packed with over 2,000 Odd Fellows descended on the depot. Over 1,000 people came in on just two trains, the longest passenger trains that had ever arrived at Sycamore. The depot grounds swarmed with men in colorful uniforms waving equally colorful banners to the tunes of ten different brass bands. Early morning rains might have ruined the occasion, but thanks to the efforts of Sycamore's chairman of the City Committee on Streets and Walks—also Alonzo Ellwood—all the roads had been recently regraded and regraveled (at great expense to the city). The new roads justified their high price because they made the city safe and mud-free for marching. And march the Odd Fellows did, most of the day, up and down almost every city street. With the exception of a parade cannon exploding and removing a man's jaw, the event was a huge success. At midnight, 28 passenger cars escorted everyone back to their respective cities.

When the *True Republican* reported on the event, it included a supposed verbal exchange between two visiting Odd Fellows:

> "Stand aside and let us into the hotel; we want to get a drink," said a Rockford man as he made his way through the crowd on Odd Fellows day.
>
> "Hotel?" said a by-stander; "that ain't no hotel. It's the railroad depot."
>
> "Railroad depot!" exclaimed the visitor; "It's big enough to be a hotel. Why, it's worth more than all the depots in Rockford!"

In its December 8, 1880 issue, the *Chicago Tribune* published the following short article mocking the SC&C:

The great length and importance of this [rail]road makes it necessary to have six general officers to operate, which is just one and a half to the mile. The number of general officers (or bosses) is two less than the total number of other employees, or one and one-third employee to each boss.... The total number of passengers carried was 10,811, and the average number of miles traveled by each was five. Inasmuch as the road is only 4.9 miles in length it is presumed that the passengers walked from the end of the track to the depot to make up the average of five miles.

Who Designed the Depot?

While local historians generally credit Chauncey Ellwood for bringing the new SC&C depot to Sycamore, we don't actually know who designed the building. When constructing larger homes and buildings, Sycamoreans often turned to Chicago for their architects. The three following Chicago architects, and one local architect, designed several buildings in Sycamore around the time the depot was built. All four men make good candidates for the depot architect, not only because they designed buildings of a similar style throughout Sycamore, but because they all had ties to the Ellwood family. So if one of these men did not design the depot, all of them certainly influenced its design through their other work throughout Sycamore.

Gurdon P. Randall

Chicago architect Gurdon P. Randall received his training in Boston. His early work focused on churches and railroad buildings. After moving to Chicago, he designed private residences, churches, public schools, university buildings, and courthouses throughout the Midwest. From the 1860s to the 1880s, he made several trips to Sycamore, either to oversee projects he had designed or to sell his latest home blueprints. In addition to the schoolhouse he designed in 1865 (see page 51), Randall also designed homes for Reuben and Alonzo Ellwood.

George O. Garnsey

George O. Garnsey is best known for designing the Illinois state capitol building in Springfield. After the Chicago Fire in 1871, he planned several prominent buildings throughout that city. In DeKalb, Garnsey is best known as the architect of the historic Ellwood Mansion, which he designed for Isaac Ellwood in 1879. Garnsey also drew up plans for a DeKalb home for Isaac's brother Hiram. In Sycamore, Garnsey designed the Old Congregational Church and several of the historic homes on Somonauk Street. He also designed Sycamore's elegant opera house on State Street. As a further connection to the Sycamore & Cortland Railroad, in 1879 Garnsey designed St. Peter's Church on Somonauk, the construction of which was overseen and fully funded by S&C president James S. Waterman.

John W. Ackermann

John W. Ackermann came to Chicago in 1864 and worked as a draftsman for George O. Garnsey. He assisted his boss in the design of the Illinois state capitol building. In Sycamore, Ackermann designed the George P. Wild house on Somonauk Street and the elegant Winn's Hotel on State Street (see page 67). He also designed Chauncey Ellwood's house on Somonauk Street. All three buildings had strong Italianate features that can be found on the train depot.[1]

Isaac Ellwood's house in DeKalb (c. 1880), designed by Chicago architect George O. Garnsey

[1] Author's note: C&NW historian Charles H. Stats, who has done extensive research on Sycamore's railroads, informed me that he believes Ackermann designed the depot. I share his theory, though neither of us has uncovered definitive evidence to prove it.

The Local Option: James Shannon

A local mason and building contractor, James Shannon, sometimes designed and built his own buildings without the aid of an architect. Based out of Batavia, then Sycamore, then Batavia again, James Shannon executed contract work throughout northern Illinois. He specialized in large buildings, such as factories or multi-use buildings that took up entire city blocks. He built the latter type in downtown Batavia, Sycamore, and DeKalb. In 1877, Shannon built the large factory for the Reuben Ellwood Manufacturing Company just south of the S&C's second depot. In late 1880, just after the brick depot was finished, Shannon began constructing Isaac Ellwood's massive barbed wire factory in DeKalb (see page 67). Both factories were constructed from Truman Van Galder's bricks, the same bricks used to build the depot. It is possible, but uncertain, that Shannon did the brick and stone contract work on the depot. It is also possible that he designed the depot, based on his past experience designing some of the buildings he constructed.

The Chicago & North Western Comes to Town, 1883-1886

Had an inhabitant of this county, thirty years ago, composed himself for a Rip Van Winkle slumber, truly, upon awaking now, he would imagine himself in another world advanced far beyond his comprehension.

True Republican, Nov. 12, 1884

In November 1880, with the new train depot nearing completion, Sycamore, Cortland & Chicago (SC&C) president James Waterman met with officials from the Chicago, Milwaukee and St. Paul Railroad (CM&StP) to discuss running a new line through Sycamore. He promoted Sycamore's proven location as a business center—highlighting, no doubt, the city's fine new depot—and he sweetened the deal by offering the CM&StP the use of the SC&C's five miles of track to Cortland. It is unclear if Waterman was offering only the right-of-way to the company's tracks or if he wanted the CM&StP to purchase the company outright. Based on the SC&C directors' maneuvers during this time, the latter seems the most likely answer.

Waterman's deal with the CM&StP never came to fruition, but after the SC&C finished its new depot, the company's directors could look to the future and focus on their three goals to secure

Sycamore's status as a railroad and business center: build a north-south line through town, connect the town to another railroad to create competition with the Chicago & North Western (C&NW), and sell the SC&C to a larger, more stable company. The first two options seemed the most feasible. Rumors of a second railroad had bombarded the town since the branch line's completion over two decades before. Sycamoreans knew that a new line would force the C&NW to cut its rates. When reports rolled in from other cities that railroad competition had driven down their ticket prices, the *True Republican* declared: "Railroad War! May there never be peace."

Local papers carried regular reports of railroad surveyors spotted in the vicinity. Hotels and restaurants welcomed such men, not only to show them local hospitality, but also to glean any information as to whom they worked for and where they were surveying. At the behest of their employers, the surveyors usually remained tight-lipped, but occasionally they let slip that they were mapping a railroad to Rockford, Belvidere, Aurora, Freeport, St. Louis, or any number of cities. However, Sycamoreans couldn't always trust this information, because the railroads occasionally sent out false survey parties to conceal their intentions or confuse the competition.

In early 1881, the SC&C stockholders met with a new railroad company looking to build a line between Milwaukee and St. Louis by way of Belvidere and Sycamore. As usual, nothing came of it. So many railroad companies approached the city about building there that Sycamoreans could barely differentiate the business from the bluff. Most residents decided to hold their enthusiasm until a company made concrete efforts.

The SC&C Bounces Back

While rumors of new railroads came and went, Sycamore's little railroad continued to experience great success. Within two years of building the new depot, the SC&C's profits rose by 50 percent. The company had to hire more depot men to load and unload all the freight arriving daily. While the SC&C remained stuck dealing exclusively with the C&NW, Sycamoreans still benefited from increasing railroad competition nationwide,

which forced all railroads to cut their freight and passenger rates. Sycamoreans could now travel from Chicago to New York for $10. They could purchase round trip tickets to California for $29. If the traveler couldn't decide where to go, he or she could purchase a 1,000-mile open-ended ticket for $25.

One by one, local businesses continued to connect their stores to the depot by telephone. They continued this piecemeal process until May 1883, when the National Bell Telephone Company delivered a carload of cedar telephone poles and galvanized wire to the train depot. The company's employees immediately installed telephone service to the principal businesses all over town. National Bell provided all the equipment free of charge. It made its money off the usage fees: 15 cents for a five-minute call in-county; 20 cents for five minutes outside the county (which meant a half-hour call to Chicago cost nearly as much as taking the train there). Within days, Sycamore's businesses had phone contact with almost every town in the county and several towns throughout northern Illinois. More importantly, a Sycamore merchant could call a Chicago business in the morning, place an order, and receive his goods at the depot on the afternoon train.

Rival Interests

In January 1883, the papers caught wind of yet another railroad project to connect Sycamore to Belvidere, only this time the project would be undertaken by a small, private railroad, similar to the SC&C. When this plan also fell through, the SC&C directors decided to take matters into their own hands. In April of that year, they voted to increase the company's capital stock to extend the line north to Genoa (and later to Belvidere), where it would link up with the CM&StP and provide railroad access to Rockford. If the SC&C directors went through with this plan, it would be the railroad's first extension since its inception. Belvidere's local paper, the *Northwestern*, viewed the idea favorably and encouraged its citizens to purchase the stock.

Another interested party also viewed the idea favorably. The Chicago, Burlington & Quincy Railroad (CB&Q) had been angling to gain a larger foothold in the region. It offered to purchase the city of Sycamore's shares of the SC&C, which amounted to a quarter of the company. As often happened in the hyper-competitive railroad world, the CB&Q's sudden interest caught the attention of the C&NW, who did not want another railroad encroaching on its territory. In June 1883, the C&NW stepped forward and offered to purchase all of the SC&C's stock. To prove its commitment and to ward off any counter offers, it offered to pay double what the stock was worth.

Changing Hands

In June 1883, unseasonably cold and wet weather forced Sycamoreans to break out their overcoats and flannels in the middle of summer. The abnormal weather threatened the region's crops with ruin and turned farmers' dispositions gloomy. In mid-June, however, the winds suddenly shifted and Sycamore enjoyed several weeks of fine weather. This good fortune brought bountiful crops and a boom in the milk business, which made fresh butter plentiful and cheap. The whole town benefitted, especially the SC&C, who profited off the surplus in outgoing freight. While Sycamoreans breathed a sigh of relief and rejoiced in their healthy harvest, the SC&C directors negotiated the much-anticipated sale of their company.

On Saturday, June 16, 1883, the C&NW completed negotiations to purchase all of the stock of the SC&C for $80,000—double the shares' value. The C&NW agreed to the purchase "on condition that all passenger trains on said Sycamore and Cortland Railroad, now being operated and all connections with passenger trains on Chicago and North Western Railway which are now made by said Sycamore and Cortland Railroad shall be maintained and continued." In other words, the railroad would continue operating as usual, but as a proprietary line of the C&NW. Private shareholders—mostly the SC&C's board of directors—held 300 of the company's 400 shares.

They agreed to the deal outright and signed the contract on Monday, June 18.

The town itself, however, owned a quarter of the company's shares, valued at $20,000, and it could not sell those shares without public approval. To seek that approval, town clerk W. E. Sivwright called a special town meeting for Saturday, June 30, to vote on the issue. In the meantime, several C&NW officers arrived in town to look over their new purchase.

Sycamoreans generally agreed that this sale would benefit the city and provide more access to nearby markets, but they proceeded with some trepidation. They were concerned about handing over control of their locally owned and operated railroad to a "foreign corporation" that had no direct ties to the needs and interests of the city and in which no Sycamorean had any voice or control. But the *True Republican,* who had often spoken out against the power of the railroad conglomerates, backed the sale, noting that the $20,000 would be used to fund local schools. It suggested using the money for a new seminary with boarding facilities, which could bring in students from around the country and give Sycamore a reputation as a center for education. The city could also use the money to improve the high school so Sycamore's students could be more competitive when applying to college. The *True Republican* also noted that three-quarters of the company had been sold already anyway, so it made sense for the town to sell the rest of the shares.

The *True Republican* also took the opportunity to mock the wealthy—and now wealthier—railroad directors, referring to them as "the noble army of dead heads."[1] The paper claimed that

C&C Stockholders

ock in the SC&C changed hands regularly over the ears. At the time of the C&NW buyout, the *True Republican* reported the following list of SC&C ockholders (value of 1 share = $200):

ockholder	Shares	Value
euben Ellwood	120	$24,000
hauncey Ellwood	100	$20,000
ty of Sycamore	100	$20,000
mes Waterman	42	$8,400
hn Waterman	16	$3,200
harles & William Marsh	5	$1,000
veral small holders	17	$3,400
tal	400	$80,000

[1] "Dead-head" was a derogatory term describing those who sought free train rides or passes as a matter of privilege, even though they could afford to pay for them. Many people despised "dead-heads" who sought free tickets due to their social or business connections. A similar term, "dead-beat," described someone who sought a free ride because he or she couldn't afford to pay: a freeloader.

Chauncey Ellwood "mournfully" stated, "It will be a long walk for me to Chicago," implying that the directors had become so averse to purchasing their own tickets that they would rather walk than pay the fare. It also chided Reuben Ellwood with this humorous anecdote:

> When Reub went off to St Paul some years ago and then asked for a pass out on the Northern Pacific, because of his being Treasurer of the SC&C RR, the amazed official asked, "Isn't yours a pretty short road to be taking you so far from home?" "Well yes," says he, "it's pretty short, but am I to blame for that? It's just as broad as any of your roads and I'm as big a man as any of your treasurers." He got his pass.[2]

The paper later noted that the "dead heads" need not fret over the loss of their free passes, because the C&NW had assured them that their passes would be honored until the end of the year.

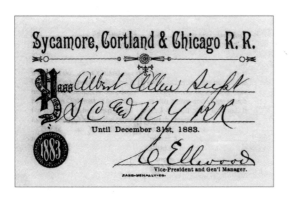

One of Chauncey Ellwood's coveted railroad passes.

At the public meeting, several of the SC&C's directors made the case for selling the town's shares. The *True Republican* described Chauncey's oratory as a "queer mixture of business sense and buffoonery that keeps his audience always in a merry humor." Much of the meeting was just for show, because Sycamore's residents had generally agreed beforehand that the sale would go through. After the town clerk tallied the votes, the results showed just that.

The SC&C and the C&NW still needed to work out a few particulars. On Monday, July 2, a special train with a "palace car" pulled up outside the Sycamore depot. It carried the president of the C&NW, Albert Keep, who had traveled from New York to Sycamore to sign the paperwork that would finalize the SC&C transfer. The company's general manager and several other leading businessmen accompanied him. The task took several hours, as each stockholder had to surrender his stock personally to receive on-the-spot cash for his shares. All stockholders were present with the exception of SC&C President James S. Waterman, who lay in a Chicago hospital, where he had been suffering from a severe stomach ulcer for nearly a month. It can be assumed that his brother John oversaw the transfer of his shares.

---

[2]Slightly modified versions of this story have appeared in Sycamore newspapers over the years, often interchanging Reuben and Chauncey.

When the C&NW handed over $20,000 to the city of Sycamore, Reuben Ellwood made a formal show of asking Albert Keep if he understood that he now owned the entire Sycamore, Cortland & Chicago Railroad. Keep replied that he did. With the transfer complete, the SC&C's directors convened their final meeting. Vice President Chauncey Ellwood presided as each director resigned his position and the C&NW named each man's successor. Everyone adjourned to a fine dinner at the Ward Hotel (formerly Winn's Hotel), where Keep assured Sycamore's "business men of large views and great sagacity" that the C&NW would prove a benefit to the city. Then the C&NW men hopped on their train and returned to Chicago.

James Sears Waterman

On Thursday, July 19, 1883, little more than two weeks after the sale of the SC&C, James S. Waterman died in the Chicago hospital he had occupied for six weeks. He was 63 years old. He had come to Sycamore in 1838 at only 18 and quickly become one of the village's leading citizens. He had worked tirelessly for twenty years to bring a railroad to Sycamore, and when the S&C was finally completed in 1859, he was its largest shareholder. In Waterman's obituary, the *True Republican* put its biases aside to praise this early pioneer's instrumental impact on the city:

> In his death Sycamore has lost one of the earliest, strongest and warmest of its friends. He may very properly be regarded as its founder, for he took part in the selection of its site, was its earliest merchant, its largest landholder, its first banker, and its wealthiest inhabitant, and all through the forty-five years of his residence here has been always ready and eager to do anything and everything necessary to promote its growth and prosperity.

Waterman's funeral was held in St. Peter's Episcopal Church, the church he had helped design and paid for out of his own pocket. John C. Waterman, already suffering from ill health, never recovered from the loss of his little brother. He passed away on October 19, 1883, at the age of 69. In a span of only a few months, Sycamore lost two of its most productive and dedicated pioneers.

After the SC&C

After the transfer, few noticeable changes took place at the depot. The C&NW retained the depot agent, Elry Hall, and all of the depot employees. Everyone still referred to the branch line as the "Sycamore & Cortland."[3] Within a few months, the company promised to replace the train's old

---

[3]Author's note: The newspapers also went back to calling the line the Sycamore & Cortland (S&C), dropping the lately added "Chicago." I will do the same for the book's remainder.

coaches with two new ones. When the time came for the new coaches to arrive, however, only one showed up, and it was smaller, older, and in worse condition than the originals. A furious Elry Hall sent it straight back to Chicago. Other than this minor difficulty, the C&NW proved to be a company of its word, and life at the depot returned to normal.

Over the next year, the C&NW added new coaches, altered its timetable to include more runs, replaced the iron rails with heavy steel, and fenced-in the tracks, all of which made freight and passenger service to and from Chicago more amenable to Sycamore's needs. Now that Sycamore had transferred its local railroad service to the security and stability of a large company, it was free to concentrate on another of its railroad objectives, that elusive north-south line that forever seemed just out of reach.

> Visitors to the depot during the cold weather of Saturday were alarmed by reports like the discharge of musketry in the freight room. Sixteen barrels of beer, in eighth and quarter kegs, and several barrels of bottled beer, consigned to Fred Woltz, had been caught in the cold snap and frozen, and these reports came when the kegs burst or the corks flew out . Two hundred dollars worth of beer is a total loss.

From the January 9, 1884 issue of the *True Republican*.

A Greater Plan

Throughout the spring and early summer of 1884, local newspapers continued their speculations on the numerous new railroads rumored to be coming to town, all the while printing accounts of clandestine surveyors canvassing the nearby fields and groves. The *True Republican* asked its readers to be on the lookout for surveying parties "running lines through their farms" and to report any such activity to the paper immediately. At one point, the paper reported that no fewer than five railroads were planning to build new lines through Sycamore: the Northern Illinois; the Chicago, Milwaukee & St. Paul; the Bureau & Northwestern; the Joliet, Aurora & Northern; and the Chicago, Freeport & St. Paul.

In June, the newspaper announced that its reporters had cracked the case. The C&NW had created a subsidiary company, the Northern Illinois Railroad (NI), to construct and operate a north-south line to connect the Spring Valley region (55 miles south of Sycamore) to Belvidere (20 miles north). As of yet, no one could confirm whether the new route would include Sycamore. The most direct route would have bypassed both DeKalb and Sycamore to the west and run through Malta. However, several Sycamoreans and DeKalbans believed the C&NW would run the railroad slightly east to accommodate the large manufacturing industries in both cities.

The C&NW's purchase of Sycamore's branch railroad had been part of a much greater plan. The company wanted to dominate northern Illinois shipping and to expand its already vast empire. To do this, it made several large land acquisitions throughout the region, including the purchase of 16,000 acres of coal-rich land near LaSalle and Peru, in the Spring Valley region surrounding the Illinois River. The region's coal deposits had been discovered as early as 1679, when Catholic priest and missionary Father Louis Hennepin, who accompanied Robert de La Salle on his expedition of the region, noted a coal mine on his map of the Illinois River, near the present-day city of Ottawa. Hennepin's tiny note became the first record of coal in North America. Two hundred years later, these coal deposits had the potential to power all of the C&NW trains in northern Illinois. However, the C&NW needed a north-south line to connect its mines to a northern outlet. It set its sights on the small but expanding city of Belvidere, which provided rail connections to Rockford, and from there branched out to Wisconsin, Minnesota, and the Dakota Territory.

Sycamore's manufacturing interests had long been looking for an easier route to Belvidere. At the time the C&NW took over the S&C, if any Sycamoreans needed to travel or ship freight to Belvidere, their only options were to provide their own transportation, take a series of indirect connections by train, or hire out a stagecoach from John Hoag, whose decrepit horses were said to be on their last legs. By horse or stage, the trip could take a full day. Using the train, passengers had to go to Chicago first, which turned the 20-mile trip into a 90-mile trip that—with multiple transfers—took several hours. A direct route to Belvidere would provide a great convenience for Sycamore and had the potential to make the seat of DeKalb County one of the largest transfer points in the region.

A New Line Secured

The NI broke ground on the line's southern end on April 29, 1885, yet Sycamoreans still waited anxiously for news about the railroad's ultimate route. When the railway company finally approached the city with terms for building the line through Sycamore, city leaders hastily convened a meeting to examine the contract and to select a soliciting committee to raise funds. The *True Republican* called on Sycamore's residents to contribute something—anything—to secure the railroad, as they had done almost three decades before. "We must be liberal," the paper claimed. "If anyone supposes [the new railroad] will come to Sycamore without liberal help… they will make a grave mistake."

The issue fell on Sycamore's shoulders during the 1885 mayoral election, in which both candidates centered their platforms on bringing a new railroad to town. Incumbent and former manager of the S&C, Chauncey Ellwood, who still had strong ties with the railroad companies, easily won his re-election by claiming that his experience and connections would guarantee Sycamore the new railroad.

The pressing need to secure this railroad is seen in the *True Republican's* sudden shift in favor of the railroad companies it had so long attacked. The paper began praising the large railroad conglomerates and called on all Sycamoreans to "recognize the fact that the life-giving railroad has multiplied by ten our population; has multiplied by twenty our wealth; has made every farm worth double, perhaps quadruple the price it would have brought without it; has built into prosperous cities the impoverished little hamlets; and brought enlightenment and wealth where would have been ignorance and desolation." The paper then condemned those who would attack the railroads in the name of social justice and workers' rights. Such men, it claimed, were just looking for political capital by influencing "shallow minds."

It is possible that the C&NW exerted some editorial influence at the paper. It is also possible that the editors really had changed their opinions about the railroads; everything they said about the

railroads' benefit to the region was true, after all. But the most likely reason for the *True Republican's* flip-flop was the burning desire to get a north-south line to run through Sycamore. If the city's largest newspaper stood against the C&NW's interests, as it had in the past, then this railroad might never materialize, and Sycamore would suffer as a result.

Because Sycamoreans understood the importance of this second line, which was projected to bring in $6,000 a year in tax revenue, they quickly raised the necessary funds to build the new railroad. Within days, surveyors, engineers, and contractors poured into the depot. Building materials piled up outside. Small shanty towns and tent villages cropped up on the outskirts of Sycamore and DeKalb to house the workers. The makeshift housing became a common addition to the landscape throughout the summer. For a time, the C&NW considered turning the tracks sharply east just north of DeKalb, which would have allowed the line to connect with the S&C tracks north of Cortland, but the NI soon abandoned this plan and began building the first direct line between DeKalb and Sycamore. The tracks would join the S&C line at a junction just south of Sycamore so that the new line could still use the depot. From the depot, the line would continue north on Sacramento Street, crossing State and Exchange Streets before following Brickville Road north out of town and curving northwest to reach Belvidere.

Reuben Ellwood

In July, the jubilation over the new railroad was cut short when Sycamore suffered the unexpected loss of one of its most prominent citizens. U. S. Congressman Reuben Ellwood, Sycamore's first mayor and a co-founder of the Sycamore & Cortland Railroad, suffered a sudden illness that left him confined to his bed. A few days before, a witness reported seeing him leave his factory near the depot and begin staggering down the S&C tracks toward Cortland. He was said to be in a "bewildered" state before collapsing on a pile of lumber. His family brought in a prominent doctor from Chicago by special train. The doctor's train made the trip in one hour and twenty minutes, the fastest time ever recorded between the two cities. A team of physicians worked around the clock, treating Reuben Ellwood for "liver inflammation and other complications," which later turned out to be cancer of the pancreas. The doctors admitted they could do little more than ease his pain. "Reub," as he was affectionately known, passed away on July 1, 1886, at the age of 64.

The following Sunday, over 3,000 mourners from across northern Illinois arrived at the depot on special trains to attend the largest funeral in Sycamore's history. "He was a man of great heart, and wherever he went he had a host of friends," the *True Republican* reported. "The people of

A portrait of Reuben Ellwood commissioned by Congress after his death.

Sycamore and its immediate vicinity came out almost unanimously to testify to their loss." His obituary in the *New York Times* described him as "a robust man, large in stature, large in heart, and large in his business capacity."

There is an interesting historical footnote to this unhappy affair. While the expert team of doctors tended to Reuben Ellwood, they were assisted by a young Sycamore man who had ambitions to attend medical school. His name was Albert Philip Ohlmacher, 19-year-old son of Chris Ohlmacher, the tinsmith who had crafted the train engine weathervane that stood atop the depot. One doctor was so impressed with young Ohlmacher's work that he arranged for him to attend the prestigious Rush Medical College in Chicago. Ohlmacher went on to have a diverse and distinguished career as a physician, pathologist, bacteriologist, and chemist. He published numerous papers in all areas of his interests, and his work in bacteriology is credited with contributing directly to several life-saving vaccines.

New Accommodations

Work on the north-south line continued throughout the summer of 1885. A constant stream of cars carrying gravel, ties, and rails came up the S&C and deposited their materials at the depot. By October, supply trains came in on the new railroad from the south, carrying the materials needed to finish the line to the north. Although the NI was built to accommodate freight—mostly coal and lumber—it provided much-needed passenger service as well. To better manage both services, the C&NW built a short spur line on the depot's east side for passenger use while the original tracks on the depot's west side remained in use for freight.[4]

The NI completed its 76-mile north-south line on October 25, 1885. Soon after, Sycamoreans marveled at all the freight trains passing through their town from places many had never seen before: St. Louis, northern Wisconsin, Minnesota, and the Dakota Territory. At the NI's peak of operation, a coal train departed the Spring Valley mines every hour, making traffic through Sycamore very lively and also very congested. Sycamoreans found several of the city's major intersections north of the depot inconveniently blocked for the first time. They also had to adjust to the sudden presence of hundreds of coal cars from the south and lumber cars from the north passing through town nearly 24 hours a day. Some NI trains stretched over 200 cars long, so long that the engines often stalled for want of power to pull such heavy loads.

The first passenger car ran on the new line on December 9, 1885, when several C&NW directors travelled the full distance from LaSalle to Belvidere on an inspection tour. The *True Republican* praised the directors for going out of their way to accommodate DeKalb and Sycamore with their new railroad, noting that "the time has gone by for intelligent people to regard railroad corporations as powerful and remorseless tramplers upon the rights and wishes of the public."

---

[4]The C&NW later reversed this system and used the depot's east-side spur line exclusively for loading and unloading freight.

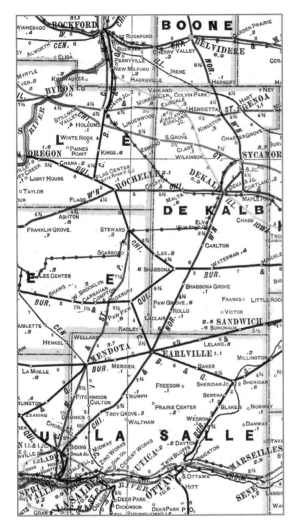

This 1907 railroad map shows the Northern Illinois route between Spring Valley and Belvidere.

Sycamore's latest advancement. The tracks ran alongside the S&C line until about a mile south of town, where the line branched off and curved southwest toward DeKalb. "The traveler finds a remarkably smooth, pleasant track, over a rich prairie country," the reporter wrote. "It is seldom that a new road is so good a road." His journey took him through the stations at DeKalb, Elva, Newton, Old Shabbona, Rollo, Earlville, Triumph, and Troy Grove before ending at the C&NW coal fields in Spring Valley, just west of Peru and LaSalle. The reporter noted that Spring Valley had all the "foundations for a thriving place," but because it was inhabited mostly by coal miners, they were "underground most of the time and [made] little show on the streets."

A few weeks later, a similar report highlighted a trip north to Belvidere, noting that the day-long journey by wagon had shrunk to only 95 minutes of a "very pleasant afternoon." This northerly excursion took the reporter through new stations at Henrietta and Herbert before arriving at Belvidere. The writer gave his readers a flattering account of Belvidere's accommodations and improvements—minus a few negative comments about Belvidere's saloons with their "blear-eyed occupants"—and warned Sycamoreans that they needed to step up their advertising before Belvidere stole away all of their business.

When the railroad opened to regular passenger service in mid-December, a *True Republican* correspondent rode the rails south to report on

But Sycamoreans did not need to feel threatened by Belvidere. Having the new north-south line created the expected economic boost, and Sycamore experienced another period of considerable growth. New businesses opened, new blocks and houses went up, and the town enjoyed a sharp population increase. The *True Republican* compared the new developments to those brought on by the S&C a quarter century before and found that this new growth showed signs of quality over quantity. The earlier economic boom had necessitated quick, cheap housing and businesses to secure the nation's frontier. Now the city focused on sturdy, elegant brick structures that improved a town already firmly established in the region.

To accommodate not only the people of Sycamore, but all residents of DeKalb County, the C&NW adjusted its timetables to improve connections with the new line. Now almost anyone in the county could travel to the county seat in under two hours. Because many of these travelers took the time to eat and do a little shopping while in town, Sycamore's economy saw marked improvement.

An 1888 timetable for the C&NW's S&C and NI lines out of Sycamore.

Within four months, over 9,000 passengers had taken advantage of the one passenger train running on the new line. The route's popularity led the company to add a second passenger train by year's end and prompted rumors that the C&NW would abandon the S&C line. The C&NW put such rumors to rest when it ordered extensive improvements to the tracks at Cortland. By April 1886, twelve passenger trains a day departed from Sycamore's depot: six on the NI route and six on the S&C route. To accommodate all of the new traffic coming through Sycamore, the C&NW re-laid the tracks around the depot and re-graded and re-graveled the switchyards.

This 1916 map created by the Interstate Commerce Commission shows the C&NW's section house on Exchange Street, just west of the C&NW tracks.

The C&NW made other improvements to its depot facilities as well. It added new sheds north of the depot to store equipment for section work crews. The company also purchased a house just west of the tracks on Exchange Street so that section workers had overnight accommodations. The C&NW section house operated like a bed and breakfast, complete with kitchen, dining room, and bedrooms with bunk beds.

In early December 1885, the C&NW contracted for a new well and "monster windmill" just north of the depot. The whole project was set to cost $2,500, but over the next few months, the project constantly confounded its contractors. Just when they thought they'd hit the water table, the windmill pumped the well dry and they had to dig down farther. The water that did come out had a strong sulfur and iron smell and later became popular as an "excellent tonic mineral water" that, among other things, treated "kidney complaint." It wasn't until May 1886, nearly six months after work began, that the windmill pump pulled up a consistent water supply. The entire endeavor cost the contractor twice what he earned. Six months later, the well failed again and the C&NW hired a different contractor to bore a second well near the old one. This well proved to be more successful.

The 20-foot diameter windmill was a "Haliday Standard" made in Batavia, Illinois, by the United States Wind Engine and Pump Company. The small shed between the freight house and water tank was used by the C&NW section crews to store tools and equipment.

"Our railroad facilities are unsurpassed," the *True Republican* declared. "Yet we expect to improve them by the addition of another railroad." By the end of 1886, this notion was more than just conjecture on the newspaper's part. While new railroad construction continued cutting into the west, the final phase of Sycamore's major railroad development was about to begin. A new railroad—a rival to the all-powerful C&NW—had set its sights on Sycamore. The city's mighty brick depot—barely six years old but already accommodating two lines and working to capacity—would no longer serve as Sycamore's only outlet to the outside world.

C&NW Locomotive 37 sits beside the depot water tower in 1893.

Sycamore's Railroading Dynasty

Ed Rose on top of Sycamore's first locomotive (c.1865)

During the latter half of the 19th century, Edwin "Ed" Porter Rose created a railroad dynasty in and around Sycamore. The Rose family became associated with the railroads for over a half century, and the Sycamore & Cortland Railroad could not have operated without them.

Ed Rose was born in Erie County, New York, on April 11, 1827. His family came west in 1843 when he was 16 years old. He met his wife, Sarah Jeannette Russell of Cortland, and in Sycamore they raised eight children, seven of them boys. In 1865, Ed became conductor of the S&C. He also built a home on the north side of Grant Street, just west of the depot. He remained conductor for ten years before leaving to operate a coal business, which he set up near the depot. He returned to his old position five years later, around the time the new depot was under construction.

When the C&NW took over the S&C in 1883, Rose kept his position as conductor. When the Northern Illinois line brought more trains through town, Rose remained as the conductor of the local train, only now he added runs to and from DeKalb. To distinguish the local train from the other trains now passing through town, the C&NW referred to it as the "Sycamore Local," but Sycamoreans knew it by a different name: "Ed Rose's Train."

Ed Rose put his sons to work at the depot at early ages. They performed menial tasks, such as sweeping the floors, washing the windows, and organizing papers. The oldest son, Chauncey, learned to use the telegraph. In 1871, the 18-year-old became the telegraph operator at the Cortland depot. The next son, Lamont "Mont" Rose, performed general tasks around the Sycamore depot office until he advanced to ticket agent in the late 1870s and then to telegraph operator in the early 1880s. The third son, Elmer, became a brakeman on his father's train.

On a typical day, Conductor Ed Rose would take his train out of Sycamore. His son Elmer would operate the brakes. His son Mont would telegraph a message to Cortland to let them know the train was on its way. And yet another son, Chauncey, would receive that message. Almost all aspects of the S&C's daily operations were run by a Rose.

Mont Rose was always dedicated to his duty. One day in March 1881, the telegraph went down, so Mont walked the telegraph messages to his brother in Cortland. Along the way, he checked the entire telegraph line for damage. In 1886, Mont and his wife, Lillian Rowley Rose, moved into the depot's upper rooms. It was common for depot's to have someone living on the premises, but this was the only time that anyone lived in the Sycamore depot. Mont and his wife occupied the depot's second floor until 1891, when they moved into a home Mont built next to his father's house on Grant Street, where they lived just a few houses down from the S&C's longtime engineer, John Tucker.

Ed Rose retired in 1901 after 31 years as Sycamore's local train conductor. Chauncey became Cortland's depot agent in 1902 and retired in 1915, after 45 years of railroad service. Mont worked as telegraph operator until around 1910, retiring after over 30 years of service. Elmer retired from the C&NW after 45 years. Two other brothers, Edwin and Frank, also made careers as railroad men working for the C&NW. In all, five of Ed Rose's seven sons dedicated their lives to the railroad.

On December 8, 1892, the *City Weekly* provided this fitting profile of the railroading patriarch:

> Other conductors may come and go, but Ed remains. We don't know how many years he has run the Sycamore and Cortland train, but a good many. That means that he is competent and trusty, that he always runs on schedule time, makes four trips a day regularly, never kills anybody, and if the company could, it does not get along without him.

The Great Western Moves In, 1886-1892

It is evident from the number of schemes in process of evolvement, that an era of railroad expansion west of Chicago is certain beyond question.

The Chicago Times, July 22, 1886

While Sycamoreans awaited the completion of the north-south line, outside forces worked to pull the city into a much larger railroad scheme. Several companies vied to complete a profitable new route between Chicago and St. Paul, Minnesota. The most popular proposed route was a line between St. Paul and Dubuque, which would then connect with either Freeport or Rockford, but the exact route from those cities to Chicago was anybody's guess. Railroad companies interested in the route deployed their surveyors throughout the region. Newspapers peppered their local columns with rumors and speculations as to which towns would get the railroad.

"This is an area of extraordinary activity," the *True Republican* reported. "The new excitement in railroad building has just begun." Several Sycamoreans saw the benefit a new railroad company in Sycamore could bring to the town. Not only would a second railroad compete with the Chicago & North Western (C&NW) and drive down passenger and freight rates, but there was also the possibility that with two major railroads,

Sycamore would be designated a Chicago suburb. This designation would reduce rates even further and bring new businesses and residents to town.

Sycamore's leaders also had an ambitious plan to make their city a prominent manufacturing center. In this age, manufacturing was "the life of all prosperous towns," but before the 1880s, manufacturing had been limited mostly to cities, because companies couldn't profit without ready access to shipping. With the last decade's rapid railroad expansion, however, several companies began relocating their operations to smaller communities—like Sycamore and DeKalb—that readily competed against each other to secure such businesses. After Sycamore failed to attract a safe and lock manufacturer, the *True Republican* denounced the lack of public support and asked, "Are there none to fill the place of Reuben Ellwood and [James] S. Waterman as organizers? We used to denounce those men vigorously when they were in active life, but now we miss them. If they had been alive… we would have had not only the safe and lock company, but other factories."

Public organizing wasn't the only hindrance, however. Sycamoreans knew their town could not prosper without a competing railroad. "Competing railroads are what make a manufacturing town," the *True Republican* wrote, but the *DeKalb Chronicle* best summed up Sycamore's predicament (and its own): "All talk of manufactures is nonsense while the town is under the heel of the Northwestern."

Securing the New Line

In late December 1885, the chief engineer of an unnamed railroad arrived in Sycamore on foot, having braved the bitter cold all the way from Freeport to survey his company's proposed route. While in town, he chose the location for a railroad depot on North California Street, three blocks north of State Street, then continued his walk to Chicago. Despite this man's dedication to his duty, his company never built a line through Sycamore. That honor eventually fell to a young and ambitious corporation out of St. Paul, the Minnesota & Northwestern (M&NW), owned by A. B. Stickney. For the past few years, Stickney had defied the railroad monopolies by signing contracts and securing rights-of-way all across the Midwest. His grand ambition was to create a vast network connecting St. Paul to Chicago and Kansas City, Missouri. Stickney began his scheme by building a route from St. Paul to Dubuque. To connect this route to Chicago, he set his sight on the old Chicago, St. Charles and Mississippi Air Line, the failed railroad from the 1850s that had surveyed its route from Chicago to Freeport before going under (see pages 17-18). Outside of St. Charles, several miles of the line had been graded and a bridge had been partially built. If Stickney could secure the rights to this route, some of his work would have already been done for him.

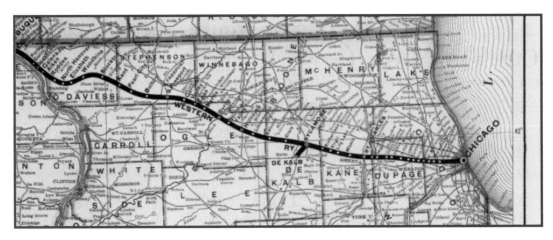

The M&NW's route through northern Illinois

Alpheus Beede (A. B.) Stickney was born in Wilton, Maine, on June 27, 1840. At 21, he headed west to the Minnesota frontier, where he worked as a teacher, lawyer, and school superintendent. In 1869, he entered the railroad business, where he worked as a supervisor, general manager, vice president, and legal counsel. In 1885, he began the railroad enterprise that would become the Chicago Great Western. The *True Republican* once said of him, "What manner of man is this Mr. Stickney the head of this Minnesota & Northwestern Railroad system? He gives evidence of possessing one of the biggest brains, the most courageous, far seeing and brilliant minds engaged in railroad construction."

Illinois granted the M&NW a license to operate within the state on February 27, 1886. Towns along the old Air Line route buzzed with rumors as to the M&NW's final plans. The company employed two survey teams to work at either end of the proposed route, one moving east from Freeport while the other moved west from Chicago. On March 27, the M&NW's chief engineer arrived in Sycamore and immediately surveyed the land on the city's north side. He later headed to the courthouse to review area maps, all the while dodging questions from reporters eager to learn his company's intentions. Over the next few weeks, more surveyors appeared near Sycamore, but their presence still did not confirm that the town would get the railroad. In late May, St. Charles officials received word that the new line would pass through their city. This news gave hope to both DeKalb and Sycamore, who each saw themselves as the line's next stop. The *DeKalb Review* claimed that this line would "be the making of St. Charles."

Even though the C&NW's mutually beneficial north-south line had been open only a few months, the M&NW's impending location reopened the rivalrous wounds between DeKalb and Sycamore. Both could not have the east-west railroad, but both wanted it. When the *DeKalb Review* suggested that Sycamore should fear the new line because other cities on its route would sap Sycamore's trade, the *True Republican* fired back: "The wish is oft times father to the thought."

John L. Pratt

For many of Sycamore's business leaders, the M&NW's route through Sycamore was never in doubt. The company had hired prominent Sycamore attorney John L. Pratt to secure the rights-of-way between Freeport and Chicago. Pratt was heavily involved in local politics and had close ties with most of Sycamore's business leaders, including the Ellwoods. In 1883, he had sat on the last board of directors for the S&C. After the M&NW completed its railroad, Pratt stayed on with the company and relocated to St. Paul. By 1890, he was in charge of the company's lands, including all rights-of-way and station grounds. He remained with the company until his death in 1910.

To better its chances at securing the M&NW route, DeKalb prepared to send a committee of concerned citizens to St. Paul to meet with Stickney personally. When the committee learned he would be visiting Chicago, they met him there instead, argued their case, and offered him $100,000 to build his railroad through DeKalb instead of Sycamore. Stickney informed the committee that he had no intention of bypassing Sycamore, as long as Sycamore could offer reasonable prices for the rights-of-way. The newspapers and business leaders of Sycamore knew that the town would offer whatever prices the M&NW wanted, so they celebrated the good news. Two rival railroads would soon be operating within their city.

Building Commences

Just as Sycamore celebrated its good fortune, another railroad stepped into the arena. The Chicago, Freeport & St. Paul (CF&StP) claimed it was building a railroad connecting Chicago and St. Paul by way of Sycamore and Rockford (conspicuously bypassing Freeport, despite the company's name). Beyond Rockford, the line would veer into Wisconsin and run through Monroe, Dodgeville, and Black River Falls. The CF&StP advertised its route as shaving 20 miles off the M&NW's Chicago-St. Paul run, a claim that could earn the company millions in shipping profits in this era of cutthroat railroad competition. The CF&StP also threw a wrench in the M&NW's plans by claiming all rights to the old Air Line route outside of St. Charles.

In spite of the CF&StP's claim, the M&NW barreled forward with its project. It sent agents to canvas towns, collect deeds and contracts, and secure the necessary rights-of-way along the route. Preliminary construction began in early June 1886, with the company claiming it would have its trains running between Chicago and St. Charles by September. The initial work employed over 1,000 men. The CF&StP tried to block the M&NW through various legal maneuvers, all to no avail. Its skittish investors eventually abandoned the project, though a persistent few continued to harass the M&NW with legal threats that never materialized.

In early July, the M&NW awarded the grading contract to the St. Paul firm Shepard, Winston & Company. To the delight of Sycamore's business leaders, the firm made Sycamore its headquarters, which meant that most contractors and subcontractors would also relocate to Sycamore, hire in Sycamore, and spend their money in Sycamore. Contract workers could earn anywhere from $3.50 to $7.00 a day, depending on experience. This wage far exceeded the pay for farm work, which was wanting "in these dry times." Contracting firms raked in thousands

in profits. The *True Republican* proposed the question: "Who wouldn't be a railroad contractor in this wonderful year for railroad building?"

The ink on the contracts had barely dried before Sycamoreans saw the "dust flying" in a flurry of railroad activity. Survey teams staked the new line while contractors broke ground and began grading the roadbed. More teams arrived in Sycamore daily, thronging the streets before finding lodging in various hotels or setting up camp just outside of town.

Amid all this hustle and bustle, the papers carried word of a third railroad projected to connect Chicago and Freeport, this one under the control of the Illinois Central Railroad (IC). The *True Republican* declared, "It is a piece of folly to build another railroad from Chicago to Freeport." This railroad would bypass Sycamore entirely, but many saw it as little more than a bluff by the IC to earn favorable rates on the use of the M&NW's line. The IC eventually opened this line, which continued from Freeport to Madison, Wisconsin, in 1889.

The regular reports of rival railroads racing against the M&NW only spurred the company's progress. It struck a deal with the C&NW to have its building materials shipped into Sycamore on the S&C line and unloaded at the depot. The C&NW rearranged and re-laid the tracks around the depot to accommodate the carloads of construction material that soon would be steaming into Sycamore.

By mid-October, daily shipments of railroad materials poured into the city. One massive shipment contained 156,000 ties and 50 carloads of steel rails. North of the C&NW depot, the M&NW built a Y-junction in the Northern Illinois line to get the materials to the construction site on the north side of town, between Sacramento and Main Street. Throughout construction, this whole area remained buried under "a whole forest of ties and a whole mine of steel rails." It was an exciting place for Sycamore's children to gather and watch all of the activity. At any given time, there were between five and ten work trains stopped there. In all, over 1,200 cars hauled construction materials into Sycamore to build the new railroad.

Track-laying outside Sycamore commenced on December 4, 1886. Contractors worked day and night, with the night crews surrounding their work sites with torches so they could labor straight through to dawn. Late-night travelers noted the strange glow these work sites cast upon the horizon.

Winter's onslaught brought about several delays. Heavy snowdrifts blocked the construction trains while intense cold and freezing rains further slowed progress. Despite the difficult conditions, the M&NW completed the line from Chicago to Sycamore on Friday, January 28, 1887. When the construction train rolled into Sycamore around noon, workers spiked the last rail, the engine blasted its horn, and a jubilant crowd paraded the work crew to the Ward Hotel, where the men received a lavish dinner. The papers marveled that only six months had passed since construction began. The M&NW predicted that its regular trains would be running through town by spring.

On February 25, the materials for Sycamore's second depot arrived at the construction site two blocks north of the courthouse, between Maple and Main. At the time, the north side of town ended one block north of the courthouse. There were no businesses, no factories, and very few homes. It was just a wide-open stretch of farms, prairies, and pastureland. The M&NW's surveyors had staked out the site close to the Genoa Road so the depot would catch the city's north-side business and offer convenience to farmers and merchants who entered Sycamore from that direction.

Carpenters completed the one-story, heavy-timber structure in only two weeks. Its 22-by-90-foot dimensions housed a freight room, ticket office, and both ladies' and gentlemen's waiting rooms. The ticket office sported an attractive

The Minnesota & Northwestern depot, pictured here in the 1940s when it was operated by the Chicago Great Western.

bay window, yet O. T. Willard, one of the depot's earliest employees, described the office as being crowded, cluttered, and wholly unorganized. The M&NW built its depot to be functional, not aesthetically pleasing like the C&NW depot. It followed a standard design and offered reasonable accommodations, but it was never popular among Sycamoreans. Within four years of the depot's construction, residents were already calling on the M&NW to build a new one (which it finally did, 60 years later in 1951).

To complete the ballasting along the M&NW line, the company used gravel from pits east of Sycamore, near St. Charles. At the project's onset, 100 men were hired to work the pits. However, because of the railroad's demand for 100 to 200 carloads of gravel a day, the workforce quickly increased to over 300 men who worked both day and night. Many of these men came from outside the city. They funneled money into the local economy, but also frequently engaged in drunken, disorderly conduct. The papers reported several instances of disgruntled workers going on strike, getting into fistfights, or passing out in city alleys. "Black eyes, bloody noses and chewed ears are a common sight," the *True Republican* reported. Sycamore saw a little more peace on its streets in early July when the M&NW completed graveling and shut down the pits.

The M&NW's first freight trains began running through Sycamore in early June, but delays along the line prevented passenger trains from running until the end of July. The first M&NW passenger train, the west-bound *St. Paul Express*, arrived on Sunday, July 31, at 9:24 p.m. Several hundred Sycamoreans gathered at the depot to celebrate the train's arrival and to glimpse the M&NW's well-advertised, elegant travel accommodations, which included sleeping, dining, reading, and drawing cars far beyond anything available to the average traveler on competing lines. The *True Republican* described the locomotive as "resplendent in glittering brass and new paint," with cars that were "a dark color and finished in gold." The next morning, another large crowd, accompanied by the Sycamore Brass Band, returned to the depot to celebrate the arrival of the first east-bound train, the *Chicago Express*. Regular service began that day with three passenger trains and five freight trains running each way. When the M&NW completed the full line, its trains could make the 420-mile trip between St. Paul and Chicago in 14 hours, or as the *Chicago Tribune* put it in an

August 4, 1887 headline: "St. Paul But a Night's Journey Away." Besides gaining access to the St. Paul/Minneapolis market, Sycamore finally had direct access to the heart of Chicago, exactly 55.7 miles away.

In late October, the editor of the *St. Charles Valley Chronicle* visited Sycamore on the M&NW and gave the following account:

> Walking into Sycamore from the M&NW station one gets a most favorable idea of the place. Broad streets, elegant residences and ample shade trees make the town look very inviting, and give it an air of comfort and social cultivation in strong contrast with many other places…. The Minnesota & Northwestern [Railway] Co. has done well by Sycamore, as the convenient and roomy station building and the extensive stockyards and feeding grounds of the company testify. The business of the [rail]road is evidently increasing, and both the railway company and the city are to be congratulated. The new [rail]road brings Sycamore and St. Charles much nearer together than they have been heretofore and the people of both cities will no doubt profit by their improved facilities.

Progress and Problems

The new railroad brought the expected boon to Sycamore's economy and pushed the city further into the modern age. After the M&NW's arrival, several new businesses, residences, and churches sprang up around town. Stores on State Street began operating under the warm glow of an exciting new technology, the electric light. The city built a new water works, put down asphalt sidewalks to replace the outdated—and often dangerous—pine-board sidewalks, and improved the drainage and lighting on the city streets. A new steel manufacturing business took over the recently closed Marsh Harvester Works, returning the "rap-a-tap of the workman's hammer" to that once-thriving facility. The steel factory joined Sycamore's other prosperous manufacturing concerns: a preserve works, a soap works, a paint works, a farm implement factory, a furniture factory, and businesses producing carriages and horse tack.

DeKalb's business leaders saw the progress of their sister city and wanted to share in the wealth. They remained, however, at the mercy of the C&NW. Now they could see firsthand how much a new railroad would benefit their town. The M&NW, in turn, also wished to "tap" DeKalb. President Stickney traveled there to meet with Isaac Ellwood. They discussed building a branch line to connect DeKalb to the new M&NW depot in Sycamore. DeKalb's business leaders strongly supported the plan, as did several people in Sycamore, but the project did not come to fruition for another seven years.

Although the M&NW started off strong, the company still saw its share of problems. In mid-October 1887, M&NW station agent M. C. Shields, who had been at the job for only three months and had become quite popular in the community, shocked those who knew him by suddenly resigning. He claimed that the M&NW demanded too much work from too few employees. The company refused to hire more help, which resulted in local freight being mishandled and delayed. Shields' replacement, R. F. Scoffern, worked for just one day before sending in a letter of resignation for the same reasons, though he ended up sticking with the job for a couple months. The depot went through two more agents in a matter of months before Shields returned to the job, but the railroad's refusal to hire extra help continued to cause a high turnover rate at the depot. When O. T. Willard became the postal operator in early 1889, he noted that the office atmosphere was "not what you would call congenial." On the whole, however, the company's shipping business was booming. On some days, over thirty freight trains passed through Sycamore. The company had to lease engines from other railroads to keep up with the freight demand.

More local problems arose when the M&NW installed extra tracks to accommodate its stockyards, making the grounds around the depot a quagmire of crisscrossing rails. Four sets of tracks now crossed Main Street, Sycamore's major northern artery. Anyone entering or departing

Sycamore from the north often found the road blocked or the tracks hazardous to cross. The local papers carried several stories of terrifying near misses as wagon teams tried to make their way across the tracks. The *True Republican* declared that this hazard would drive the northern trade from the city.

With two busy railroad lines now passing through town, Sycamore paid another price for its success: tramps. DeKalb had dealt with tramps for years because of the city's location on a direct line to Chicago, but Sycamore had never had a throughline, so "train hoppers" never had a reason to go there. Sycamoreans soon began to notice an increase in strange faces, break-ins, and petty robberies. In mid-1888, the *True Republican* declared, "Tramps abound," and remarked that "Sycamore has never before been infested with so many tramps as this summer."

The M&NW's chief strength lay in shipping for the booming western livestock trade. To accommodate this growing trade, the company purchased and rented large tracts of land in and around Sycamore's north end to use as stockyards and pasture. Northeast of the new depot, the M&NW constructed sheds and a two-acre stockyard to hold 10,000 sheep. From these stockyards, the company shipped over 100,000 sheep a year. The M&NW's stockyards regularly expanded until massive sheep sheds dominated the city's north side. A visitor approaching Sycamore from the north might have experienced a surreal sight: undulating fields that appeared to be "covered with a carpet of animated wool." The stockyards became a fixture in that part of town for over 70 years until they were torn down in 1958.

According to the *Genoa Issue*, however, the smell of these stockyards provided "one more insult to every person who enters Sycamore from the north." The paper claimed that the city would "open the next season with a grand smelling match between the old soap factory, which has been doing its best for years to stink people off the road, and these new stockyards.... Let those coming to town from the north guess which smells the strongest."

Besides the stench, the stockyards created a new hazard to traveling Sycamoreans. Farmers had to drive their sheep and cows through Sycamore's streets to get to the stockyards. When residents heard the drivers' shouts, they knew to scatter and seek safety indoors or on sidewalks and porches. The sudden surge in livestock traffic brought more than the threat of trampling; it brought more mud in the rainy season and dust in the dry season, forcing Sycamoreans to once again fret over the condition of their roads.

Massive stockyards like those in Sycamore became a common sight all along the M&NW line. They were part of Stickney's ambitious plan to corner the country's livestock market. His company developed several innovative shipping cars designed specifically for livestock. He could take the large, healthy, grass-fed cattle from the western plains and ship them to the East Coast. By 1892, he'd built stockyards and wharves on the Staten Island waterfront so that he could ship his livestock all the way to Europe.

Stickney Solidifies His Empire

M&NW stockholders held a meeting on December 5, 1887 to consider whether they should merge their company with the Chicago, St. Paul & Kansas City Railway Company (CStP&KC). The move was more of a financial reorganization than a merger, because Stickney controlled both railroads. The sale passed by vote and in January 1888 the M&NW officially changed its name to the Chicago, St. Paul & Kansas City Railway Company. This was a more apt title, considering the company's achievements and long-term ambitions, but the *True Republican* described it simply as "too long."

The CStP&KC completed its line to Kansas City on February 1, 1891. The company quickly forged alliances with several western railroads to

Jim the Talking Crow

In the early 1890s, a pet crow named Jim would hang out in a lilac bush near the Maple Leaf depot and mimic the people who passed by each day. He greeted some with a "good morning" or "good-bye" and often repeated orders the telegraph operators shouted from the depot. He was also known to hurl profanities that he picked up from the railroad men, which would confuse or scare those who were new to town. Upon the crow's death in December 1899, the *True Republican* reported that the bird's owner was already training a replacement "in the questionable ways of his predecessor."

facilitate travel and shipping west of the Missouri River and south into Texas. With this last vital connection complete, Stickney's whole system became known as the Maple Leaf Route or Maple Leaf Line, because its railroads branched out on the map like the veins of a maple leaf. Sycamoreans distinguished between their two depots by referring to the CStP&KC's depot as the Maple Leaf depot and the C&NW's depot as the Northwestern depot.

In April 1892, the CStP&KC added a new passenger train that ran only between Sycamore and Chicago, stopping at the principal towns along the way. The Sycamore Local, as it became known, departed early each morning and returned in the evening. Each run took approximately one hour and forty-five minutes. The company later added an afternoon run, and by July the Sycamore Local averaged 400 passengers a day. The engine remained in Sycamore each night, sheltered in the new roundhouse the company built just east of North California Street. The Sycamore Local solidified Sycamore's place as an important Chicago suburb and railroad town. It also showed that the CStP&KC had long-term plans for the city. In addition, the Sycamore Local allowed the company to steal business from the C&NW, whose Chicago-bound passengers still had to transfer trains in either Cortland or DeKalb.

In less than a decade, Stickney had followed through with his plan to link his railroads to the Midwest's most thriving gateway cities. His vast railroad network—referred to collectively as the Stickney System—dominated the heavy freight hauling market, mostly in livestock, coal, and iron ore. This railroad upstart had dared to challenge the entrenched companies that had dominated Midwest shipping for three decades, and won. In the summer of 1892, all of Stickney's grand maneuvers culminated in the reorganization of the whole Stickney System. He restructured his various railroad enterprises into a powerful new conglomerate, the Chicago Great Western (CGW). On Friday, July 1, 1892, the CGW officially took control of the CStP&KC and created

what Stickney called "the model [rail]road of this country." The *True Republican* noted that the CGW was "a system of railroad as nearly perfect as men and money can make." And its main line traversed not only DeKalb County, "the garden spot of the world," it ran right through Sycamore.

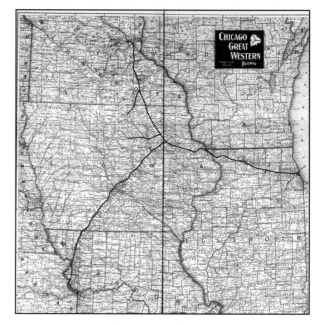

The Maple Leaf Route

The CGW incorporated the maple leaf into it's logo

O. T. Willard, Sherman Paxton, and the Nickel Plate Telegraph Company

O. T. Willard was born in Sycamore on July 1, 1867, in a house on the northeast corner of High and Locust streets. He was the son of Hosea Willard, one of Sycamore's early pioneers, who came to the little village in 1846 and built several of the town's homes, churches, and businesses. O. T. attended Sycamore schools, but his true love was telegraphy, a skill he taught himself. Through his interests, he formed a close bond with a group of boys also interested in telegraphy: Boyd Middleton, Harvey Orton, George Dutton, and a new kid in town, Sherman Paxton.

Sherman H. Paxton was born in Iowa on November 26, 1864. His father, James Paxton, had served in the Civil War with Company D, 3rd Regiment, Iowa Cavalry. James moved the family to Sycamore in 1879. Sherman always liked to tinker with new technologies, so when he started high school in Sycamore, he soon found himself hanging out with O. T. Willard and friends.

The boys' hobby turned into a serious opportunity when George Marsh, son of Charles Marsh, co-founder of the Marsh Harvester Company, offered to give them the four miles of telegraph line that connected the factory in Sycamore to Charles Marsh's home near DeKalb.[1] The only catch was that the boys had to remove the old line themselves. O. T. Willard and Dick Divine, son of Sycamore Mayor R. L. Divine, collected the 20,000 feet of wire using a special reel they had attached to the back of a wagon. It took them five trips to collect all of the wire, which they stored in giant bundles in Divine's barn.

The friends strung the line in a north-south direction through the western half of town. The line connected to the C&NW depot, where Paxton personally installed the wires, probably under the supervision of telegraph operator Mont Rose. It is unknown if the boys received—or even asked for—permission from the city to install the line.

---

[1]When the Marsh brothers installed this line in the 1860s, it was the first telegraph line in Sycamore. In 1879, they no longer needed it, because they had recently connected the same two locations with Sycamore's first telephone line.

When they completed it, they adopted their own set of codes and regulations and created their own business: The Nickel Plate Telegraph Company. They elected Sherman Paxton as the first president.

The Nickel Plate Telegraph Company included eight stations,* each with a working key and sounder:

1. Charlie Arnold's house on Charles Street (South Terminal)
2. Dick Divine's house on Edward Street
3. O. T. Willard's house at Somonauk and Waterman streets
4. Arthur Martin's house on Park Avenue
5. The C&NW Depot
6. Boyd Middleton's house on the south side of State Street
7. Rowe, Norris, & Patch grocery store on the north side of State Street
8. George Allen's house on West Exchange Street (North Terminal)
* The company later connected their line to the courthouse at the city's request

At night, the boys used the telegraph to challenge each other at checkers. They numbered the squares on their boards so they could wire each other their moves. They also organized checkers tournaments where one group of players set up at the depot and the other group set up at the Rowe, Norris & Patch grocery store on State Street.

During the 1880 presidential campaign, city officials asked the boys to extend the line to the courthouse, which would allow the courthouse to receive regular news bulletins relayed from the depot. On Election Day, O. T. Willard stationed himself in the courthouse and took down the election returns. The boys were paid "quite liberally" for the service.

It is unknown how long the Nickel Plate Telegraph Company remained in operation. Not long after it was set up, Paxton took a job as a printer with the *Sycamore Free Press* and later with the *True Republican*. In 1885, both he and Willard found themselves working at the C&NW depot. Paxton made deliveries for the American Express Company, which operated out of the depot. Willard fulfilled his dream of becoming a telegraph operator when the C&NW hired him to train under Mont Rose. He also learned train order operations under Chauncey Rose at the Cortland depot. He worked for two years as a substitute telegrapher at depots up and down the NI line.

After Paxton's father died in 1887, Paxton left his job at the depot and took a similar position at the U. S. Express office in Peoria. He later moved to Rockford, but made regular trips back to Sycamore to visit friends and family. Sherman eventually moved to Los Angeles, where he worked as an engineer and inventor. For the remainder of his life, he tinkered with telegraph equipment, an obsession that he carried with him from his days in Sycamore.

When the M&NW began building its line through Sycamore in 1887, Willard took a position as the first telegraph operator on the line. His telegraph "office," a six-by-ten-foot shanty in the mud alongside the tracks, was located at the company's gravel pits between Sycamore and St. Charles. When the pits closed for the winter, the M&NW sent Willard to St. Charles to help them set up their new depot.

Willard returned to Sycamore in 1889 and began working in the M&NW depot as office help, postal operator, and assistant to depot agent M. C. Shields. On his second day in the office, Willard spilled a pint of ink over Shields's paperwork. Shields inspected the damage, glared at Willard, then calmly responded, "Well, kid, they say a bad beginning makes a good ending, so I guess you'll make good all right."

A year later, Willard took over as the depot's night telegraph operator. He soon worked his way up to day operator and then assistant station agent before the CGW transferred him in 1895 to help set up their new station in DeKalb. The company promoted him to agent of the DeKalb depot in 1905, a position he held for the next 32 years. After 50 years of service, Willard retired from the CGW on May 19, 1937.

Outside of his railroad career, Willard founded Sycamore's first Boy Scout troop in 1910 and remained active with the group for the rest of his life. He also became the city's foremost local historian, writing a column for the *True Republican* that recollected Sycamore's early history, including the minutiae of everyday life so often absent from the newspapers of that period (many of the stories in this book would not have been possible without Willard's dedication to local history).

In the 1930s, Paxton wrote several letters to his old friend Willard, recalling the Sycamore of their youth. Willard reprinted the letters in his column. At Willard's request, Paxton wrote more recollections of early Sycamore life and Willard featured them in his column for several months. In September 1947, at the age of 83, Paxton made one last trip to Sycamore to visit old friends and old stomping grounds. He dropped in on Willard to reminisce over their time with the Nickel Plate

Telegraph Company and at the C&NW depot, which Paxton recalled as "probably the finest depot west of Chicago in northern Illinois." They probably shared a good laugh over one of Paxton's favorite depot stories, which he had shared in the December 23, 1939 issue of the *True Republican*:

> Some of the boys around the depot put up a April Fools joke on Ed [Rose]. They took a small box about a foot square, made of heavy lumber…. [T]hey nailed the box to the floor of the baggage car then nailed on the top. When they met the Chicago train at Cortland, they transferred the express from one car to the other, which was always a hurry-up job. When they came to the small box, Ed grabbed it and was much surprised to find he could not lift it. Then Mr. King, the agent at Cortland, jumped up into the car and tried to help Ed…. All of this time, they were holding up the Chicago train, which was a serious matter; they then looked at the address on the box and were dismayed to find it addressed to "Miss April Fool, Fool Creek, Ky." Well, the Chicago train had to make up several minutes.

Sherman Paxton (1864–1948) worked as an express manager in the C&NW depot from 1885–1887. Sometime during that period, he signed his name on a wall in one of the depot's second-floor offices. The faded signature was still visible when interior renovations began in 2011. (Author's collection)

O. T. Willard (1867–1952)

(Sycamore History Museum)

Competition and Calamity, 1887-1897

With these railroads… there is no city as near Chicago as we are that has better facilities for distributing manufactured goods.

True Republican, April 27, 1887

While all eyes were on the Chicago Great Western (CGW),[1] the Chicago & North Western (C&NW) implemented several improvements to compete with its new rival. Soon after the CGW began operations in 1887, the C&NW extended its tracks on the depot's east side to better facilitate the neighboring lumberyard. To compete with the CGW's faster trains and direct route to Chicago, the C&NW introduced new engines on both its Northern Illinois (NI) and Sycamore & Cortland (S&C) lines. It also replaced most of the railroad ties along the old S&C line and supplied the line with new passenger and baggage cars.

The fate of the S&C's locomotive, *Sycamore II*, remains unknown, but it is possible that the C&NW removed it from service soon after the CGW's arrival. The engine would not have matched the speeds of the CGW's newer engines, so the C&NW probably replaced it when the company replaced the other older

[1]Author's note: To avoid confusion, I will refer to all incarnations of the Chicago Great Western as the CGW, even if I am referring to an earlier time when it operated under a different name.

From the May 25, 1887 issue of the *True Republican*

> The Northwestern railroad is about to uniform all its conductors. Ed Rose rather objected; but last Saturday a couple of men met him at De-Kalb, and measured him from head to foot. In about 30 days he will appear resplendent in blue cloth, brass buttons and gold epaulets, all overtopped by a neat sleeping-car-porter style of cap.

Ed Rose would have worn something similar to this uniform worn by C&NW conductor Harlie E. Shull. Sycamore's regular passengers gave Rose a "rousing reception" the first day he wore his new uniform.

engines on its lines. The *Sycamore II* could have been transferred to another line on the C&NW, or it could have been sold to a small railroad startup out West. The latter possibility would have followed the pattern of older railroads selling used equipment to newer railroads as the country expanded west, which is how the S&C procured its first engine back in 1859.

Some of the C&NW's changes rankled local officials. To compete with the CGW's new stockyards, the C&NW built new stockyards along its tracks north of State Street. This move earned the enmity of Sycamore's city council, which had passed an ordinance forbidding stockyards within city limits. Before building, the C&NW asked the city council for permission, but when permission was denied, it built the stockyards anyway. The need to compete with the CGW outweighed the need to appease local officials.

The company also met with harsh criticism when it began locking up the depot long before the last passenger train departed at midnight. The *DeKalb Review* reported on a party of prominent women who had traveled to Sycamore for a lecture and were forced to roam the streets after dark while awaiting their train. "And yet Sycamore pretends to be a first-rate town," the paper criticized. A few days later, the same paper reported how several masons who had attended a meeting in Sycamore were

forced to stare at two warm fires burning inside the depot while they and their fellow passengers waited out in the cold. The *True Republican* sided with the DeKalb paper and argued that the county's citizens had a right to expect better accommodations at the county seat. It also pointed out that most other depots throughout the county remained open at night, including the CGW depot. It is unknown whether the C&NW responded to the criticism or made any changes, but the DeKalb and Sycamore newspapers contained no further complaints.

Despite the criticisms, the C&NW still played an invaluable role in the community. In the early morning hours of December 17, 1887, a barn on DeKalb Avenue went up in flames. The city's fire alarm system failed, even though it had cost the taxpayers a considerable sum. John Tucker, the quick-thinking engineer of the C&NW's local train, ran his engine out of its engine house and blasted its whistle. Sycamoreans, who knew that the train whistle blew like clockwork, were instantly roused by this irregular blast and summoned the fire companies to extinguish the blaze.

In 1888, the C&NW introduced new steam whistles on some of its trains. These whistles were meant to sound more melodious and less harsh than the old ones. The *True Republican* described the sound:

A locomotive with this new-fangled tooter, with its unearthly howl, blood-curdling scream and demoniacal wail, is enough to make an inoffensive boy's hair stand on end and his eyes start from their spheres, while the agonizing complaints and thundering cuss-words will scare a cow so far off the track that the owner would have to insert a "strayed" notice in the papers for her return.

Nevertheless, the paper noted that the new whistles were a great improvement over the old ones.

On May 20, 1891, a Cortland contributor to the *True Republican* reported that Cortland was in need of a new depot. Three weeks later, on June 10, 1891, he got his wish. The C&NW's Cortland depot caught fire from the sparks of a passing train and burned to the ground. Most of the freight inside the building was destroyed, as were two nearby businesses. Cortland's longtime depot agent, John King, set up a temporary office inside a box car while the C&NW built a new depot (pictured above). The plans called for something considerably smaller than the previous building, illustrating how Cortland had never grown into the prosperous railroad center everyone thought it would become when the G&CU built the original depot in the 1850s.

Price War at Last!

Immediately after the CGW commenced operations in 1887, local businesses began transferring their freight to the new line. Some of the shift was economical: the CGW offered cheaper rates than the C&NW. For example, Isaac Elwood found it cheaper to haul his barbed wire from DeKalb to Sycamore by horse to ship on the CGW than to ship the barbed wire directly from DeKalb on the C&NW. Some of the shift was geographical: the CGW depot was closer to businesses on the city's north side. Some of the shift, however, arose from long-standing grudges against the C&NW, which had monopolized shipping in Sycamore for over a quarter century.

To combat the sudden freight and passenger exodus, the C&NW had no choice but to lower its rates. The CGW responded in kind; the C&NW matched. The CGW then announced that it would designate Sycamore an official Chicago suburb, making passengers traveling between those two cities eligible for reduced suburban rates. (At that time the suburban rate was one cent per mile, or fifty-five cents to Chicago.) The C&NW was forced to reduce its rates even further.

The price war was exactly what Sycamore had always wanted. Both companies continued cutting their passenger rates, shaving off a few cents at a time. By September of 1887, Sycamoreans could buy a roundtrip ticket to Chicago for one dollar, a quarter of the C&NW's price before the CGW arrived. However, these bargain rates couldn't last. Prices soon crept back up, but they never surpassed the old C&NW rates from the days when it monopolized the local market.

With two rival railroads operating in Sycamore—and three lines between them—the city had 20 passenger trains arriving each day. This gave Sycamoreans plenty of travel options. To secure Sycamore's business, the railroad companies offered a variety of specially priced "excursion tickets." Popular excursions included trips to the Fox River and to Madison and Lake Geneva in Wisconsin. The railroads also offered excursion rates for picnics, political rallies, holidays, fraternal society meetings, and special events. They offered cheap and competitive rates to the West, including the "Homeseekers Excursion," which gave the purchaser several months to redeem a return ticket. "Homeseekers" could look for work and a new home before returning to collect their personal belongings and, usually, their families.

The Chicago Columbian Exposition

By the 1890s, an era of unprecedented railroad expansion in the Midwest was coming to a close. Without new lines to bring in revenue, railroad companies had to look for other ways to increase their profits. They saw an opportunity in the 1893 World's Fair. This major, months-long event would attract millions of visitors from around the world. Newspapers claimed it would be the "most significant and greatest exhibition ever seen by man." However, the final location had yet to be determined. Several American cities wanted to host the exhibition, most notably Chicago and New York.

Chicago had been lobbying to secure the World's Fair since 1888. The city's leaders knew the advantages the fair could bring to the region. Besides the massive revenue, the fair could show the world that there was more to the United States than her eastern cities and more to Chicago than the stench of her stockyards. The midwestern railroad companies knew that a World's Fair in Chicago would bring a huge boost to their industry. They would carry not only the passengers to the fair, but also the materials required to build it and the supplies necessary to run it. Several railroad companies established a united front and donated massive amounts of money to the lobbying effort.

In Sycamore, Mayor Chauncey Ellwood called a meeting to discuss how the fair could benefit Sycamore and how the town could assist Chicago in securing the event. Everyone agreed to lend their support to Chicago's bid, because the fair would provide plenty of jobs for Sycamoreans, especially contractors, who would build it, and farmers, who would feed the visiting masses.

On February 5, 1890, after months of vitriolic attacks in the newspapers of each candidate city, the U.S. House of Representatives chose Chicago to host the World's Fair. In Chicago, "men, women and children yelled themselves hoarse, and crowds quickly supplied themselves with fish-horns and other ear-splitting implements and paraded the streets." It was not only a victory for Chicago, but a victory for the railroads. Chicago never would have earned hosting rights without its extensive railroad network. Now it was time to put that network to the test and pull off the biggest event in the region's history.

Immediately after the announcement, agents from the C&NW and CGW canvassed Sycamore to secure lodging for World's Fair patrons. They signed contracts with hotels, boarding houses, and several homeowners who would rent rooms exclusively to visitors who traveled on one railroad or the other. These contracts allowed the railroads to offer excursion deals that included food and lodging. They marketed Sycamore as a destination for visitors who wished to experience Chicago, but then escape the city's overcrowded accommodations and stay in a small, country setting. Despite the distance, lodgers could take an early train into Chicago each morning and return to Sycamore each evening.[2] The railroads' scheme worked. Several large traveling parties made Sycamore their headquarters for the duration of the fair.

The World's Fair became known as the Chicago Columbian Exposition, because it celebrated the 400th anniversary of Columbus's landing. With the exhibition looming, railroads tried to lure new passengers through price cuts. Sycamoreans took advantage of the reduced rates to visit the exposition's construction site. Though it was little more than piles of materials spread among mounds of upturned earth, everyone marveled at the site's vast scale. Over the next few months, visitors returned to the site time and time again, in awe of the 7,000 workers swarming over the skeletal frames of half-finished buildings. Many believed they bore witness to the most momentous event of the century. In October 1892, over a hundred Sycamoreans joined the crowd of 100,000 who attended the exposition's dedication ceremony.

[2]This arrangement was one of the main reasons that the CGW introduced the Sycamore Local in 1892.

A ticket and souvenir map to the Columbian Exposition in Chicago. (Library of Congress)

Several Sycamoreans found employment at the exposition as contractors, administrators, ticket collectors, carriage drivers, guides, guards, and entertainers. Other Sycamoreans started their own "World's Fair Club," which met every Saturday at the courthouse to discuss and distribute educational materials that further explored the fair's exhibits. Sycamore's children scrimped and saved to purchase the commemorative World's Fair coins and stamps released by the US Mint and US Post Office, the first time either organization had released such items.

The fair officially opened on Monday, May 1, 1893. That morning, a special World's Fair train steamed up to Sycamore's CGW depot to carry a throng of excited Sycamoreans into Chicago. The entire train was adorned with flags and bunting. Large oil paintings depicting World's Fair buildings hung from the tender and boiler. Each painting was wrapped in streamers and evergreen wreaths and had a large maple leaf in the center, surrounded by the words "Take the Maple Leaf Route to the World's Fair." If the C&NW offered similarly decorated accommodations, the newspapers did not mention it.

A newspaper image of the CGW's World's Fair train in Sycamore.

The C&NW and CGW waged a fierce battle for World's Fair patronage. Besides slashing their rates, both companies adjusted their timetables to cut down on the travel time into Chicago. They also put additional trains on their lines to accommodate the extra traffic and to provide more flexible arrival and departure times. In Sycamore, however, the CGW held the advantage, because it still had the direct route to Chicago.

During the first month, the fair saw over 100,000 visitors each day. As it progressed, this number grew to over 300,000. Hundreds of Sycamoreans made the journey each week, and the local papers printed lists of those who attended. For the month of October, the CGW reported that it had transported 60 Sycamoreans to the fair each day. As the fair began to wind down, local businessman James Branen—who would later become a railroad man in his own

right—sponsored a free trip to the exposition for 215 of Sycamore's children. Branen chartered a CGW excursion train specifically for children who had not yet had a chance to attend the momentous event.

Even though the CGW dominated the World's Fair business in Sycamore, the C&NW still carried over 2.5 million passengers into Chicago during the event, ten percent of the fair's estimated 25 million visitors. The *True Republican* reported, "If one asks the names of those from Sycamore who attended the Fair… just hand them a city directory and let them read it."

The Pullman Strike

While the World's Fair brought a huge boost to the Midwest's economy, it did not provide the financial windfall the railroads had hoped for. Many railroad companies, including the C&NW, had cut their rates so low that they actually lost money during the exposition. Before the event ended, the C&NW was already reducing its workforce and cutting back on its passenger and freight runs. The problem highlighted just how much the railroad industry had saturated the market and overextended itself. Competition had driven rates so low that many railroads proved unprofitable. The employees suffered first. Companies tried to make up lost profits through layoffs, reduced wages, and longer working hours. In May 1894, 4,000 workers at the Pullman Palace Car Company in Pullman, Illinois, went on strike over reduced wages. The American Railway Union entered the fray and the strike grew to involve 250,000 workers in 27 states. The two-month strike resulted in $80 million in property damage, 30 deaths, 57 injuries, and prison sentences for labor organizers.

Railroad workers in Sycamore did not join the strike, but the strike did have a minor impact on the city. Service on the Chicago trains on both lines became erratic and trains sometimes arrived hours late or not at all. Sycamore's manufacturers and merchants worried about the safety and regularity of their shipments, but the delays were tolerable and there were no reports of Sycamore freight being lost or damaged. On more than one occasion, some of Sycamore's boys gathered at the CGW depot and yelled insults at the trainmen, calling them "scabs," but whenever the sheriff showed up the group quickly dispersed. In the strike's waning days, no trains were coming in on the C&NW's lines, so the company sent its employees home and shut down the depot for over a week. This was the only time in the depot's history that it was shut down while the railroad was still in operation.

A Merry Milk War

The Pullman Strike did little to curb the competition between the CGW and C&NW. Since the CGW opened, it had been slowly and successfully luring Sycamore's milk shippers over to its line. By 1894, the CGW dominated milk shipping, which had grown into a major business for DeKalb County. But in October 1894, the company suddenly fired Will Harris, the milk conductor on the CGW line, supposedly over a paperwork error. Harris had become popular among Sycamore's milk shippers, who immediately petitioned for his reinstatement. Several local businessmen even traveled to Chicago to appeal to CGW executives in person. When the company still refused to reinstate Harris, almost all of the milk shippers in Sycamore switched their business over to the C&NW. The C&NW happily added a new milk train on its line to accommodate them. It also hired a new milk conductor: Will Harris.

A C&NW milk train stopped at Cortland in 1900.

The DeKalb & Great Western

Throughout the railroad rivalry, the C&NW had been able to exploit one major advantage over the CGW: access to DeKalb. It offered local service over the NI line. In the early 1890s, the C&NW improved this service by offering the "triangle run," which ran from Sycamore to Cortland to DeKalb, then back to Sycamore. It sometimes made this run in reverse. The C&NW's local service became increasingly beneficial to the growing number of commuters between DeKalb and Sycamore, which saw a huge increase in 1892 when Abram Ellwood, son of Reuben Ellwood and also Sycamore's mayor, moved his father's factory to DeKalb. Many of his employees chose to continue working for the company and commuted to DeKalb each day from the C&NW depot.

The C&NW's lock on local traffic ended in March 1895 when the CGW announced that, with the help of several DeKalb investors, it would finally build the branch line between Sycamore and DeKalb that Isaac Ellwood had been trying to organize for seven years. The DeKalb & Great Western (D&GW) would branch off of the CGW's main line in Sycamore, run south alongside the C&NW's NI line, then branch off north of DeKalb and run through the city's manufacturing district. It was designed to tap the business from the big

wire and steel mills in both Sycamore and DeKalb. It also ran right by Abram Ellwood's DeKalb factory, creating competition for the C&NW's commuter business.

A 1936 view of the Cyclone Fence Company (formerly the Abram Ellwood Manufacturing Company) in northeastern DeKalb, looking north toward Sycamore. The C&NW's and D&GW's parallel lines ran right past this factory and accommodated several commuters from Sycamore.

Most Sycamoreans approved of the new connection with their sister city. For DeKalb, the new line would provide access to a competitive railroad for the first time. The line also came at a beneficial time for DeKalb. The state was looking to build a new normal school in northern Illinois, and DeKalb was one of several cities in the running to obtain it. Access to two major railroads added considerable leverage to the city's bid.

The CGW struck the C&NW another blow when it announced that the D&GW would include short spur lines to the Sycamore Preserve Works, Lattin Coal Sheds, Stark Brothers Hay

Press, and other businesses around the C&NW depot that had shipped freight almost exclusively with the C&NW.

The contract to build the D&GW went to J. A. Caughren. In June 1895, his team of 75 men began grading the roadbed and laying the ties. The DeKalb newspapers gave regular updates on the progress of the city's new depot. Besides building the depot, work crews constructed a freight house, turntable, and multiple side tracks. Harry Jackson, who had worked for ten years at the C&NW depot in Sycamore, left his position to take over as station agent of the D&GW depot in DeKalb. The CGW sent O. T. Willard to assist Jackson in opening the depot. For several weeks, they operated their makeshift office out of a boxcar.

In July, while track crews toiled to lay the new rails, the board of supervisors for the Northern Illinois State Normal School chose DeKalb as the site for the new school. One hundred and fifty Sycamoreans traveled to DeKalb by train to celebrate the good news. Gaining the Northern Illinois State Normal School was the most significant and enduring event in DeKalb's history. The school eventually evolved into Northern Illinois University, which, today, is the county's largest employer and most recognized institution.

Passenger service on the D&GW began on Sunday, September 29, 1895. Each run took approximately 15 minutes and a round trip cost just 25 cents—the price the S&C had charged for a one-way trip to Cortland almost four decades earlier. The line offered six trips a day between the two cities, including two on the Sycamore Local to Chicago, which now started each run in DeKalb before transferring over to the CGW's main line in Sycamore. With the addition of the D&GW, 38 passenger trains ran through either Sycamore or DeKalb each day. Thirteen of those trains ran to Chicago, and all but one made the trip in less than two hours.

The D&GW opened just in time for the Normal School's cornerstone ceremony. It was one of the largest events in DeKalb's history. On Tuesday, October 1, thousands of people from around the county descended on DeKalb. In most towns, including Sycamore, schools and businesses closed so that everyone could attend the celebration. Sycamore sent 2,200 of her own people, more than half taking either the C&NW or D&GW (the rest traveled by horse, wagon, or bicycle). In DeKalb, over 200 tents decorated the school grounds. Visitors heard speeches from Isaac Ellwood, Governor John Altgeld (for whom the original Normal School building is now named), and many others. Everyone then enjoyed a parade, baseball and football games, and an evening of fireworks that were "the best ever witnessed outside of the World's Fair gates."

Sycamore newspapers estimated the crowd size at between 10,000 and 15,000 people (though the DeKalb papers estimated 45,000).

The Northern Illinois State Normal School in 1899. Today, the building is named Altgeld Hall and houses administrative offices for Northern Illinois University, including the president's office.

In November 1895, the D&GW added a new passenger train that departed Sycamore at 6:20 a.m. to get workers to their factory shifts in DeKalb. To the chagrin of the C&NW, this train made a stop to pick up passengers at DeKalb Avenue, a block southwest of the C&NW depot. The CGW deliberately chose this location to poach the C&NW's south-side commuter traffic, which might not have used the D&GW because of the distance to its north-side depot. In January 1897, the D&GW erected a small passenger depot to accommodate these same customers. Sycamore's third depot stood on the southwest corner of

Grant Street and Mill Street (present-day Stark Avenue), one block west of the C&NW depot. Passengers waiting at one depot were able to see those waiting at the other. The D&GW passenger trains continued to run to the CGW depot on the city's north side, but they made an extra stop each way at the Grant Street Station.

The C&NW fought back by adding extra runs on the Sycamore, Cortland, and DeKalb "triangle." It also replaced the old passenger cars with brand new ones. But with rival depots now only a block apart, customers could compare rates, timetables, accommodations, and several other factors when choosing a service. They also benefitted from another round of price cuts brought on by the new depot. The CGW had outmaneuvered the C&NW again, because the C&NW had no leverage to attract passengers from the city's north side. Years later, O. T. Willard called the D&GW "the best paying six miles of track" on the entire CGW line.

Sycamore's First Railroad Disaster

In the 1890s, newspapers carried regular accounts of railroad injuries and deaths. Based on the sensational headlines that ran almost daily, it seems that railroad passengers and workers regularly fell off of, in front of, and under trains. The papers seemed to delight in sharing the gory details of each accident. In 1893, after a particularly gruesome railroad-related death in DeKalb, the *True Republican* boasted that no one had ever been killed by the railroad in Sycamore. While this was true, Sycamore had still experienced its fair share of railroad accidents.

The Stark Brothers Hay Press Fires

On Monday night, September 2, 1895, Sycamore experienced one of its largest fires when the Stark Brothers Hay Press, just west of the C&NW depot, went up in flames. The building, all of its machinery, and over 60 tons of hay were completely consumed. A freight car already loaded with hay was also destroyed. The intense heat scorched several houses on Grant Street north of the hay press, including the home of C&NW conductor Ed Rose. The heat also broke several of the depot's windows and scorched the cornices, but the building survived due to its brick walls and slate roof. The Stark brothers quickly rebuilt their business. On Wednesday, April 15, 1914, nearly 20 years after the fire, the second hay press also burned to the ground. Although floating firebrands damaged buildings over a block away, the depot again escaped without serious damage.

According to O. T. Willard, minor accidents "were of an almost daily occurrence." Several workers smashed their arms, hands, or fingers while coupling the cars (both Ed Rose and his son Elmer had done so on a number of occasions). In March 1890, a CGW train derailed just east of the city, its cars "piled up and strewn about in such a promiscuous manner that they afforded quite an attraction for a small army of sightseers." In November 1892, two trains collided in the CGW railyard; a freight car burned and a locomotive was heavily damaged. Two CGW trains collided again in January 1894, just east of Sycamore. Both trains were total losses and several cars burned, but as with the earlier incidents, no one was killed or seriously harmed.

Sycamore did not experience a railroad-related death until December 1895, when a section crew worker from Rockford was performing maintenance on the D&GW tracks two miles south of the city and was struck and killed by a passing train. Two months later, Ed Rose's Sycamore train backed over and killed a man crossing the tracks near the C&NW depot at DeKalb. It was the first death associated with the Sycamore train in its four decades of service. The C&NW, conductor Ed Rose, and engineer John Tucker were immediately cleared of wrongdoing, but the day after the accident the entire region was blanketed in a layer of black snow.[3]

Three months later, Sycamore experienced its worst railroad disaster. Just after midnight on Monday, May 4, 1896, a 22-car CGW freight train became separated as it entered Sycamore from the east. The separated back half contained five oil tanks filled with either kerosene or gasoline. The engineer, not realizing what had happened, stopped the front half of the train to take on water at the CGW water tank. Just as he hopped to the ground, the separated cars, still travelling at regular speed, slammed into the front cars and knocked the train forward several car lengths. The train's fireman had been standing on the tender, filling the locomotive's tank with water. When the collision occurred, he leapt up, caught hold of the water spout, and pulled his legs up while 10 to 12 cars lurched beneath him.

The night engineer at the city waterworks, James Paxton, younger brother of Sherman Paxton, heard the crash and rushed outside. He could hear and smell the gas pouring onto the ground from the ruptured oil tanks. Then he saw the train's conductor, L. C. Price, exit the caboose to investigate the damage. Paxton observed that Price carried a lighted lantern and warned him that one of the oil cars had ruptured and he shouldn't go near it. Price ignored the warning and continued on, swearing to himself about leaking cars. Paxton feared what might happen next and returned to the waterworks pump house to watch through the window. Moments later, a massive explosion sent a fireball hurtling a hundred feet into the air. The *True Republican* described the sound as "a hundred locomotives… blowing off steam at the same time."

By the time the fire companies arrived, the flames had consumed several cars, the other oil tanks were threatening to blow, and the stockyards north of the tracks and a coal house were on fire, as was the pump house that would supply the water necessary to extinguish the blaze. One fireman took a hose to the pump house roof and battled that blaze alone so his comrades could concentrate on extinguishing the railyard and stockyard fires. One by one, the rest of the oil tanks burst, blasting hundred-foot shafts of flame into the air. The massive columns of black smoke, eerily illuminated by the raging inferno, could be seen from miles around. The *City Weekly* called it "the fiercest fire that ever raged in Sycamore." A night policeman

---

[3]Black snow is a meteorological effect caused by high winds kicking up fine, dry soil and mixing it with snow. It is a rare but natural occurrence, and must have seemed ominous to those involved in the Sycamore Local's first fatality.

in DeKalb saw the glow and sounded the alarm because he thought the fire was burning in the northern outskirts of that city. DeKalb's firemen rushed toward the glow until they realized it was over six miles away.

Sycamore's firemen battled the blaze for two hours before finally getting it under control. When they searched the smoldering rubble, they found Price's body not far from the oil tanks, burned beyond recognition. He was identified only by the gold watch given to him by the railroad.

The pump house escaped with minimal damage. The stockyards were saved, but several sheds and some fences had been consumed. Several freight cars were destroyed, but the train crew had been able to uncouple several cars at the back of the train and push them away from the flames while the engineer used the engine to pull some of the front cars to safety. The Sycamore Local's dining car had been left on a side track next to the oil tanks. The $10,000 car was completely destroyed. Total damages were estimated at $25,000. Everyone was in agreement, however, that the damage and loss of life would have been far worse without the intervention of Sycamore's dedicated volunteer fire department.

Sycamore's volunteer firemen in 1897

Public Safety and a Major Depot Renovation

While Sycamore's railroad competition was good for the local economy, the numerous tracks and crossings made the city's streets increasingly hazardous for the public. In the late 1890s, Mayor Frederick B. Townsend spearheaded a movement to improve the safety of the city's major railroad crossings. The railroads and the Sycamore City Council had clashed over this issue for several years. The city wanted the railroads to install gates and electric signals at its major crossings, especially where the C&NW crossed DeKalb Avenue and the CGW crossed Main Street. When the railroads ignored or objected to several requests, the council passed ordinances requiring the upgrades. When the railroads still balked, the city finally threatened them with fines. Townsend met with officials from both railroads to resolve the matter. The companies finally placed flagmen at the intersections while they slowly installed the gates and signals over several months.

When Townsend met with the C&NW's division superintendent in late 1896, he also suggested that the C&NW renovate its depot to include two separate waiting rooms, one for men and one for women. The C&NW followed Townsend's suggestion and in January 1897 it put the depot through an extensive interior renovation, the first in 17 years. The C&NW took the large and open first-floor waiting room and divided it into two waiting areas separated by a ticket and telegraph office. The office formed a horseshoe shape with service windows on each side. The south room became the ladies' waiting room and the north room became the men's waiting room. The C&NW may have made this renovation because the CGW had included separate waiting rooms for men and women in its depot ten years earlier. It also may have been trying to stay current with the times. The division of men's and women's facilities had become a common feature of public buildings across the country. One underlying reason was that men were filthy—always smoking cigars,

spitting tobacco, and covered in grime from a hard day's work—and a woman's delicate sensibilities should not be exposed to such unsavoriness. Men most likely enjoyed the freedom to smoke as they pleased, to ignore the mud on their boots, and to spit in any of the readily available spittoons that occupied their side of the depot. Both waiting rooms were outfitted with comfortable new rocking chairs. The *True Republican* noted that these long overdue improvements would be "greatly appreciated by the traveling public... especially by the citizens of Sycamore."

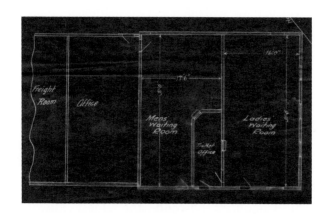

C&NW depot waiting rooms after the 1897 renovation

Except for the addition of men's and women's restrooms in 1916, the depot's interior layout remained relatively unchanged from 1897 until the major renovation of 2010 to 2012.

Canine Confounds Trainmen

On Saturday night, March 7, 1896, a small dog stirred up considerable excitement outside the C&NW depot. It had been checked as baggage on a passenger train passing through from Spring Valley. When the train pulled up to the depot, the dog leapt from the baggage car and darted around the depot platform. The dog's owner departed the train and called to the dog to no avail. The ensuing chase entertained several onlookers as the dog ran circles around a breathless and increasingly angry train and depot crew. The dog eventually dashed around the depot's corner and took off for parts unknown. The train was forced to leave without it and the railroad most likely had to make restitution to the owner.

Chauncey Ellwood

On the night of May 6, 1897, Sycamore said goodbye to another of its pioneering railroad men. Chauncey Ellwood, the eldest Ellwood brother, passed away at the age of 80. During his long tenure in Sycamore, he worked as a lawyer, operated a flaxseed mill, sold boots and shoes, served as postmaster and mayor, managed Elmwood Cemetery, served as director of Reuben Ellwood Manufacturing and the Marsh Binder Company, and managed the Sycamore & Cortland Railroad. He often said that his role with the S&C was the most rewarding of his long career.

Chauncey had always been one of the most popular men in town. He kept an office behind the post office where his friends liked to gather, smoke cigars, and discuss business and politics. Many decisions that forever shaped Sycamore undoubtedly were made in that office.

Chauncey had also been a popular character among Sycamore's youth. According to local legend, when a school teacher once asked her students, "Who holds the highest office in the United States?" an eager young girl shouted, "Chauncey Ellwood!" Sherman Paxton remembered that all the boys "had a warm spot in their hearts for Chauncey." In the late 1870s, some Sycamore boys wanted to challenge Cortland's boys in a baseball game, but they had no way to get to Cortland. Paxton asked Chauncey if he could "pass our team down to Cortland and back." Chauncey said he'd do it, but only if Paxton could guarantee that his team would "bring back the bacon." Chauncey stood the team up in a line on the depot platform and chalked his initials on the back of each boy's coat. He then told the conductor, George Sivright, to watch out for the boys and make sure they got home all right. They did, and Paxton happily reported that they had "brought back the bacon." Chauncey was so pleased that he had Paxton tell the boys that if they behaved, they could expect more passes. The *True Republican* often criticized Chauncey for being liberal with his free passes, but many Sycamore boys lamented the day the C&NW took over the railroad and their free rides to Cortland came to an end. For them, Chauncey's chalked initials had been worn as a badge of honor.

By the end of the 1890s, most of Sycamore's "old guard" was gone, but a new generation of young businessmen would carry on their legacy and entrepreneurial spirit. Some of these men were about to introduce Sycamore to the region's latest railroad fad, which would usher in the last era of expansion in the city's rich railroad history. Sycamore's railroad rivals were about to face a whole new kind of competition: the electric railroad.

Last of the S&C Men

While Sycamoreans dreamed of securing the latest in railroad technology, the city began losing the old railroad men who'd kept the steam engines running since the Sycamore & Cortland days. Within a span of three years, the C&NW lost five longtime employees or contractors, all veterans of the S&C Railroad.

On June 17, 1899, 74-year-old John Tucker passed away after a short illness. Tucker had worked as a train engineer for various railroads since the age of 18. He moved to Sycamore in 1865 and immediately secured work as the engineer on the S&C's first locomotive. He stayed on for the next 34 years—18 years with the S&C and another 16 years with the C&NW. He was one of the only employees to have worked at all three S&C depots. He had a reputation for giving free rides and tutorials in the locomotive's cab to any boy who showed an interest in railroading (O. T. Willard fondly recalled taking some of these trips). Tucker manned his post on the Sycamore train until four days before his death.

Less than a year later, depot agent Elry Hall retired after 29 years of railroad service—23 in Sycamore. He became agent at the S&C's second depot in 1877 and stayed on through the construction of the new depot and the C&NW takeover. While still a depot agent, he went into business running the town's electrical plant, which became known unofficially as Hall Electric. He later sold the plant and became a partner in a shoe store.

In October 1900, Harry Little retired after 35 years of service as one of Sycamore's popular local draymen. In the early 1860s, he operated a horse-drawn carriage on the S&C line to make up for the S&C's scheduling conflicts with the G&CU (see pages 45-46). He became a drayman in 1865, transporting freight, baggage, and mail between the S&C depot and downtown businesses. He continued his draying business after the C&NW took over, and added trips to the CGW depot when it was built. According to the *True Republican,* he was one of the most recognized figures in town. He was "constantly on the streets, coming and going, all day every day." Harry Little "came in contact with everybody and everybody had a pleasant word with Harry." When one of Little's horses died suddenly in 1882, several Sycamoreans pitched in to buy him a new one. In the 1890s, well into his 60s, Little shocked everyone when he purchased a bicycle and rode it all over town, a practice which, until that time, had been reserved for the young.

In February 1901, Sycamore's beloved, longtime conductor, Ed Rose, retired from the C&NW after 30 years of railroad service. He had worked for 12 years as conductor of the S&C's engine and continued in that capacity another 18 years after the C&NW takeover. Like John Tucker, Rose operated the original Sycamore engine. Upon Rose's retirement, the *True Republican* reported that Sycamore's middle-aged men couldn't remember a time when Ed Rose didn't run the local train.

Cortland's depot agent, John King, retired in September 1902 after 38 years of service in that position. While technically never an S&C employee, as the C&NW agent in Cortland, he had worked directly with the company almost since its inception. To those Sycamoreans who regularly rode the rails, King was a well-known and respected figure. He had also served as Cortland's postmaster, village board president, and county board delegate. He was replaced by Chauncey Rose, the oldest of Ed Rose's railroading progeny.

These men were not the last of the old S&C employees still working for the railroads in Sycamore, but they were the most well-known. They had all worked for or with the company since its earliest days, when it was the only railroad in town and a source of local pride.

Enter the Electrics, 1897-1911

There is quite as much, or more, talk about electric roads now as ever, and some of the roads are being built.

True Republican, August 8, 1900

While Sycamore's steam railroads fought for the local market, a new technology, the electric railroad, entered the fray. Electric railroad cars were slower than steam engines, but cheaper to operate and equally capable of transporting passengers and some freight. Companies could construct the lines quickly, because the rails were lighter, the ties were smaller, and the tracks usually ran on existing streets. Electric cars caught on with the public because they were quieter and cleaner than steam engines, provided convenient schedules, and easily reached rural areas that had long been bypassed by the larger railroads.

Railroad trade magazines predicted that someday these "light railroads" would connect every community to the country's vast commercial markets, completing a national network that modernized all towns and left no one living in isolation. For many, electric railroads heralded the next major leap in the country's industrial evolution.

The Geneva Lake, Sycamore & Southern Electric Railway Company

In northern Illinois, the Rockford and Fox Valley regions were the first to start connecting their communities by electric railroads. A group of Sycamore businessmen followed their progress with great interest. Headed by James Branen, these men joined with several outside investors.

In 1897, they launched an ambitious electric railroad project that included Sycamore on a line from Geneva Lake in Wisconsin to the Illinois River at Streator, Illinois. From the south shore of Geneva Lake, the line would run through Harvard, Marengo, Genoa, and Sycamore. South of Sycamore, it would bypass DeKalb and run through Cortland, Hinckley, Sandwich, and then on to Streator. The men named their company the Geneva Lake, Sycamore & Southern Electric Railway Company (GLS&S). They even created a company tagline: "From Lake to River." When they unveiled their plan in March 1897, the *True Republican* hailed it as a way for Sycamore to "keep pace with the times."

James Branen (1848–1910)

Born in Ireland, James Branen's parents brought him to New York when he was less than a year old. At the age of twenty-one, he moved to Sycamore, where he embarked on several business ventures and served five terms in the state legislature. He served as Sycamore's mayor from 1901 to 1903.

The company had 15 directors, all from towns along the proposed route. The four directors from Sycamore also served as the company's chief officers: James Branen, President; John Whalen, General Manager; George Morris, Secretary; and George Brown, Treasurer. The directors envisioned their railroad as Chicago's "outer beltline." The north-south line would cross ten east-west railroads running into Chicago. The company would build transfer

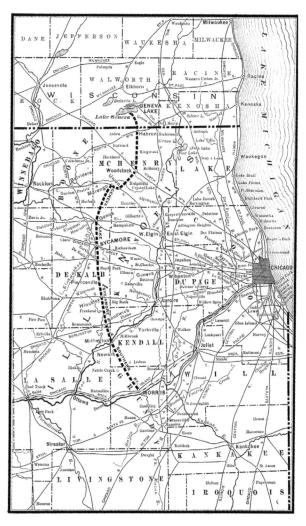

When the GLS&S released this map of the 110-mile proposed route in May 1898, the route had been significantly altered from the company's original plans. To the north, the town of Woodstock had been substituted for Harvard, and to the south the terminus had been removed from Streator and relocated at Morris.

In 1898, the GLS&S released an 84-page prospectus that summarized the company's mission, business prospects, and probable cost of operation. It also included 75 high-quality images of prominent homes and businesses found in towns along the proposed route.

depots at each crossing so passengers and freight could switch to any other railroad with ease. At Geneva Lake, it would create its own 30-acre park on the lake's south side, free to those who arrived via the electric railroad. The company promised that the whole project could be completed in about six months.

Sycamoreans had several reasons to champion this new railroad. The company's founders hailed from Sycamore, so they would most likely locate the railroad's general facilities there, which would provide jobs at the business offices, car barns, supply depots, and repair shops. Sycamore would also house

one of the large electric plants needed to power the line. This plant would allow the city to improve its current electric service, which was often inadequate. The line would cut into the C&NW's and CGW's local passenger and freight profits, forcing another price war. On top of these benefits, Geneva Lake had been a favorite destination for northern Illinoisans for decades; Sycamoreans welcomed a direct line to the popular vacation spot.

Sycamore got its first taste of electric railroads on March 20, 1898. A large crowd gathered at the CGW depot to witness an electric railcar passing through town on its way to a new line in Cedar Falls, Iowa. The car ran on an electric motor powered by a small gas engine and it averaged 20 miles per hour. Everyone marveled at the "odd little car, propelled by its own power," especially how it made no noise other than a light hum and produced no smoke. It didn't even have a smokestack.

Securing the right-of-way between towns proved more difficult than the GLS&S's directors had anticipated. They spent much of the next two years in horse-drawn buggies and wagons, canvassing the towns along the route. In April 1899, when construction still hadn't started, Sycamore elected local businessman David A.

Syme as mayor on his campaign promise to bring Sycamore an electric railroad—whether it be the GLS&S or another line.

The company's surveyors made repeated visits to Sycamore. They were often followed by a revolving door of directors who promised construction would begin soon and cars would be running in six months. For three years, Sycamore was always six months away from seeing the electric railroad completed. After surveyors visited again in the summer of 1900, the *True Republican* finally admitted that Sycamore's residents had lost faith in the project. A few weeks later, the GLS&S announced that it had re-incorporated under the name the Illinois & Wisconsin Railway Company (I&W). This new incarnation promised to preserve the original route, which it would complete in about six months. Little was heard from the I&W after that.

Despite the failure of the Geneva Lake line, it still played an important role in Sycamore's railroad history: it got Sycamoreans fired up about electric railroads. So when a Chicago businessman showed up and proposed building an electric line between Sycamore and DeKalb, Sycamoreans threw their full support behind the project.

The Sycamore & DeKalb Electric Railway

The Sycamore & DeKalb Electric Railway (S&D) was the brainchild of Chicago businessman Edwin B. Magill, an experienced railroad man who had worked as an official for the Chicago, Burlington & Northern Railway. His banking firm, Magill Brothers, was also building an electric railroad in Belvidere, so he had the credentials to back up his promises. His company planned to run the S&D line from the courthouse in Sycamore to the Northern Illinois State Normal School in DeKalb. The *True Republican* immediately backed the project, stating that "the [rail]road will certainly be a great thing for our city and should be encouraged by all."

On September 15, 1899, Sycamore's city council approved the ordinance for Magill's line. Under the ordinance, he had to complete construction in two years or forfeit his franchise. He immediately began securing rights-of-way along the route, but the whole project hit a snag in mid-October when the DeKalb City Council introduced a franchise ordinance "so ridiculous and hoggish" that the S&D refused to accept it. The disagreement arose over the distribution of electricity. The DeKalb Electric Company, which operated the city's power plant, had exclusive distribution rights in DeKalb. The company's directors felt that they should have exclusive rights to supply electricity to the S&D as well (originally, both Sycamore and DeKalb would have provided an equal share of the electricity). They also demanded that the S&D's directors sign off on this agreement without knowing how much the electricity would cost. The S&D's directors refused and negotiations dragged on for months.

The S&D and the DeKalb City Council eventually reached an agreement, which required the S&D to buy out the DeKalb Electric Company and modernize the equipment. The S&D moved its headquarters from Sycamore to DeKalb and changed its name from the Sycamore & DeKalb Electric Railway Company to the DeKalb County Light, Heat and Traction Company. Survey work for the tracks began in February 1900, but the company ran into financial trouble and construction still had not started more than a year later. The *True Republican* began to express doubts about the project.

In May 1901, almost everyone had given up on Magill's electric railroad when work crews suddenly appeared in DeKalb and began installing the poles that would support the railroad's overhead electric wire. The *True Republican* called these "shiny white poles, wabbling unsteadily about… the real birth of that long heralded enterprise." After the Chicago contractor installed the poles on several DeKalb streets, however, he abandoned the project and took off somewhere back east. It is unknown if the contractor stole money from the project, but the company continued to suffer severe financial shortages.

Magill scrambled to raise more money to hold the project together. He asked DeKalb and Sycamore to extend his franchise expiration dates because work would not be completed by the two-year deadline. Both cities agreed to the extensions if Magill provided each with a $1,000 deposit guaranteeing that the work would be completed by the new deadline. Magill had 30 days to deposit the checks, but he never showed in either city. Sycamore's mayor declared Magill's franchise void. DeKalb's mayor did the same. After two years of excitement and anticipation over the new railroad, the *True Republican* declared the whole project "dead as a door nail." The only actual work done was on the poles that stood "naked and useless" in DeKalb's streets.

On October 16, 1901, the *True Republican* passed final judgment on Magill and his failed enterprise: "He has only helped the newspapers to fill their columns with interesting reading."

Dueling Neighbors

By the turn of the century, everyone in DeKalb County knew that something had to be done about Sycamore's aging and outdated courthouse. In Sycamore, two schools of thought arose on how to handle the issue: renovate the old courthouse or build a new one. Renovations seemed expensive and impractical, but DeKalb and Sycamore residents knew that to build a new courthouse would revive that age-old question: Why not build it in DeKalb?

The county-seat conflict had always festered under the surface of DeKalb-Sycamore relations, but DeKalb had made no serious attempts to seize the county seat since the 1860s. Back then, DeKalb had been a prosperous and rapidly expanding town, but still considerably smaller than Sycamore. Now DeKalb had the manufacturing, transportation, and educational facilities to make it a county-seat contender. Even the *True Republican* acknowledged that DeKalb had experienced more prosperity in the last two decades than any other town in the county. In December 1901, the courthouse struggle came to a head.

Sycamoreans called for unity over the courthouse issue. The *True Republican* reported that in the last decade "we have had no bitter contests and our people have stood together for everything that benefit[s] any part of our county. … An inauguration of a period of bitter strife will result in checking further progress." The paper used the electric railway—despite its failure—as an example of the two communities working together. However, it glossed over the fact that many Sycamoreans blamed the electric railroad's failure on DeKalb. They claimed that DeKalb's business leaders had bankrupted the company by forcing it into a bad deal for a bad electric power plant that had been losing money already. Despite these allegations, the *True Republican* called for peace, noting that the business interests of both towns were deeply intertwined and "the cry of war, wherever it comes from, is thoughtless and silly."

War did come, however. DeKalb waged a vicious battle to seize the county seat, and newspapers on both sides heaved volleys of vicious accusations. Both cities accused the other of corruption, manipulation, and subterfuge. On January 22, 1902, the DeKalb County Board of Supervisors voted on the matter and determined that the county seat would remain in Sycamore. Many in DeKalb refused to accept this decision and called for a county-wide vote. Despite DeKalb's continued efforts, the vote never took place, but the animosity between cities continued for several years. Sycamore's new courthouse opened on March 1, 1905.

Sycamore's new courthouse, seen here around 1918 during a parade for departing WWI soldiers.

The DeKalb-Sycamore Electric Railway

While DeKalb licked the wounds of its lost courthouse bid and both cities lamented the loss of the electric railroad, three different organizations swooped in to take control of Magill's deserted franchise. One group called itself the DeKalb, Sycamore & Northern Traction Company and wanted to connect Sycamore and DeKalb to a line it had already built in Rockford. Another group proposed to connect the two cities to Aurora. A third group called itself the DeKalb-Sycamore Electric Railway (D-S) and

it didn't offer to extend connections anywhere beyond DeKalb and Sycamore, but it did offer something better: it would have the railroad completed before year's end. The other two companies could make no such claim.

Sycamore's mayor called a public meeting on March 10, 1902. Hundreds of Sycamoreans turned out at the city's opera house to hear proposals from each company. Almost everyone favored the D-S line, but a few holdouts expressed suspicion because the DeKalb City Council also favored this line. Anger and mistrust over the courthouse issue and previous electric railroad debacle still ran deep. This faction argued that DeKalb would never have granted a franchise to the D-S unless it was somehow against Sycamore's interests. The skeptics held little sway, however, because when it came time to vote, almost everyone voted to grant the franchise to the D-S.

As part of the deal, the D-S agreed to purchase, expand, and update the electric plants in both DeKalb and Sycamore.[1] Both plants would supply the new line's electricity. The company's headquarters would be in DeKalb, and DeKalb businessman John W. Glidden (nephew of barbed wire inventor Joseph Glidden)

---

[1] The Sycamore electric plant was known as Hall Electric, because it was owned and operated by Elry Hall, who had served for 23 years (1877-1900) as the station agent at the C&NW depot (see page 44).

would manage the whole operation. The anti-DeKalb faction opposed the takeover of the local electric plant because they believed that the electric railroad—with its headquarters in DeKalb and with Glidden's involvement—was a DeKalb company. They didn't want Sycamore's electricity under the thumb of DeKalb. The D-S and the newspapers assured concerned citizens that the company was just as much a Sycamore enterprise as a DeKalb enterprise.

The contract for building the railroad went to the L. E. Meyers Company of Chicago. Its crews began work in mid-May 1902, but a summer of heavy downpours and labor shortages delayed construction. Between DeKalb and Sycamore the tracks ran on a graded strip of land alongside the main road. Within each city's limits, the company laid its tracks at ground level so that wagons, carriages, and bicycles could easily cross at any point.

In DeKalb, the D-S located its terminus at the Normal School's west entrance. In Sycamore, the original ordinance called for the D-S tracks to connect with the CGW tracks on Main Street, just east of the CGW depot. This location would have allowed D-S passengers easy access to the CGW, but a 135-foot water standpipe—considered an eyesore from the moment it was completed in 1888—stood in the middle of the State and Main intersection and didn't allow enough room for the

D-S tracks to turn north. As a result, the tracks stopped at the intersection of State and Main, in front of the courthouse. Passengers who wished to connect with the CGW had to walk the last three blocks north.

The standpipe in the middle of the intersection at Sate and Main.

The company desperately wanted to finish the railroad before winter. By November, contractors had finished the tracks in DeKalb and the rural route between cities. On November 2, the D-S's two passenger cars arrived in Sycamore on the CGW line. Each dark green car was 42 feet long, with the name DeKalb-Sycamore Electric Co. painted in gold letters on each side. They also had DeKalb painted on one end and Sycamore painted on the other. The name would face whichever city the car was traveling toward. Each car's interior was divided into two compartments—smoking and non-smoking. The seats were made of woven cane. The *True Republican* gave its own succinct description: "The interior is tastefully finished in natural woods and harmonizing, comfortable upholstery, and there are many windows of fancy glass. The exterior proportions are graceful and pleasing."

With the cars in town and the line almost complete, everyone waited anxiously for service to begin. In Sycamore, work crews installed the last of the wiring, but the tracks on State Street had gaps in two places. For months, the D-S directors had requested permission to cross the CGW line on State Street and the C&NW line at State and Sacramento, but neither company had responded. Instead, they placed guards at each crossing to watch over the tracks day and night. The D-S directors delayed building the crossings as long as possible, but in mid-November, they were all that remained to complete the line. The D-S ordered its workers to move in and build. The local papers reported that "trouble is brewing." Everyone in Sycamore waited to see how this duel would play out.

Battle of the Railroad Crossings

Neither the C&NW nor CGW had much incentive to allow the electric railroad to cross its tracks. This new line would siphon off most of their local traffic, as electric railroads had done to steam railroads throughout the region. Both railroad companies had posted watchmen at the crossings as early as September. When the weather turned cold, the watchmen used old railroad ties to build makeshift guardhouses near the intersections. In October, the C&NW began scheduling a night shift at its depot so that employees could be called at a moment's notice if the D-S workers tried to build overnight. The C&NW also began keeping the local engine fired up outside of its engine house at night so that it could block the intersection if work crews appeared.

The *True Republican*—and most Sycamoreans—sided with the electric railroad. The paper declared, "There can be no long delay and the electric railroad cannot be prevented from crossing, for all parties concerned are aware that the electric has as good a right to the street as have the other [rail] roads." Some Sycamoreans called for a boycott of whichever railroad didn't allow the electric line to cross. In November, the CGW backed down and signed a contract with the D-S that allowed the electric line to cross its tracks on State Street. Its watchmen departed the intersection and the D-S built its crossing. The C&NW, however, still did not respond to the company's repeated requests.

An electric railroad supporter wrote to the *True Republican*, blasting the C&NW for obstructing the new line. The writer acknowledged the good the C&NW had done for the city, but likened the company's current actions to throwing "stones in the way of Sycamore's progress." He or she then called on Sycamore's business leaders to enact a boycott on the C&NW: "If the Northwestern gets 'funny' over the electric, then… it might be well for those who are striving for the upbuilding of a greater Sycamore to order their shipments over the Great Western."

Under the close watch of the C&NW's guards, the D-S work crew laid all of the rails up to within a few feet on both sides of the C&NW's tracks. The D-S could still get by without installing an actual crossing—the electric car could ride over the C&NW's tracks—though this could cause a bumpy and possibly dangerous passage. To finish the line, it needed only to complete the electric circuit by connecting its rails by copper wire, which it could run under the C&NW's tracks. The C&NW was determined not to let the D-S do even this. Each night, it moved an engine to a side track just north of State Street to keep watch.

Soon after, a late-night prankster slipped past the watchmen, took several whacks at the tracks with an iron bar, and slipped back into the night. Several C&NW employees swarmed from the depot and guardhouse to investigate, only to find the streets quiet and empty. It is unknown if the prankster was someone from the D-S testing the C&NW employees' response or someone who just wanted to watch the flurry of activity. Either way, it showed that the C&NW was serious about protecting its crossing.

The D-S workers didn't make their move until December 8, 1902. That evening, three workers approached the C&NW tracks on State Street and began digging so they could run their copper wire beneath the rails. The C&NW depot agent, John Owen, spotted them and immediately ordered his engineer to block the crossing. The engineer ran his locomotive into the intersection and vented a blast of steam that enveloped the D-S workers and forced them to retreat. When the air cleared, the D-S workers tried to approach again, only to be met by another blast. This back-and-forth battle of shovels and steam went on for several minutes and quickly attracted large crowds on all corners of the intersection.

The city marshal soon arrived and informed the C&NW employees that their train could block the intersection for only ten minutes, the maximum allowed by city ordinance. The engineer complied and moved the engine out of State Street. The three D-S workers ran to the tracks and dug as fast as they could. After a few minutes, the engine rolled back into the intersection and blasted them with more steam. The engine remained in place for ten minutes, moved out of the intersection, then moved back again. Each time the train moved, the electric railroad workers rushed forward and dug under the tracks. The crowd cheered them on and even began hurling insults at the C&NW employees.

After an hour, the C&NW workers realized that the D-S men were actually making progress, so they brought up their own work crew to drive posts deep into the ground alongside the tracks, preventing the D-S workers from digging any farther. With all of their efforts blocked, the D-S workers retreated for the night.

The C&NW must have considered itself victorious, because when the D-S workers returned early the next morning, there was no one watching the intersection and the men quickly ran the wire through a sewer pipe that ran under the gutters at the road's edge. The pipe was several feet out of the way, but it allowed the workers to connect the rails on both sides of the C&NW tracks.

The next issue of the *True Republican* carried the headline: "ELECTRIC GOT ACROSS." Even with the full line connected, the C&NW still would not grant permission for the D-S to cross its tracks. To prevent the electric car from getting across, it installed a metal bar in the crossing that would derail the car. The general consensus around Sycamore, however, was that the D-S had gotten the better of the C&NW.

Electric Service Begins

After five years of expectations and disappointments, Sycamore's first electric railroad made its inaugural run on Saturday, December 13, 1902. Three evening runs followed. All four runs were free of charge. Saturday's runs had not been advertised in advance, but word quickly spread that the electric line was in operation. When the company's regular schedule began the next day, hundreds of Sycamoreans gathered at State and Sacramento to catch a ride to DeKalb. Because the C&NW still would not grant the D-S permission to cross its tracks, the company could not use its terminus in front of the courthouse. It had to load and unload passengers west of the C&NW's tracks on State Street.

In both Sycamore and DeKalb, residents ran to their windows or stopped on the street at the sound of the electric car's bell "clanging through the business centers." The *DeKalb Chronicle* celebrated the long-anticipated event by declaring, "The millennium has arrived." The *True Republican* gave the following account of the first day of operation:

An early 1900s view of State Street looking west. Note the D-S tracks in the middle of the street and electric wire overhead.

> The promised improvement has been offered… time and time again and just as often the promises have turned out to be delusions that have shaken our faith in the electric [rail]road project and called out the announcements on all sides, "I will believe it when I see the cars running." If seeing is believing, DeKalb was thoroughly convinced yesterday, for the people who did not ride strained their necks to see the cars go by… The triumphal entry of trolley cars in both towns… dispelled the hallucinations that have flitted through the minds of fond dreamers… The sound of the gong, the whistle of the brakes, and the whirr of wheels of the first electric car was sweeter music in the ears… than the chiming of church bells.

The railroad was designed so that cars could leave each city on the hour—a sidetrack halfway between allowed the cars to pass—but only one car ran the first day. It departed DeKalb on the hour and Sycamore on the half-hour. Each run took approximately 20 minutes. It cost 10 cents for a ride between cities and five cents to ride locally. A car packed to capacity, including standing room, could hold a hundred passengers. The D-S estimated that 1,300 passengers rode the first day.

Within a week of opening, the D-S finally worked out an agreement with the C&NW; the electric cars could pass all the way to the courthouse. The C&NW claimed that it had never intended to block the electric line's construction, but that the only official who could have approved the track crossing had been out of town. In March 1903, the D-S leased space in the Townsend Building on State Street, alongside the railroad's courthouse terminus. The company turned the space into a mini-depot, of sorts, with a small business office and a waiting room.

One major advantage the electric line had over the steam lines was its ability to make frequent stops. These stops allowed farmers who lived between cities to catch a quick ride into one town or the other. They also allowed people in both cities to use the line locally, or to take a five-cent ride to the woods outside of town for a short picnic. Two weeks after opening, the D-S reported that it had sold over 19,000 five-cent fares.

A trolley car on the DeKalb-Sycamore Electric Railway.

A rural waiting station on the D-S line between DeKalb and Sycamore. When this photo was taken in 1941, the D-S had been out of service nearly 20 years.

A New Golden Age

In the first year of operation, the number of daily passengers on the D-S continued to increase. The numerous summertime events and festivals in DeKalb and Sycamore taxed the cars to capacity. The company's directors were so pleased with the success that they added extra cars to the line. They also began negotiating to extend service to Genoa, and from there to Belvidere and Rockford. The company had these routes surveyed and even secured land rights between Sycamore and Genoa (though it never built this line).

World's collide in this early 1900s image depicting three generations of transportation on the road between Sycamore and Dekalb.

In the summer of 1904, the company introduced open bench cars, which were unpowered trailers pulled behind the main cars. They had large open windows and doors that let in cool air and allowed unobstructed views of the countryside. The *True Republican* described the experience—and odors—of a typical ride in an open car between DeKalb and Sycamore:

Nothing will interfere with the view of the corn-fed porkers waddling about the barnyard; the chickens industriously scratching and then fleeing wildly as they barely escape from the wheels of the passing car; the exciting pursuit of the car by the farm dog, whose great bounds and ferocious wide-open mouth, soon dwindle in the distance and dust in the rear; the horses and cattle which hardly raise their heads from cropping the green of the pastures to gaze briefly and stupidly... [T]he pleasing effect of these pastoral scenes will be enhanced by the setting of green meadows, fresh pastures, fields of glistening corn and dark cool-looking woods. Passengers will also receive the full force of the breezes, which... will also bring odors direct from the fields enriched from the sheep sheds.

A D-S car at the line's northern terminus outside the courthouse in Sycamore.

The D-S became so successful that in 1906 the CGW stopped passenger service between Sycamore and DeKalb on its DeKalb & Great Western (D&GW) line. Ticket sales had plummeted after the electric line opened. The D&GW still garnered plenty of business running freight on the line, but passengers arriving at Sycamore's CGW depot who wished to continue on to DeKalb now had to walk three blocks south to catch the D-S car in front of the courthouse. To make the transfer easier, the CGW started selling D-S tickets at its depot. The D&GW most likely shut down its small Grant Street passenger depot at this time.

The electric railway brought more than just a new railroad to Sycamore. The D-S also owned and operated the city's electric plant, which it

expanded and updated with the latest technology. Besides supplying power for the electric railroad, the company secured contracts to provide power, water, and heat to the whole city. In June 1903, the D-S finished a 900-foot well that gave Sycamore the "purest and most palatable drinking water" in all of DeKalb County. In early 1904, it began running power lines to farms along the electric railway between DeKalb and Sycamore, providing electricity to many of these locations for the first time. The D-S modernized Sycamore's entire infrastructure, which helped expand the city and attract new investors.

The Sycamore City Council bolstered the improvements by updating the sewers, paving the roads, and adding more streetlights. By 1905, Sycamore had added a new courthouse, library, and business block on State Street. The C&NW contributed with its own improvements. At the turn of the century, it had put in new walks and platforms around the depot. In 1904, the company worked with the city council to pave Sacramento Street in brick and install new gas lamps on the depot platform (the C&NW purchased the lamps and the city paid for the gas). This was the first time the C&NW depot had exterior lighting at night. The *True Republican* noted that the new lights offered considerable courtesy to "the passengers alighting from the night trains." The company later added cement sidewalks to replace the wooden walks. In 1906, the depot was "thoroughly overhauled." The company installed a new windmill, performed "repairs of all sorts," and added coats of white paint on the interior and red paint on the exterior. The red paint covered the bricks, limestone foundation, and limestone trimmings. A new lumberyard moved in east of the depot, and a coal company constructed the largest coal shed in the county directly northeast of the depot.

With so many modern improvements, Sycamore attracted several new businesses and manufacturers. The Borden Condensed Milk plant opened alongside the C&NW's tracks on the city's southern outskirts, which encouraged Sycamore to extend its streets, sewers, and electrical lines in that direction. Soon after, Turner Brass Works

moved its Chicago plant to Sycamore. Other companies followed, and the new factories created a construction boom. Times were especially good for contractors. The *True Republican* noted, "If you do not want to work, Sycamore is an uncomfortable place… for you will be bothered by people trying to get you to work for them and help them share in the general activity." The paper referred to the manufacturing district along both sides of the C&NW tracks as Sycamore's "mile of industry." The C&NW had to improve old tracks and build additional ones to facilitate all of the extra freight coming and going from the new factories. So much freight went through the depot each day that in 1907 the C&NW built its only major depot expansion: a 100-foot-long freight shed attached to the north end of the original freight house.

In 1907, the C&NW added a 32-by-100-foot extension to the depot's freight house.

DeKalb experienced a similar boost to its economy. With DeKalb and Sycamore united by three different lines, a new era of business and social interaction brought the two cities closer than ever before. Some business leaders and local officials even talked of working together to set up new manufacturers along the electric line. Such factories would employ men from both cities, and businesses and neighborhoods would eventually extend to these factories until both cities and their interests were fully intertwined. This prospect did not occur as quickly as some business leaders envisioned it, but it is the reality—to some extent—the two cities enjoy today. Even though it didn't happen immediately, the idea alone sent property along the electric line soaring from $100 to $500 an acre.

In October 1906, a group of investors wanting to share in Sycamore's success bought out the DeKalb-Sycamore Electric Railway Company and reorganized it under the name DeKalb, Sycamore & Interurban Traction Company (DS&I). The company split the railway and power plants into separate businesses. In June 1908, it added new cars to the line, which allowed runs to leave each city every half hour. The company also announced plans to extend new electric lines from DeKalb and Sycamore in all directions. First, it would focus on building a northern route, toward Belvidere and Rockford and possibly into Wisconsin. But if it wanted to be the first electric railroad to secure such a route, it would have to hurry. Other companies already had their sights set on Sycamore.

The Woodstock & Sycamore Traction Company

Sycamore's residents had become numb to the rumors, speculations, and empty promises from businessmen who claimed they could connect Sycamore to every town in northern Illinois by electric rail. So they probably didn't get too excited in September 1907 when yet another electric railroad scheme hit the local papers. This new company claimed it could build the long-fabled electric line between Geneva Lake and Sycamore, but it would start by building a more conservative 37-mile line from Sycamore to Woodstock.

Incorporated on October 31, 1907, the Woodstock, Marengo, Genoa & Sycamore Electric Railroad Company planned to build an electric railroad through all of the towns in its title. The company's officers, made up mostly of businessmen from Chicago and Columbus, Ohio, visited Sycamore in October 1907 to promote the railroad and encourage investors. A few weeks later, they spent a day riding over the proposed route in a procession of automobiles. This means of transportation was a far cry from that of a decade earlier, when the officers had spent weeks riding over the proposed line in wagons and buggies. After the inspection, the directors met with investors in Sycamore and declared that their new railroad would open inside 12 months. They then climbed into their automobiles and drove back to Chicago.

Over the next few months, the company secured rights-of-way along most of the route. On April 8, 1908, it wisely shortened its name when it reincorporated as the Woodstock & Sycamore Traction Company (W&S). The W&S planned to build the railroad along the highways, as the DS&I had done. Many farmers donated the right-of-way, knowing that the electric line would increase their property value and provide easy access to travel and shipping. The *True Republican* supported the new railroad, declaring it the best prospect of all the companies trying to build in the area. "Let everybody hustle to secure this [rail]road," it wrote. "Already one farm has been sold at a nice price just on the strength of this [rail]road being built."

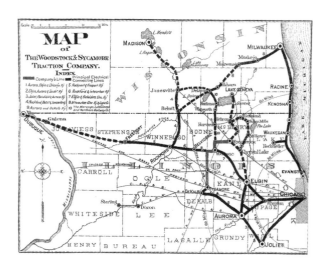

The W&S released this promotional map showing not only the company's line between Sycamore and Woodstock, but all of the electric railroad lines in northern Illinois that passengers would be able to reach by way of the W&S.

Problems securing the rights-of-way delayed construction for over a year, but in the summer of 1908 the company's chief engineer surveyed and staked out the entire line between Sycamore and Woodstock. Throughout the summer, company officers went on several automobile tours to solicit investors and assure everyone that the railroad was still a sure thing. Several local businessmen, including former mayors Fred Townsend and David A. Syme, invested thousands in the enterprise. They breathed a collective sigh of relief in late August 1908 when grading work finally began between Sycamore and Genoa. By year's end, contractors had graded most of the line between Sycamore, Genoa, and Marengo. In

May 1909, the company announced that it would use cars that ran on gasoline. The company had decided to forego the trolley-style electric car—like that used on the DS&I line—which would have required running poles and electric lines along the full route at a cost of $4,500 per mile. The company planned to convert the line to electric at a later date. In the meantime, it ordered two cars from the McKeen Motor Car Company of Omaha, Nebraska. The cars became known as the 711 and 709. The company ordered a third car, the 707, in 1911.

The grading reached Sycamore in November 1909, when work crews began on the frozen ground north of the CGW's tracks on Main Street. In April 1910, with grading and fencing mostly complete between Sycamore and Genoa, the company built a switch track to the CGW line so it could transport ties and rails and start building north from Sycamore. The first shipment included 200 tons of rails and 4,000 ties.

The W&S "first spike" ceremony. Fred Townsend stands in the middle.
He is wearing a hat and bowtie and resting a sledgehammer on his shoulder.

To celebrate the laying of the first rails, the company held a "first spike" ceremony on Wednesday, May 4, 1910. Over 300 people gathered just south of the bridge over the Kishwaukee River on North Main Street, where the W&S line branched off to meet the CGW, and where laying of the rails would commence. The railroad was already graded and fenced, and the ties lay for as far as the eye could see. Fred Townsend drove the ceremonial first spike halfway into a railroad tie. W&S president C. G. Lumley drove it in the rest of the way. Lumley then gave a speech, promising that this railroad would be the best in the state and a credit to Sycamore. He also acknowledged the prejudices his company had overcome due to the failure of the Geneva Lake line a decade earlier. Townsend, Syme, and George Brown, a local lawyer working for the W&S, followed with their own rosy remarks. Brown had been treasurer and one of the founding directors of the failed Geneva Lake line, so for him, this ceremony was a sublime moment 10 years in the making. After the ceremony, many of the guests and investors returned home in their automobiles.

A work crew of 85 men labored through the summer to lay the remainder of the ties and steel rails. Fresh supplies arrived at the CGW depot daily, where a work train on loan from the CGW shuttled the materials to the crews at the end of the line. The first McKeen car arrived in Sycamore over the CGW on July 3, 1910. The railroad was incomplete between Sycamore and Genoa, but on July 4 the company decorated the car with American flags and offered complimentary rides to a point about four miles north of Sycamore.

The Woodstock & Sycamore Interurban Traction Company made its first full run on Saturday, July 23, 1910. The trip consisted of company officials traveling to Genoa to meet with officials from the Illinois Central Railroad (IC), who had refused to let the W&S cross its tracks in that city. If the W&S couldn't cross the IC, it would have to stop its cars almost half a mile from Genoa's downtown. It also couldn't continue its route on to Marengo, which was graded and ready for ties and rails. The two companies failed to reach an agreement and the matter had to be shelved for the time being.

Despite this inconvenience, the W&S made its first regular run a week later on July 30. Over 1,600 passengers took advantage of the new service. Each 15-minute run packed the car beyond capacity, averaging between 80 and a hundred passengers. By evening, "Genoa was filled with Sycamoreans and Sycamore was well filled with Genoese." The company donated a percentage of the day's fares to the Sycamore Hospital.

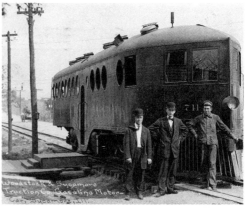

The W&S car on the line between Sycamore and Genoa. The red, all-steel car stood 55 feet long—12 feet for the operator's compartment and 43 feet for passengers. Large porthole windows lined the sides. The *True Republican* described it as "a unique looking conveyance" resembling "an inverted boat." In later issues, it referred to the car as a "warship." The interior was finished in mahogany and lit by acetylene gas. The car was built to hold about 75 passengers. Each leather-upholstered seat accommodated three passengers and a semi-circular seat at the back sat 10 passengers. It cost approximately $20,000.

When the W&S began its regular schedule the following Monday, the car left each city every two hours and made seven runs a day. Because the car was heavier than most electric cars, passengers noted its smoother ride, without the sudden jolts often experienced on the DS&I. In the first month, the line carried 9,012 passengers. The second month, this number dropped to 5,426, which was a better representation of the average monthly patronage going forward. The company released a statement to its investors in May 1911, reporting that in the first eight months of operation it had sold 42,675 fares. By this time, the W&S had resolved its crossing dispute with the IC in Genoa by veering its tracks west and building a viaduct under the IC's line. But W&S officials still faced a long uphill battle to complete their line and turn it into a profitable enterprise.

INTERURBAN CAR KILLED 35 SHEEP

Large Flock In Road Belonging To Foy & Townsend Struck By Woodstock Sycamore Car On Sunday.

The car on the Woodstock-Sycamore interurban railway ran into a large flock of sheep about two miles north of Sycamore on Monday afternoon, and after the car had been stopped and the result was noted, it was found that some 35 of the foolish animals had ended their active existence if not all their usefulness.

From the November 8, 1911 issue of the *True Republican*

Sycamore's two electric railroads were the last major expansion in the city's railroad history. By the end of 1911, the electric railroads had proved, at least temporarily, to be a success. They had brought Sycamore closer to its neighbors, and they had effectively competed against the C&NW and CGW and come out on top, securing the majority of local railroad travel. Overall, Sycamore's railroad advantages and connections had never been better. Including both steam and interurban lines, over 50 passenger trains ran through the city each day, and the numerous freight trains offered a huge incentive for any businesses or factories looking to relocate. Despite the city's newfound optimism, its business leaders did not predict that the nation would soon embrace a wholly different transportation technology, one that would seal the fate of Sycamore's railroads and undermine the entire industry: the automobile.

The Electric Park

Electric Park shelter house

Baseball field at Electric Park

In January 1903, Sycamore farmer Henry Groves, who was known to wield a walking stick with "spectacular flourish," announced that he would build a recreational park a mile and a half south of Sycamore on 20 acres of land alongside the D-S electric line. Groves Park, as it became known, opened with great fanfare on June 25, 1903. The electric cars from both cities were packed to capacity as they carried over 700 visitors to the event. Partygoers paid just 10 cents to travel from Sycamore and 15 cents to travel from DeKalb. Admission to the dance was included in the cost of the round-trip ticket. At the pavilion, hundreds of electric lights illuminated the large dance floor and dazzled the visitors. The *True Republican* called the celebration "the largest dance ever held in DeKalb County, without a doubt."

Groves Park also offered visitors a baseball field, covered amphitheater, picnic grounds, and a promenade for strolling. Groves designed the park to host a variety of wholesome social events, including baseball games between DeKalb and Sycamore, church and society picnics, youth dances, and holiday celebrations. Liquor sales were not allowed.

Just over a week after opening, the park's first Fourth of July celebration turned into an unmitigated disaster. Thousands of revelers from DeKalb and Sycamore attended, but a heavy rainstorm canceled the fireworks and drove everyone under the pavilion. Because the pavilion had only a packed-dirt floor, the place soon turned into a sloppy, sucking mud pit.

The rain wasn't the only problem that day. The D-S horribly underestimated the number of people who wanted to attend the event. The *True Republican* heaped heavy criticism on the company and gave the following account of the day's indignities:

> The cars were crowded so that breathing room was at a premium. At the end of the line in Sycamore a mad rush was made for every car, and the crowd was allowed to rush aboard before those who were in could get out, so that there was dire confusion and some not able to make their exit were even carried back over the line. Women had their best hats knocked off into the mud, and crying women with crying babies were jostled and crushed. Others who were agile enough made their escape from the windows. Many passengers hung on a narrow ledge outside the cars in order to get a ride.

After three years, Groves sold his park to the D-S, which wished to turn it into a "high-class resort." The company updated the attractions and added a hardwood dance floor in the pavilion. It also hired local and traveling bands to play each night. Palmer's Orchestra was a local favorite and always drew large crowds. Additionally, the company built an indoor theater and brought in a professional theater group and a variety of vaudeville acts. It also introduced Sycamore and DeKalb to "moving pictures," which, previously, had been available only in Chicago. Throughout the life of the D-S, the electric park, as it was now known, remained a popular destination for dances, picnics, ball games, and holiday celebrations.

The original dance pavilion burned down on May 11, 1921. The owners suspected arson by "blue law fanatics" who disliked that the park was open on Sundays. No one was ever caught. A new dance pavilion opened in April 1923, just a year before the DS&I discontinued service. Even after electric railroad service ended, the electric park remained a popular entertainment destination for Sycamoreans and DeKalbans. The park's popularity, however, came to an abrupt end on June 11, 1930, when the second pavilion burned to the ground. Arson was again suspected but never proved. The park hosted a few more picnics and ball games, but the owners never rebuilt the pavilion and the park shut down for good in 1931.

For a time, the neighborhood near the park was known as Electric Park Corner. Today, the park's only remaining legacy is Electric Park Drive, a small residential street south of Sycamore that runs between DeKalb Avenue and Coltonville Road.

End of an Era, 1901-1984

The motor car has become an indispensable instrument in our political, social, and industrial life.

President Warren G. Harding, 1921

On July 9, 1901, a special event took place in Sycamore that foreshadowed the long, slow decline of the city's railroads. A well-known local actor, playwright, theater director, and all-around showman named Fred Raymond motored into town in his shiny new automobile. Fred's car, the first of its kind seen on the streets of Sycamore, caused a sensation when it sped through town "at a pace that made the old inhabitants dizzy." One person who rode in the car described feeling "uneasy and apprehensive" when it reached 20 miles per hour.

Over the next two years, Sycamore's residents saw the occasional automobile pass through, but no one else in town owned an automobile until 1903, when several wealthy businessmen purchased cars of their own. The number of automobiles in Sycamore increased slowly, but not significantly, for the rest of the decade. Railroad leaders viewed these new contraptions as mere novelties—playthings for the rich or for eccentric entertainers like Fred Raymond. No one foresaw the threat they posed to the thousands of

Muddy roads plagued automobiles as much as they plagued the horses and wagons of the previous century. Until towns and counties could improve their roads, railroad travel would remain superior.

miles of railroad—both steam and electric—that dominated shipping and passenger service across the nation.

In late 1903, the courthouse construction and the new electric line overshadowed another significant event that would spell doom for local railroad service: Sycamore started paving its streets. Sycamoreans had dreamed of such an improvement since the pioneers first trudged through the thick prairieland. In October 1903, contractors poured cement curbs and gutters and began laying asphalt on State Street. Several roads branching north and south from State Street were paved in brick, including Sacramento Street past the C&NW depot. Paving the roads within city limits took several years, but when the process was complete, Sycamore never again had to deal with the choking dust, muddy holes, and hazardous ruts that had plagued its streets for three quarters of a century.

By 1910, the *True Republican* boasted of Sycamore's smooth, paved roads. With travel by automobile becoming easier and prices for mass-produced automobiles falling, more and more cars made their way onto Sycamore's streets. Nationwide, Americans had purchased over 500,000 automobiles. By 1915, that number jumped to two million, with automobile manufacturers producing nearly 800,000 new cars a year. The large railroad conglomerates, already weakened by electric railroads and government regulations, saw their profits plummet.

Northern Illinois' railroad lines suffered a serious blow in 1913 with the opening of Lincoln Highway, the nation's first transcontinental highway. It ran for 3,389 miles from New York to San Francisco and passed through over 700 cities. Automobile and tire manufacturers helped fund the project because they knew it would boost

sales. In 1915, future etiquette expert Emily Post travelled the full length of the Lincoln Highway and wrote about her experiences for Collier's Magazine. Her articles plus her follow-up book, *By Motor to the Golden Gate*, created a huge interest in cross-country automobile travel.

In Illinois, Lincoln Highway ran from the Indiana border just south of Chicago to the Mississippi River at Fulton. The 180-mile stretch passed through the heart of DeKalb. The proximity to such a major highway influenced residents from across DeKalb County to purchase automobiles. Local passenger service on the C&NW and the two interurban lines—already in decline—took another steep drop.

As the number of passengers deteriorated, so did public perception of railroads. In previous decades, the blast of the locomotive's whistle or the clanging of its bell represented progress and prosperity. But by the 1910s, many Sycamore residents began to view railroads as a nuisance. They complained about the noise, dangerous crossings, blocked intersections, soot in the air, and tramps in the streets. To counter these perceptions, one civic-minded organization set out to improve the railroad's place in the community.

The Sycamore Woman's Club

In 1908, a group of 35 socially conscious women founded the Sycamore Woman's Club, a group dedicated to "active work along the lines of improvement in sanitary conditions, municipal cleanliness, both material and moral, good citizenship, and the beautifying of the city." The group's earliest missions targeted city sanitation and beautification.

The Sycamore Woman's Club, date unknown. (Sycamore History Museum)

In 1913, the woman's club proposed building a park on the empty lot directly north of the C&NW depot, which still held the remains of a mop factory that had burned down in 1910. They wanted the park to serve as an attractive entrance to Sycamore for anyone stepping off the train at the C&NW depot. The park would feature a finely landscaped path that would escort visitors directly to the city's business center. Passengers just passing through Sycamore would still get a taste of the city's beauty and sophistication when they saw the park through the train windows.

Several Sycamoreans, however, complained about the site's proximity to the depot. They claimed that dust and smoke from passing trains would pollute the park, the nearby tracks would present a danger to children, loud locomotives would interrupt conversation, and hobos would take up residence there. These valid concerns showed how much attitudes toward the city's railroads had changed. A decade earlier, the public would have quickly embraced such a project, knowing that the park would have offered a good first impression of the town to visitors and investors alike. Park supporters eventually prevailed and the city completed the park in 1915. The C&NW even donated time and materials to fill in the dilapidated lot.

For sanitation, the woman's club first pressed the public schools, encouraging them to install modern toilets. Many of them did. Next, the group encouraged the C&NW and CGW to improve their local depots. The companies proved a bit stubborn, but the women persisted. Backed by the Sycamore Chamber of Commerce, they waged a long petition campaign, urging both the C&NW

This 1950s aerial view of Sycamore, looking west, shows the city park on the southeast corner of State Street and Sacramento Street, to the north (right) of the C&NW depot. The city replaced the park with a public parking lot in 1955.

the company laid new floors, put "plenty of paint everywhere," and installed two restrooms and a drinking fountain.

The C&NW held out a while longer, but in 1916 it gave in to the club's demands and installed men's and women's restrooms in their respective waiting rooms. It also installed a porcelain drinking fountain in the women's waiting room. To make room for the new restrooms, the C&NW had to move the depot's coal stove into the basement. It also had to switch around the doors and windows on the building's east side so the entrances to the men's and women's waiting rooms didn't open into the restrooms. This was the last major renovation of the depot under the ownership of the C&NW.

and CGW to improve their facilities and install indoor toilets and water fountains. They argued that such facilities not only offered sanitation and modern convenience, but showed that Sycamore could keep pace with the times.

The CGW gave in first. From 1914 to 1915, the company built a new foundation under the depot, installed a new brick platform, spruced up the landscaping, planted bushes around the building, and gave it a new coat of paint. Inside the depot,

With several successes under their collective belt, Sycamore's women focused on a more urgent matter: the looming war in Europe. The club founded the Sycamore chapter of the Red Cross, which quickly grew to over 600 members. Red Cross volunteers raised over $10,000 for the war effort. The woman's club then set to work collecting donations, knitting clothes and bandages, and packing much-needed medical supplies. They sent their packages to both the C&NW and CGW depots, where they were shipped out to join the vast network of war materials flowing east.

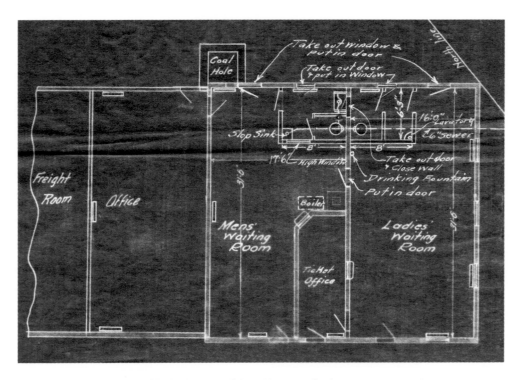

In 1916, the C&NW created a set of depot blueprints for the restroom renovation.
They are the only known blueprints of the depot still extant. (Sycamore History Museum, courtesy of Paul Rubeck)

When built, the depot's headhouse had one entrance on each side. The window with the slightly lower keystone arch was the original east-side entrance. The C&NW added a second door to the right of the original door when it split the waiting room in 1898. The doors were moved to their current position during the 1916 renovation to accommodate the new restrooms.

World War I

World War I had a profound effect on the nation's railroads. To shore up national security and streamline the shipping of war materials, the federal government took control of many aspects of the railroad industry. The changes improved railroad efficiency but cut deeply into company profits. Freight and troop movement took precedence over passenger service, which drove more potential passengers toward buses and automobiles.

On September 5, 1917, the first twelve Sycamore soldiers to depart for the war left by automobile to catch a C&NW train in DeKalb. Thereafter, almost every soldier left by way of Sycamore's C&NW depot. Before their departure, soldiers would meet at the courthouse to listen to speeches by local leaders, businessmen, and politicians, followed by music from Sycamore's brass band (see photo on page 152). Then a cheering crowd paraded them down State Street to the C&NW depot.

During the war, hundreds of troop trains stopped at the C&NW and CGW depots to take on water. Red Cross volunteers met the soldiers there with sandwiches, coffee, books, and magazines. Soldiers sometimes disembarked from their trains and marched or drilled outside the depots and in nearby streets, which always attracted a large crowd. Sycamore's young women often waited at the stations to cheer on the troop trains. When soldiers didn't disembark, some girls ran up to the cars so soldiers could pick them up for a kiss.

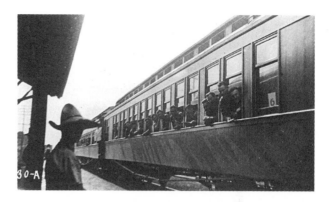

A WWI troop train stopped outside of the CGW depot (Sycamore History Museum)

In total, 500 Sycamore boys served in the war. Nine lost their lives: five in action, one from wounds, and three from disease. On Memorial Day in 1920, the city paid tribute to the nine fallen soldiers by planting trees in their honor in the city park north of the C&NW depot. The park became known unofficially as Memorial Park after World War II, when several civic and fraternal organizations added a veteran's memorial.

End of the Electrics

The Woodstock & Sycamore (W&S) line saw little success beyond its first few months of operation. Mechanical problems plagued the McKeen cars, resulting in delays and irregular timetables. The erratic service showed Sycamoreans that they couldn't depend on the W&S for reliable transportation. Patronage began to slip on the Sycamore-Genoa branch before contractors finished the Genoa-Marengo branch in 1911.

A large crowd gathers outside the C&NW depot to see-off soldiers departing for WWI. (Sycamore History Museum)

After the W&S finished its expensive viaduct under the Illinois Central line, it hit its most devastating complication. Another railroad in Genoa, the Chicago, Milwaukee & St. Paul (CM&StP), also refused to allow the W&S to cross its tracks. By this time, the tracks from Genoa to Marengo had been completed. The only obstacle preventing Sycamoreans from riding straight through to Marengo was a one-block gap in the tracks in Genoa. The company had to run separate cars on each branch of the railroad. Sycamoreans travelling to Marengo had to disembark south of the CM&StP tracks in Genoa, walk across the tracks, and board the second car to continue the trip north. While the walk was short, it still created a huge inconvenience for the passengers, especially in winter or during inclement weather. For the W&S, it was an embarrassment impossible to overcome. This situation remained for two years until the W&S spent a large sum of money to build a bridge over the CM&StP.

The erratic and unreliable service, coupled with the growing number of automobiles, resulted in poor sales and plunging profits. As passengers dwindled, the company discontinued several runs. By April 1918, it made only one run a day between Genoa and Marengo. The busier route between Sycamore and Genoa maintained three runs a day, but these few runs could no longer sustain the operation. The company ended service on May 20, 1918. Despite a completed survey and several miles of grading between Marengo and Woodstock, the company never finished that branch. The railroad's contractor, John Seymour, who had done all of the contract work since the project's beginning, had to sue the W&S for $65,000 in unpaid wages.

The W&S officially met its demise on August 10, 1918, when Sycamore auctioned the company's property at the courthouse. The auction brought in $120,000, most of it for the steel rails, which were in high demand due to the war in Europe. The company that purchased the rails had them all removed by year's end. Over half the auction money went to pay off John Seymour. The rest went to investors, who recovered only 10 percent of their original investments. Several Sycamore businessmen lost thousands of dollars on the failed enterprise. The *True Republican* called the whole project a "financial embarrassment from the outset." A fitting eulogy was provided by *Chicago Tribune* writer David Young, who wrote in a 1991 article on Illinois' interurban railroads: "The Woodstock & Sycamore Traction Company [was] arguably the most ill-conceived, useless and appropriately forgotten railroad ever operated in Illinois or any other state."

The DeKalb, Sycamore & Interurban (DS&I) fared much better than its northern counterpart, but like the W&S, it suffered from increased automobile and bus traffic. To compensate, the company's directors raised prices and reduced runs. In 1921, Sycamore's business owners no longer wanted the electric cars running through the main business corridor on State Street, so the DS&I ended its runs to the courthouse and made its new terminus outside the Ward Hotel at the corner of California and State. In 1923, the company had to take out a substantial loan to stay in business. When the number of passengers continued to decline, the DS&I couldn't repay its debts and had to shut down. After over 21 years of service, the last electric car departed Sycamore for DeKalb at 11:30 p.m. on Thursday, April 17, 1924.

The end of the interurban lines had little impact on residents of Sycamore, DeKalb, and Genoa. By this time, passengers had mostly given up on the services, preferring buses or their own automobiles. Northern Illinois' once vast network of interurban lines slowly faded away throughout the rest of the 1920s and 1930s. In almost all cases, they were quickly superseded by buses that covered nearly identical and ever-expanding routes.

Rise of the Roads

By 1920, over eight million automobiles roamed the nation's 360,000 miles of paved roads, an increase made possible by factory assembly lines, falling prices, and government initiatives to improve roads. By 1923, the number of railroad passengers had fallen to less than half of pre-war figures. That same year, city officials in Sycamore began their biggest road-improvement push since the paving of State Street two decades earlier. With new roads and an increase in automobile traffic, gas and service stations became regular features of the city landscape.

Well into the 1920s, an optimistic railroad industry remained competitive by improving tracks, updating freight and passenger cars, introducing new and more powerful engines, and modernizing depots. In some parts of the country, most notably the Great Plains, they even built new tracks to connect the region's fast-growing but far-flung farming communities. In Sycamore, the CGW moved its freight department out of its depot in December 1923. It built a new freight depot along its tracks east of Main Street. The 20-by-60-foot structure had a 150-foot-long loading platform that stood at the same height as the railroad car doors. The company did some touch-up work on its old depot, which now accommodated passengers only. These railroad improvements, however, could do little to slow the nation's shift toward automobiles and trucks.

The C&NW constructed this 8x10 foot watchtower in September 1924. It stood 12 feet above the crossing at High Street and DeKalb Avenue. It had windows on all sides so a watchman could observe traffic on the streets and the tracks. When a train approached, he operated the signals to warn oncoming traffic. The C&NW built the tower due to increased automobile traffic and because several newer buildings obstructed the view from the depot. The watchman stayed on duty only until 6:00 p.m. After that, drivers were on their own.

Sycamore's automobile traffic saw a huge increase in 1926 with the opening of Route 23, which stretched from Wisconsin to the Illinois River, following a similar path as the failed Geneva Lake electric line of the 1890s. A year later, Sycamore removed the bricks from DeKalb Avenue and several side streets—including Sacramento Street by the C&NW depot—and paved the roads with smooth asphalt. The city also ripped up the old DS&I tracks from State Street and repaved that road. In 1929, the *True Republican* boasted of Sycamore's many paved streets and how well they accommodated the city's increase in motor traffic.

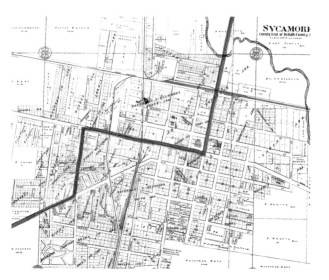

Heading into Sycamore from DeKalb Avenue, Route 23 cuts north on Center Cross Street, east on State Street, then north again on Main Street. State officials chose this route in 1926 because they didn't want the road to cross the numerous railroad tracks on DeKalb Avenue in front of the C&NW depot. They felt that this crossing was too dangerous and would delay traffic.

Another blow to Sycamore's railroads came in 1929 with the opening of Route 64, which connected Sycamore directly to Chicago. The road's first automobile travelers reported making the drive to the Chicago C&NW depot in one hour and twelve minutes. The fastest passenger train out of Sycamore made the trip in one hour and forty-two minutes. For the first time, Sycamoreans had a faster option than the railroad to reach Chicago.

The Great Depression

When the stock market crashed in October 1929, many people outside of the financial institutions, including railroad officials, saw little cause for alarm. But a year later, the Great Depression had crippled the nation, and railroad profits—from both passengers and freight—had plummeted. Nationwide, railroad companies cut expenses and laid off thousands of employees. The CGW depot in Sycamore lost about a quarter of its staff, including employees who had been with the company more than 20 years.

As the Depression wore on, companies continued reducing depot staff. At many small-town depots, the station agent became the only employee. Depots that needed to be rebuilt were rebuilt smaller. Depots that still had separate men's and women's waiting rooms would pick one as the joint waiting room and repurpose the other, usually as an office or for storage. As a further cost-saving measure, railroads began shutting down unprofitable depots and branch lines. In the early 1930s, C&NW president Fred W. Sargent addressed the issue in one of his annual reports:

In short, the railroad was built in the days of dirt roads and the horse and buggy. Stations are now more numerous than necessary, with concrete roads and the automobile. Unnecessary stations should be abandoned where the business can be handled at other stations on the same or adjacent lines. Likewise, more branch lines were built in the horse and buggy age than would have been built in the age of the automobile and concrete highways.

Local Passenger Service Disappears

For several years, the C&NW had offered only two trains a day on the original S&C line. All freight went by way of DeKalb and fewer and fewer passengers traveled by train to Cortland. By early 1930, the C&NW had reduced the service to a single evening train each day. Then it decided to abandon the five-mile spur line altogether. The branch railroad that had given birth to Sycamore's entire railroad industry saw its final run on Saturday, April 26, 1930. After 70 years of continuous operation, the old line died with little fanfare. It received barely a mention in the local papers, other than brief press releases explaining the change to the company's timetable. The C&NW used the tracks to store unused box cars, then sent section workers to remove the rails in October 1936. The company left the ties behind and several local residents dug them out of the roadbed and salvaged them. Soon after the removal, a reporter for the *Sycamore Tribune* observed that cattle and hogs grazed on the grass-covered roadbed. Nature had already reclaimed the land.

A few months after the C&NW ended service on its S&C line, it removed the only passenger train still running between Sycamore and Belvidere on its Northern Illinois (NI) line. This removal left Sycamore without any railroad passenger service north of the city. The NI line had been struggling since the late 1920s, when the coal mines in Spring Valley began shutting down. The C&NW continued regular freight service on the line until the mid-1930s, but even after it suspended this service, it continued to run freight trains over the line intermittently. Scheduled freight service returned briefly in 1936, again in 1937, and for a final time in 1940. Each time freight trains ran on the line, the *True Republican* expressed hope that it would open for good and that passenger service would be restored. Neither scenario came to pass.

When passenger service ended to Belvidere, an evening train between DeKalb and Sycamore made the only remaining local passenger runs. Back in 1905, DeKalbans and Sycamoreans chose from dozens of daily runs between their cities, but by the 1930s, as the county continued to improve the DeKalb-Sycamore road, travelers continued the switch to buses and automobiles. Local railroad patronage fell to almost nothing. Faced with dwindling profits, the C&NW pulled the last Sycamore-DeKalb passenger train on Sunday, September 26, 1937, ending 50 years of direct passenger service between the sister cities.

The local train's removal ended the C&NW depot's role as a passenger depot, and it also ended its status as a significant public building. From that point on, the depot catered only to freight. Most Sycamoreans no longer had a reason to go there, though the office still sold tickets for C&NW passenger trains departing from DeKalb.

By 1940, the C&NW and CGW had evolved almost exclusively into freight railroads. In Sycamore, the CGW still offered four passenger trains a day to Chicago, but the company sold few tickets for this service.

A hitching post on Somonauk Street (date unknown). Sycamore did not remove its last hitching posts until July 1940, when it cut down a row of metal posts still standing on the east side of South Maple Street. The city left one post behind, just in case. It is unknown when this last post was removed.

The C&NW's Last Passengers

World War II brought a huge boost to the nation's railroads. Factories across the Midwest were converted to manufacture war materials, and most of those materials were shipped to the east and west coasts by railroad. Along with the war materials, railroads transported volunteers and draftees to their respective training camps. For the first time in years, the railroads raked in substantial profits.

The first draftees from DeKalb County departed Sycamore on the evening of November 29, 1940. The four young men, none of whom were from Sycamore, stood alone on the CGW depot platform, waiting for the train that would take them off to an unknown and uncertain future. A *True Republican* columnist scolded Sycamore for its "silent, cheerless send off" and wished the men good luck and good health. Two months later, a second round of draftees departed from the CGW depot—twenty-one young men, including one from Sycamore—and the depot grounds were crowded with family members and well-wishers. Just after their departure, Sycamore organized a veterans group to gather at the depot in support of all draftees headed off to war.

On March 19, 1941, the C&NW depot saw its last moment in the limelight when a special passenger train was brought in to transport 103 members of the 129th Infantry of the Illinois National Guard to Camp Forrest in Tullahoma, Tennessee. In the early afternoon, the soldiers fell in line outside of the armory on east State Street, marched the full length of the town to Sacramento Street, then turned south and marched to the depot, where they were met by over two thousand friends, family, and supporters. The *True Republican* gave the following account:

Shortly before boarding the train, final embraces, kisses and handshakes were given, tears making their way down some faces, sadness mirrored in others—everyone seemed to realize the solemnity and historical significance of the moment.

Inside the train the boys opened the windows and waved farewell as the warning whistle of the engine was sounded. As the train suddenly moved down the track, final warm handclasps were hastily made and hands were raised aloft in fond adieu.

As the train crossed DeKalb Avenue and gathered speed down the track, the crowd stood, hushed, for a moment, their eyes following the fast-disappearing train that pounded out a farewell message with its giant wheels on the steel rails.[1]

to Chicago. In Chicago, the men transferred to the Illinois Central, which took them south. For the remainder of the war, all soldiers departed Sycamore by way of the CGW. The special troop train was the last passenger train to depart from Sycamore's C&NW depot.

WWII soldiers lined up outside of the CGW depot.

A crowd of over two thousand watches soldiers board a WWII troop train, the last passenger train to depart the C&NW depot.

The special troop train went to DeKalb, where it transferred to the C&NW's main line

The CGW Depot

The CGW depot had been an object of ridicule from the time it was built. In 1902, the *DeKalb Review* described it as "the coldest place in DeKalb County." The paper also claimed that any notions of comfort were "a delusion and a snare." The *True Republican* had long lobbied for the CGW to build a new depot. The paper argued that Sycamore, being the most important station on the CGW line between Chicago and Dubuque, should have a depot befitting that honor. The current depot was "totally insufficient for the business done here."

[1] The March 18, 1941 issue of the *True Republican* lists the names of all of the soldiers who departed Sycamore that day.

When the CGW made several improvements to the depot in 1905, such as adding a new coat of paint and a brick platform, the *True Republican* claimed that Sycamore still needed "a larger and more respectable depot than the present cheap, little wooden shed can be made into." After the C&NW added the freight shed extension to its depot in 1907, the *True Republican* called the improvement a "wide contrast" to the CGW depot, which was a "little board shanty, crowded, cold and so dirty and unsanitary that the city authorities could condemn and destroy it as a menace to the public health." After the CGW depot added restrooms in 1914, the *True Republican* admitted that the upgrades "added much to the comfort and appearance of the building," but lamented that the company did not "erect a modern building entirely suitable to the needs of a city like Sycamore."

The CGW depot, c. 1945. Over the years, the *True Republican* heaped continuous insults on the CGW depot, such as "lacking in accommodations," "long outlived its limited uses," "a detriment to Sycamore," "dingy, uncomfortable," "barn-like," "inconvenient old shanty," and "no credit to this city."

In the early part of the century, the CGW hinted that it would build a fine new brick and stone depot, but when the Great Depression set in, any such plans disappeared. In 1951, after over a half century of griping, the *True Republican* finally got its wish: the CGW announced that it would replace the original depot. Only now the company no longer needed to build the "larger and more respectable depot" the *True Republican* had always demanded. The decline in service made such a building impractical.

The CGW located the small one-story structure east of Main Street, on the site of the freight depot the company built in 1923, which was moved a block south and converted to a private residence on Plymouth Court. The new 20-by-68-foot all-steel depot was painted deep maroon with gold trim. The office had a bay window facing the tracks so employees could observe traffic. The building also contained lockers and shower facilities for its section workers. The new depot was one of several simple, inexpensive, and unornamented depots built by the CGW around this time. Many of them were similar—if not identical—in appearance. The CGW's new Sycamore depot opened on July 12, 1951.

The CGW's new depot on Page Street, east of Main Street.

In August, a moving company lifted the original 64-year-old depot off its foundation and transported it a half-mile north on Route 23, to a lot recently purchased by Lyle Bleifuss. Bleifuss remodeled the depot into a modern ranch home, which still stands on the northwest corner of North Main Street (Route 23) and Maplewood Drive.

The new CGW depot remained open to passengers for only five years. In March 1956, the CGW filed paperwork with the Illinois Commerce Commission requesting permission to discontinue its last two passenger trains between Dubuque and Chicago, the only two passenger trains that still ran through Sycamore. The CGW claimed that its passenger service had long been a "losing proposition." Don Snyder, CGW depot agent in Sycamore, claimed that his office averaged one passenger ticket sale per month, and that had been the situation for several years. In the end,

Sycamore's loss of passenger service had little effect on the town or anyone in it. Even so, a small crowd gathered at the depot on Sunday afternoon, August 12, 1956, to watch the last passenger train run through town, ending 97 years of railroad passenger service in Sycamore.

In 1958, the CGW removed the extensive stockyards that once dominated Sycamore's north side. However, the company still shipped a substantial amount of freight. In 1960, six freight trains a day passed through Sycamore on the CGW line. Between 30 and 40 carloads of freight had to be loaded or unloaded in Sycamore each day. The majority of the company's local business came from the Anaconda Wire and Cable Company, which had located most of its Sycamore facilities along the CGW line.

The C&NW Depot

In the early 1900s, the C&NW let its depot's appearance fall by the wayside. The *True Republican* had once described the building as "an ornament to the city." In 1906, it described it as "a shabby, cheerless, dark and discreditable railway station." In September 1911, city officials met with officers from the Illinois Railroad and Warehouse Commission to demand that the C&NW replace the wooden platform around the depot with a platform of cement or brick. They also demanded that the depot stay open all night, with a telegraph operator on duty, and that it install either gas or electric lamps in its waiting rooms, which had been lit previously by smoky kerosene lamps. The C&NW eventually added the cement platform and installed electricity. It also added a night telegraph operator, but only for a few months before it went back to being closed at night. Every few years, a C&NW work crew covered the entire building—brick and limestone—in another coat of red paint. According to Betty Hampa, who worked in the depot in the early 1960s, "It wasn't a vibrant red. More like the dull red of an old chimney."

In September 1916, Sycamoreans lost another reason to go to their C&NW depot. The Western Union Telegraph Company, which had operated out of the depot since the late 1860s, relocated its office to State Street. Another example of the depot's diminishing role in Sycamore's public life occurred the following month. When a special train carrying several Republican nominees for state office arrived outside the depot, between 300 and 400 Sycamoreans gathered to listen to the speeches. The *True Republican* described the turnout as a "big crowd," but it was a far cry from the thousands who would have gathered at the depot for a similar event in the 1860s through the 1890s.

In July 1942, the C&NW removed the 28 miles of tracks of its Northern Illinois line between Sycamore and Belvidere and sold them for scrap for the war effort. Depot workers unloaded freight mostly from the spur line on the depot's east side, so in the late 1940s the C&NW removed the cement platform from the depot's south and west sides. The company neglected the tracks, and the grounds surrounding the depot became overrun with dirt, grass, and scrub weeds. The building itself looked like a structure aged well beyond its usefulness. The C&NW hadn't bothered to paint it in years, which showed in the cracked and faded red paint flaking off the brick and stone.

When Overland Greyhound Bus Lines came to Sycamore in the early 1940s, the company located its ticket office and waiting room inside the Fargo Hotel lobby. In April 1946, it relocated its office and waiting room to the C&NW depot and made some minor renovations to the space. John Nachtigall, cashier at the depot, became Greyhound's Sycamore agent. City officials were pleased with the move, because the long buses no longer interfered with traffic on State Street. Business owners and residents near the depot, however, complained about the bus passengers

The C&NW depot through the years

1908

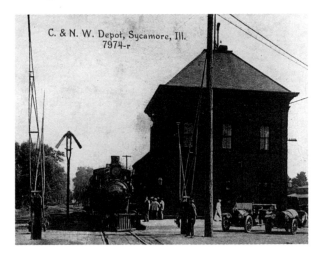

1925

1935

1950

Top Left: The large water tank and windmill were removed in October 1904. The ornamental crest railing atop the roof was also removed sometime before this photo was taken.

Top Right: In the 1920s, the depot still bustles with activity.

Bottom Left: The locomotive-shaped weathervane is gone and only part of the flagpole remains. The weathervane's fate remains unknown.

Bottom Right: The depot has fallen into a state of disrepair. Notice the Greyhound bus sign on the southwest corner. The depot served as the Greyhound bus station from 1946 until 1952.

milling about outside the building, a sight that would have been common in previous decades. Greyhound put new benches in the depot waiting room to try to solve the problem. The bus company operated out of the depot for almost six years before moving its office back to the Fargo Hotel and later to a service station across from the courthouse.

Waiting for the Greyhound bus outside of the C&NW depot (c. 1950). Standing (L-R): Mary Lou Walker, Carol Johnson, Bess Rosene. Sitting: Pat Pollett. (courtesy of Carol Johnson)

By 1957, the C&NW still hauled freight out of Sycamore, but the old brick depot had fallen into disrepair. No improvements had been made since the Greyhound renovations. The building had no running water—the plumbing leading to the bathrooms had failed years before and the C&NW never repaired it—so employees had to bring their own drinking water. In the freight house, the company stored its track maintenance materials. The upstairs rooms, which had never lived up to their original purpose as rented office space, were used for storage. Most of the windows were broken and the company had simply boarded them up. Hundreds of boxes, filled mostly with years of long-discarded paperwork, sat in piles, surrounded by stacks of unboxed papers, old furniture, and unused equipment. A similar scene appeared in the old freight office, and also in the basement. The former women's waiting room had become the main freight office, and the horseshoe-shaped ticket office between the two waiting rooms had become the depot agent's office.

Despite the depot's degradation, the C&NW continued to do a large amount of freight business in and out of Sycamore. Sycamore's "mile of industry" continued to thrive. The Preserve Works still operated at a steady clip, Holub Industries opened a new addition on DeKalb Avenue near the depot, and Barber-Greene opened its new plant southwest of town, right on the C&NW's line to DeKalb. Because most of the freight was loaded and unloaded at the facilities along the line, the depot operated under a skeleton crew.

The depot faced a serious threat on August 4, 1959, when the Sycamore Lumber Company next door went up in flames. This company stood on the same location as the sash and blind factory that burned in the 1870s. In all, five major fires and several smaller fires occurred within close proximity of the C&NW depot, but by good fortune it survived them all. The lumber company fire turned out to be arson, started by a 13-year-old boy. The damage was so extensive that the company didn't rebuild and the spur line that ran into the lumberyard had to be removed. The company sold the land to its neighbor to the east, Bert Holub of Holub Industries, makers of 800 electrical, industrial, and construction hardware products. Holub needed to expand his business to meet growing demand. He wanted his company to cover the block between Sacramento Street and California Street, but how would he accomplish this with the C&NW's old train depot in the way?

Bert Holub Buys C&NW's Old Train Depot

By 1963, the majority of the C&NW's Sycamore freight was handled directly from the factories, most of which had branch lines that ran straight into their facilities. The C&NW no longer needed the large, mostly empty depot on Sacramento Street (and it certainly didn't need the property tax bill). So in June 1963, the C&NW sold the depot to Bert Holub and Holub Industries. His purchase included the remaining tracks in the railyard, the freight shed attached to the building's north end, and the rest of the lot north to the city parking lot on State Street. He announced that he would remodel the depot into "an attractive modern structure" and use it for manufacturing and warehousing. He proposed to proceed immediately.

The sale of the depot did not mean that the C&NW quit operations in Sycamore. The railroad maintained its freight business with several local companies, so it made arrangements with Holub to rent office space inside the depot.

On August 30, 1963, the depot received its last freight shipment on the short spur that ran along its east side. (The C&NW had installed this spur in 1885 to load and unload passengers, but later used it exclusively for freight; the company then extended the tracks to serve the various coal and lumber companies that had operated next door over the years.) After a work crew unloaded the last shipment, they dismantled the track and removed the rails down to DeKalb Avenue. In September 1964, C&NW contractors pulled the rails from the street. The removal left only the main tracks across DeKalb Avenue.

At the time Holub purchased the depot, the Arrow Feed Company occupied the depot's freight shed extension. The owner, Edgar Fleetwood, had to remove his business by January 1, 1964. Because Holub intended to raze the structure to build a parking lot for his expanding company, he gave Fleetwood permission to salvage some of the shed. Fleetwood removed the loading platform on the depot's east side and much of the shed's metal roof and metal siding. A large office safe that was too heavy to move was emptied, pushed into a hole in the ground, and buried. In late December 1963, workmen piled whatever materials remained and set them ablaze. Many in town saw the smoke and feared that a downtown building was burning out of control. The *True Republican*, for one, was happy to see the "gloomy" old shed go. It remarked that "that cleansing alone is a welcome improvement."

The depot's much-dilapidated freight shed extension c. 1955

In April 1964, a wind storm tore off a six-foot chunk of the decorative sheet metal that ornamented the depot's upper cornice. Observers noted that the remaining tin sheets were "loose and flopping in the wind." The city erected a barricade around the building to protect anyone passing by. In August 1964, a contractor working for Holub began renovations on the depot's exterior. He removed the remaining tin sheets along with the cornice brackets. He also replaced the heavy slate tiles from the roof; after 84 years, many of the tiles were cracked and loose and presented a danger to the public if they fell. Finally, Holub had the entire building painted an unfortunate yellowish-grey. The major interior renovations never took place, and Holub ended up using the building for storage for the next 15 years.

The Conjunction of Two Stars

In May 1964, while Bert Holub contemplated new uses for his recently purchased depot, rumors spread that the C&NW and CGW were contemplating a merger. A month later, both companies confirmed that such discussions were taking place. To many, a merger seemed like a practical strategic move. By combining their resources, the companies could modernize, improve efficiency, and compete in the oversaturated transportation market.

If these two pioneer midwestern railroads had merged earlier in the century, this news would have had a huge impact on Sycamore, directly affecting nearly everyone who lived there. But by the 1960s, the general public had become so detached from the railroad industry that the news made few waves outside of railroad and financial circles. The merger eventually took effect on July 1, 1968. The new company was named the Chicago North Western Railway Company (CNW). The merger gave the CNW over 12,000 miles of railway in 11 states. In Sycamore, the CNW discontinued its rented office space in the old C&NW depot and made the CGW depot on Page Street its sole Sycamore freight office.

End of the Line

In September 1968, a sharp divide between Sycamore and its one remaining railroad ushered in the final stage in the city's railroad history. Sycamoreans had become fed up with the long delays caused by blocked railroad crossings and expressed their displeasure to city officials. Mayor Harold "Red" Johnson rallied behind them: "I want [the railroad] to have a ticket… People in business got work to do. They can't be sitting around." At the time, the railroad still served many of Sycamore's factories, but Sycamore's residents no longer saw long traffic delays as a necessary trade-off for the city's well-being.

Thousands of them signed a petition indicating as much. This clash with the railroad highlighted the complete reversal in Sycamore's public perception of its railroads. Once a modern convenience that brought freedom and prosperity to an isolated village, the railroad had become a nuisance, a slow-moving dinosaur that impeded movement and checked progress.

In 1972, the CNW abandoned the old CGW line west of Byron, Illinois, which diverted a considerable amount of freight traffic to the CNW's main line through DeKalb and away from Sycamore. That same year, the company sent section workers to remove the unused tracks that ran up to and alongside the C&NW depot on Sacramento Street. This stretch of tracks dated back to the original S&C line. In April 1977, the CNW discontinued service on the old CGW line between Sycamore and St. Charles after a train derailed and the company decided not to repair the damaged tracks. This stretch had been operating since the Minnesota & Northwestern built it in 1887. The once mighty CGW line had stretched from Chicago to St. Paul, but its Illinois division now ran only between Byron and Sycamore.

On May 19, 1978, the CNW closed its Sycamore freight office. The *Daily Chronicle* called this move "an almost unnoticed ending to a once illustrious chapter in the city's history."

Sycamore's last depot agent, Charles W. Finch, noted that the city would see little change. Freight shipments would continue as before, only the paperwork would be handled by the freight office in DeKalb. The CNW abandoned what remained of the old CGW main line by 1982, leaving the short branch line between DeKalb and Sycamore as Sycamore's only railroad outlet. When Sycamore's largest manufacturer, Anaconda Wire and Cable Company, left the city in 1983, the CNW lost its largest local customer. In 1984, the railroad announced that it was shutting down the branch line. The company offered to sell the line for $280,000, but the city and local businesses did not seriously consider purchasing it. Mayor Johnson said he was hopeful that the CNW would reconsider abandoning the line, but the city lodged no protest against the decision and took no action to stop it.

After 125 years, Sycamore's railroad history came to an unceremonious end. It began with the arrival of the first train on October 8, 1859; it ended when the CNW abandoned the Sycamore-DeKalb branch on October 4, 1984.

Two weeks later, on October 18, an interesting letter appeared in the *Daily Chronicle* appealing to Sycamoreans to save the railroad. It was written by 75-year-old William Boies, Sr., grandson of Henry L. Boies, who had been owner and editor of the *True Republican*, a Sycamore & Cortland Railroad founding director, and Sycamore's first local historian. William Boies called on the people of Sycamore to look into their past and consider what their ancestors went through to build a city out of unbroken prairie when "times were hard and money was scarce... [when] only dirt roads, most of them not more than winding trails, led from the village, and these became impossible after each rain." He reminded them how the Sycamoreans of old had banded together to build their very own railroad, which had saved the city and played a major role in its future growth. Like his great-grandfather before him, he called on the people of Sycamore to unite in raising the money to secure a railroad, this time the DeKalb-Sycamore line recently abandoned by the CNW. Failure to do so would deter manufacturers and businesses from ever locating in Sycamore.

Boies's argument echoed that of his ancestors and Sycamore's pioneer business leaders. But it fell on deaf ears. The railroad had saved and then established Sycamore, but Sycamore no longer needed the railroad, and no serious attempt was made to save the city's last branch line. The CNW removed the tracks from the city's streets within a year. Railroad service has never returned to Sycamore.

Marty Hampa:
Last of the Old-Time Agents

Marty Hampa in 1955, working as the telegraph operator
at the C&NW depot in DeKalb. Marty was a member of the
Order of Railroad Telegraphers, a union for railroad
telegraph operators. (courtesy of Betty Hampa)

Martin "Marty" Hampa took over as the C&NW's Sycamore depot agent in July 1958. Before coming to Sycamore, Hampa's career with the C&NW spanned over 30 years and included stints in depots all across northern Illinois. In DeKalb County, he had worked as depot agent in Shabbona Grove, Malta, and DeKalb. In Shabbona Grove, he and his wife had lived on the depot's second floor.

According to Marty's daughter, Betty Hampa, "Working for the railroad was all he ever wanted, so that's all he ever did." Marty fell in love with the railroad as a boy. He and his toy train engine were inseparable. He'd line up chairs, stand on them, and pretend he was an engineer. When he attended Valparaiso University in Indiana, he studied railroad management.

By the time Hampa took over Sycamore's C&NW depot in 1958, his office handled only freight, but still sold passenger tickets for the C&NW depot in DeKalb. The C&NW had scaled back its operation at the depot to a five-day schedule with one shift per day. When Marty wasn't filling out paperwork, he spent much of his day lifting, moving, or arranging freight. And he always worked, rain or snow.

Christmas was always the hardest. During the holidays, Marty worked seven days a week, often by himself, unloading carload after carload of merchandise in the freezing weather. He had to work on Christmas Day because of all the last-minute shipments coming in. It was backbreaking work, and Betty recalled that he would be sore for days after the holiday rush finally ended.

One of Marty's main duties was as a C&NW sales representative. He negotiated shipping rates with area businesses and worked to convince them to ship their goods on the C&NW line rather than the CGW (or by truck). As a result, Marty knew all of the local businessmen, and they all knew him. His job, however, did not prevent him from being friends with his CGW counterpart, freight agent Don Snyder. Snyder was often a welcome dinner guest at the Hampa household.

Now living in Genoa, Betty Hampa spent her early life hanging around depots with her father. She loved looking at the timetables and tried to memorize every town in Illinois. She also liked seeing someone walk out of a depot with a thick stack of long tickets, all stapled together. Such a stack indicated several interline tickets, so she knew that person was going on a long trip, maybe even cross-country, and she imagined them embarking on some grand adventure. Her family could ride on the C&NW for free with Marty's employee pass, which allowed them to travel all over the country. "Railroads were magical," Betty said. "You could sit back, relax, and just see the land. You could socialize with people in the dining and lounge cars you never would have met otherwise. You can't do that in a car, bus, or plane. At least not in the same way."

While Betty Hampa attended Northern Illinois University in DeKalb, she helped her father at the Sycamore depot after school and during summers. She sorted and filed papers and filled in shipping orders. Betty remembers that in the summer, the depot was "beastly hot—hot as blazes." It had no air conditioning, so when her father arrived each morning, he immediately opened all the doors and windows to let in some air. There were fans everywhere, which he placed strategically so they didn't scatter the stacks of paperwork. Winter presented the opposite problem. Everyone stayed bundled all day to keep warm. In the freight house, any available heat escaped the moment someone threw open the wide freight house doors. The main office had a stove to provide warmth, but the large, open room and tall ceiling made heating difficult. "Weather-wise," Betty said, "that building was a bear."

She explained that when she worked inside the depot in the early 1960s, it was no longer meant to accommodate visitors, so nobody bothered to tidy up the place. The women's waiting room was now an office filled with desks and chairs and piles of paperwork. Outside of Marty's work space, which he kept neat and orderly, the floors needed sweeping, the windows needed washing, clutter and unused junk were scattered everywhere, and a considerable amount of dust covered everything.

In spite of the depot's condition, Betty remembers there were always people there, usually waiting to collect a shipment coming in on the next train. C&NW section crews also stopped in to hang out after completing a maintenance project. Local businessmen dropped by to see Marty and to fill out shipping paperwork related to their companies. They'd sit at one of several empty desks in the freight office. Betty claimed that some of them used the depot as a "second office." Employees from surrounding businesses often dropped by for lunch and a round of cards. In the summers, everyone sat on boxes just inside the freight room doors, with the doors open to let in a breeze.

Betty has fond memories of her days working in the historic C&NW depot. She recalls that her father always carried two items with him at work: his C&NW employee handbook, because employees were tested on it every year, and his watch. The watch hung from his belt and had a train engine engraved on the back. "He would check it and wind it religiously," Betty said. "A depot agent always had to know the time."

After the C&NW sold the depot to Holub Industries in 1963, the railroad company rented space inside for a freight office. Hampa worked out of the rented office until he retired in 1966 at age 60. He had put in 40 years of service with the C&NW. "The railroad was there for him," Betty said, "and he enjoyed it." Marty Hampa passed away in 1977 at the age of 72.

Marty Hampa outside the DeKalb depot in 1970.
(courtesy of Betty Hampa)

Saving the C&NW Depot, 1978-2012

At the time the depot went onto the National Register of Historic Places, it had certainly seen better days.

In 1978, the same year the CNW closed its Sycamore office, the Sycamore Historical District Commission had the C&NW depot put on the National Register of Historic Places. One year later, Holub Industries sold the depot to Vernon Westberg, founder of Auto Meter, an automotive parts manufacturer located just northeast of the depot. In an ironic twist, the once mighty depot, brought low by the automobile, now served as a storage facility for automobile parts. The building continued in this capacity until the 1990s, when it began to deteriorate from a lack of roof and exterior maintenance. By 2005, the depot's interior wood framing began to fail from continued exposure to the elements, so Auto Meter ceased using it for parts storage and instead kept the company archives there.

Bill Schinske, vice president of engineering and manufacturing at Holub Industries, escorts the Sycamore Historical District Commission through the depot in 1978 as the commission prepares its application to the National Register of Historic Places. (Sycamore History Museum)

Coincident with the building's deterioration in the late 1990s, Sycamore's City Manager, Bill Nicklas, opened a dialogue with the building's industrial owners, seeking a private/public partnership that would at least protect the building from further structural stress. Nicklas, who holds a Ph.D. in History from Northern Illinois University, knew the importance of preserving one of Sycamore most historic and iconic buildings. The dialogue gained a sense of urgency in 2010 with the acceleration of the structure's physical deterioration. Auto Meter President Jeff King, Vice President Kent Alcott, and Nicklas presented the Sycamore City Council with a proposal that transferred the depot's title to the city of Sycamore in exchange for the city's investment in substantial exterior and structural repairs to preserve the building until a final owner could be identified. Auto Meter also stipulated a restriction on the title that the building's primary use could only be civic (and/or nonprofit) in nature, not a business use. In October 2010, the city council considered the proposal and began discussions over the depot's fate. At issue was how to finance the renovations. The majority of funding came from a private donation from Douglas C. and Lynn M. Roberts. The city of Sycamore also put up $100,000 in Tax Increment Financing (TIF) funds. The donation and TIF funds combined gave the city enough to cover initial structural repairs

In the old waiting rooms, the floor had become unstable, the ceiling was caving in, and the plaster walls had cracked and started to crumble. The building required an extensive and expensive renovation just to continue as a storage space, which would have cost Auto Meter far more than the property's commercial value. Without the needed renovations, the depot's future looked grim.

There was some debate over whether the city should spend the money to renovate this old structure, an argument that mirrored the debate back in 1858 over building the original S&C line. In both instances, the nation suffered under a deep recession, and there were those who felt that public money would have been better spent elsewhere. But any opposition to the renovation was a vocal minority, because most Sycamore residents wanted to see the historic structure preserved. On November 15, 2010, the Sycamore City Council voted to save the old C&NW depot. It became city property on December 9.

Renovations began in the depot's basement in late December 2010. After the C&NW moved the coal furnace to the basement during the 1916 restroom renovation, employees apparently discarded the burnt coal cinders and "clinkers" on the earthen basement floor, which contaminated the soil. Before any other work could be done, the contaminated soil had to be removed. This was done by Wagner Excavating of DeKalb, with the assistance of the Sycamore Public Works department. Following the cleanup, the foundation walls had to be repaired and the large wood support beams—some of which had rotted—were reinforced or replaced with steel to support the structure's wood floor.

Exterior work began in May 2011. The city council hired local contractor Steve Swedberg of Swedberg & Associates to weatherize the building. His crew replaced all of the windows and doors, put on an entirely new roof, and repaired the fascia and soffit. They also installed gutters and downspouts to direct water away from the building's foundation. To let in more natural light, French doors and large windows replaced the freight house's large sliding doors. The brick and stone exterior underwent a complete tuckpointing while some masonry had to be replaced entirely. Art Seyller of Seyller's Tuckpointing and Masonry in Genoa handled the exterior masonry work, including power washing the brick and stone to remove the layers of red paint that the C&NW had applied over the years.

With the building stabilized and weatherized, the city had to decide how it would be used. Several residents presented their ideas to the city council, including options for both commercial and non-commercial use. Whoever moved into the building, however, would be responsible for all interior renovations, including installing a heating and cooling system and updating the plumbing and electrical wiring.

Sycamore City Manager Bill Nicklas examines the exterior weatherization work at the depot in August 2011. (Shaw Media)

In September 2011, with the external work complete, the city council voted to transfer ownership of the depot to the DeKalb County Community Foundation (DCCF), a philanthropic organization founded in 1993 that has distributed over $14 million in grants and scholarships in the fields of Arts and Culture, Health and Human Services, Education, and Community Development/Civic Affairs throughout DeKalb County. The DCCF officially took title to the depot in November. To fund the extensive interior renovations, the "Friends of the Community Foundation Committee" was organized to raise $750,000 for the project. Mike Cullen and Suzanne Juday, both former presidents of the DCCF, spearheaded this successful fundraising campaign.

Daniel P. Templin, the DCCF's executive director, pledged that the renovations would honor the depot's history and connection to the community. "What a huge gift for the Foundation to be in a historically significant building so intertwined with Sycamore and all of DeKalb County," Templin told *Invironments Magazine* in late 2012. "The Depot reflects the spirit of philanthropy in DeKalb County... timeless, visible, and relevant."

The DCCF hired architect Lisa Sharp to design the building's interior. A Sycamore Depot Renovation Committee, chaired by DCCF Board Member Tim Suter, selected Russ Smith Construction of DeKalb to serve as the general contractor. Due to the building's age and deteriorated condition, most of the original interior wall framing, trim, and plaster had to be removed, but most of the interior brick was left intact and exposed to capture the depot's historic feel. The long, open freight house was converted into a community room where non-profit groups and organizations can host public and private events. The DCCF converted the two-story main building into its principal meeting and office space. Three modern offices and a conference room now occupy the second floor, returning that space to the purpose envisioned by the original

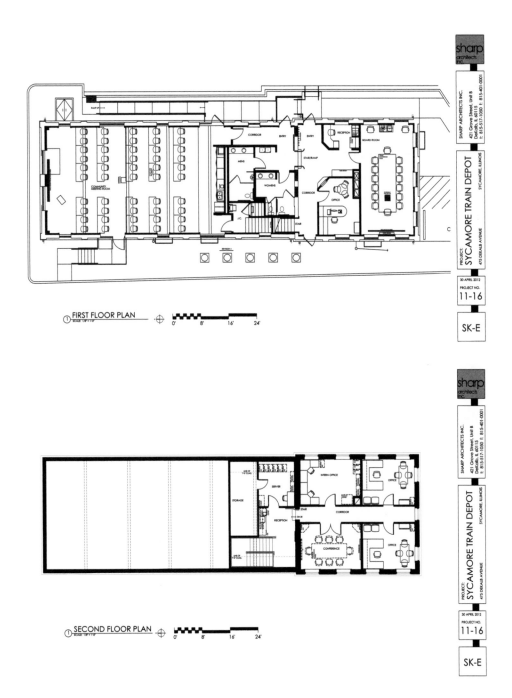

Lisa Sharp's floor plans for the renovated depot interior. (courtesy of Sharp Architects and the DeKalb County Community Foundation)

architect. On the first floor, the women's and men's waiting rooms were converted into a boardroom and reception area, respectively. The Executive Director's office now occupies the original ticket office space, complete with a fully restored ticket window adorned with the logo of the Sycamore & Cortland Railroad. The DCCF moved into its new headquarters on October 11, 2012.

A relic of the days when railroads ruled the Midwest prairies, the depot's original purpose has long since passed, but it has been born anew. From inside this storied structure, the DCCF will continue its charitable mission, and the depot will continue serving not only Sycamore, but all of DeKalb County. "It's up to us now," Templin said. "We are writing the next chapter of the building's history."

The Sycamore Train Depot—Fully Restored

Top: The fully restored train depot today, home of the DeKalb County Community Foundation. The DCCF modified its logo (top left) to integrate the depot's design. Bottom left: The DCCF's reception area now occupies the old men's waiting room. Bottom right: A large crowd gathers in the freight house for the depot's open house on November 27, 2012.

Depot Before and After Renovation

Ticket Window

Upstairs Office

Upstairs Hallway

Ladies' Waiting Room

All "before" images by the author.
All "after" images by Evan Stravers,
Sharp Architects Inc.

Freight Door Hangers[1]

Freight House

...ese freight door hangers, manufactured by the Reuben Ellwood Manufacturing Company in 1876, still supported one of the freight house doors in ...11. They were restored by Sycamore artist Lynden Bute, who also constructed the freight door (top left), restored the ticket window, and recreated ...e S&C logo mounted on the glass (previous page).

Legacy of the Chicago Great Western

The original CGW depot (1887–1951) is a private residence at the corner of North Main Street (Route 23) and Maplewood Drive.

The CGW freight depot (1923–1951) is a private residence on Plymouth Court.

The CGW's second depot (1951–1978) is a private residence at its original location on Page Street.

In the early 1990s, an abandoned 18-mile stretch of the CGW line between Sycamore and St. Charles was converted into the Great Western Trail. Each year, this multi-use trail accommodates thousan of cyclists, hikers, runners, snowmobilers, horseback riders, dog walke and nature enthusiasts. Pictured here is the trailhead at Sycamore

514   RAILROADS.

granted shall be forfeited. But should said company arrange to use the track of any other railroad company, on any portion of their route, such portion may be held to be completed within the meaning of this act. But in case such arrangement shall at any time cease then the rights of this corporation in relation to the construction of that portion of said road, shall revive.

Acceptance.   § 8. This act shall take effect from and after its acceptance by the stockholders representing a majority of the stock then held in said corporation, in such manner as shall be fixed upon by the board of directors, and shall be deemed and taken as a public act.

APPROVED February 18, 1859.

———

In force Feb'y 19, 1859.   AN ACT approving and legalizing the construction of the Sycamore and Cortland Railroad Company, and to incorporate the same.

Preamble.   Whereas the Sycamore and Cortland Railroad Company became a body corporate and politic on the 29th day of June, A. D. 1858, by filing articles of association with the secretary of state, in accordance with the provisions of sections one and two of an act entitled "An act to provide for a general system of railroad incorporations," approved November 5, 1849; and whereas the said Sycamore and Cortland Railroad Company did, on the 23rd day of June, 1858, elect, as a board of directors, to manage the affairs of said company, the following persons, to wit: John C. Waterman, Henry L. Boies, Reuben Elwood, Edward L. Mayo, William J. Hunt, Horatio F. Page, Orlando M. Bryan, Morris Walrod, Daniel B. James, Enos L. Cheesbro, jr., Benjamin Page, Timothy Wells and Harmon Payne; and whereas, also, it is found inconvenient and impracticable to construct and put in operation and operate said road without greater powers than are granted in and by said act to provide for a general system of railroad incorporations; therefore,

SECTION 1. *Be it enacted by the People of the State of Illinois, represented in the General Assembly,* That the said

Corporators.   John C. Waterman, Henry L. Boies, Reuben Elwood, Edward L. Mayo, William J. Hunt, Horatio F. Page, Orlando M. Bryan, Morris Walrod, Daniel B. James, Enos L. Cheesbro, jr., Benjamin Page, Timothy Wells and Harmon Payne, and their associates, be and they are hereby created a corporation, by the name of "The Sycamore and Cortland Railroad Company," for thirty years; and, as such, shall possess the rights, powers and franchises usually possessed by such corporations, and also all the privileges, pow-

From *Laws of the State of Illinois Passed by the Twenty-First General Assembly, Convened January 3, 1859.* Springfield: Bailhache & Baker, 1859 (pages 514-516).

ers, rights and franchises at any time heretofore possessed or acquired under and by virtue of their incorporation under the aforesaid act entitled "An act to provide for a general system of railroad incorporation;" and by that name and style shall be capable in law, of taking and holding, by gift, purchase or otherwise, leasing, selling and conveying estate and property, whether real or personal or mixed, so far as the same may be necessary for the purposes of completing, running and enjoying said railroad privilege to its fullest extent, and no further; to have a common seal, which they may alter or change at pleasure.

§ 2. The business of said company shall be managed by **Directors.** thirteen directors; and the persons named in the first section of this act shall be the first directors thereof, and so continue until a new board shall be elected under this charter; which shall take place as soon as a majority of the stockholders shall call such an election; which shall be done by the secretary giving ten days' notice, in any paper published in De Kalb county. And the directors elected at the time set shall hold over until the first Monday in January following or until a new election of directors shall take place; which election shall take place on the first Monday of January next, and on the first Monday of January of each year thereafter; and the secretary of said company shall publish a notice of such an election for ten days previous to the election.

§ 3. The said company may construct and complete **Location.** their road from Sycamore, in the county De Kalb, to Cortland, in said county, or to extend said road, in any direction, to connect with the Galena and Chicago Union Railroad Company or its branches, in such manner and on such terms as the respective companies can agree.

§ 4. The board of directors of said company shall have **Charges.** the right to fix and regulate, from time to time, the charges for all freights and fares over said road.

§ 5. Should said company experience any difficulty in **Right of way.** obtaining the right of way over any lands over which it may be necessary or convenient to run said railroad, and in case said company shall not be able to obtain the title to any lands or premises which may be necessary for the purposes of said road and its appendages, by purchase or voluntary cession, the same may be obtained in the manner provided by the 92nd chapter of the Revised Statutes of this state, entitled "Right of Way:" *Provided*, that after the appraisal of damages, in pursuance of said act, and upon deposit of the amount of such appraisal in the office of the circuit court of the county of De Kalb, the said company shall be authorized to enter upon such lands, for the construction of said railroad: *Provided, also*, that said company shall be authorized to take a strip of land, not to exceed

516   RAILROADS.

one hundred feet in width, for the purposes of a grade and track for said railroad.

By-laws. § 6. Said company shall have power to make, ordain and establish all such by-laws, rules and regulations as may be decided expedient and necessary to fulfill the purposes and carry into effect the object of said railroad corporation, and for the well ordering and securing the affairs and interests of said company, not inconsistent with or repugnant to the constitution and laws of the United States or of this state: *Provided*, that all such by-laws that may be adopted shall be printed and distributed among the stockholders of the company.

Borrow money. § 7. That the said company are authorized and empowered to borrow, from time to time, such sums of money as, in their opinion, may be deemed necessary to aid the construction of said road, and pay any interest therefore, not exceeding ten per cent., and to pledge and mortgage the said railroad and its appendages, or any part thereof, or any other property or effects, rights, credits or appendages of said company, as security for any loan of money and interest thereon, and to dispose of the bonds issued for such loan at such rate or on such terms as the board of directors may determine.

Injuries. § 8. That any person who shall willfully injure or obstruct the said road, or any of its appurtenances thereto, shall be deemed guilty of a misdemeanor, and shall forfeit, to the use of the same company, a sum threefold the amount of the damages occasioned by such injury or obstruction—to be recovered in an action of debt, in the name of said company, with costs of suit, before any justice of the peace having jurisdiction of the same or before any court of record of this state.

Streams and roads. § 9. That said corporation may construct their said road and branches over or across any stream of water, water course, road, railroad, highway or canal, which the route of the road shall intersect, by putting the same in repair.

Public act. § 10. This act shall be deemed and taken as a public act, and shall be construed beneficially, for all purposes herein specified and intended, and shall take effect from and after its passage.

Approved February 19, 1859.

From the front page of the *True Republican,* August 18, 1880:

SYCAMORE UNDER THE CORNER STONE

The Hon. Chauncey Ellwood, of the S. C. & C. R. R., has requested us to prepare a sketch of the town of Sycamore, its manners and customs, to be deposited in the corner stone of the new depot, so that when future generations may unearth it, a thousand years hence, say about the time when Macaulay's New Zealanders shall be brooding over the ruins of St. Paul,[1] they shall get an idea of what manner of people inhabited the City of Sycamore in the year of our Lord, 1880; and as such a record in order to have value, should be not common place laudation, but a veritable record of fundamental facts, we offer the following:

Sycamore is a city of about 600 buildings containing 3030 inhabitants mostly sitting with their gable ends to the street.[2]

It was founded in 1838 by Capt. Barnes, Deacon Kellogg and Curtis Smith; we will add that all rumors to the contrary are unfounded, and if those worthies should meet here now to see its present condition, they would be dumbfounded.

The popular business of Sycamore is making agricultural implements and shaving notes. Those who make the machinery make the town, and those who shave the notes make the money. This division of labor and profits gives general satisfaction.

There is also a lively business done here in running for office, about half the inhabitants subsisting in this manner; of the balance there are several who work for a living; but these are not regarded as of much account. They make less money and gather little honor. It is considered more profitable to sit in a comfortable store, shop or office, smoke fine cigars, tell stories and sell goods, or charge as much for an hours talk and advice, legal or medical, as working men can earn in a week. This is regarded as a better thing. The people who work pay enough for these things to keep the principal inhabitants jolly, fat and lazy. This division of labor and profit seems to give general satisfaction; at least there is no effort for a change.

---

[1] A cliché of the time, coined by historian, poet, and politician T. B. Macaulay in the mid-18th century. The New Zealanders he referred to would visit the remains of a future London and gaze upon the ruins of St Paul's, knowing only that they were looking upon the remnants of a long-forgotten culture. Writers invoked Macaulay's New Zealanders to show how easily society could collapse and be forgotten or replaced.

[2] This line is a parody of one attributed to 18th century geographer Jedediah Morse, who supposedly described Albany, New York, as a city of "1,000 houses and 10,000 inhabitants, all standing with their gable ends to the street." Late 19th century newspapers and writing primers often repeated the line as an example of poor grammar. The dwelling houses, not the inhabitants, stood with their gable ends to the street.

GOVERNMENT

The city has a complicated form of government.

There is, first, the City government, which consists of a Mayor who bosses around generally and is "a bigger man than ole Grant;" also eight Aldermen whose duties consist in levying $10,000 a year in taxes and licenses with which to lay down a few boards for sidewalks which soon rot out, also to muss over a little of the black soil into roads, which are unfathomable mud in a wet time. Of late, however they have drawn some gravel on the roads which process is much opposed by the old fogies, who fear that now the roads will last so long that there will be nothing for the city fathers to do, and the city government will rust out.[3] The more onerous part of the duties of these city fathers however, consists in going as dead-heads to all the shows,[4] and appearing on parade on the 4th of Julys, at big funerals and other varieties of amusement. They also have charge of the Fire Department; that is, they order it to squirt water occasionally to amuse the people. At such times the fire department is in excellent order. In case of a fire however, it is generally out of either steam or water. This arrangement appears to give general satisfaction.

In addition to the city government they have also a town government, whose duties consist in levying from $5,000 to $10,000 of taxes.

In addition to the town government they have also a school board who levies from $7,000 to $10,000 of taxes which enables the school superintendent to maintain a military discipline among the schools and impart some "larnin."

In addition to the city, town and school government, they have also a county government which levies some $2,000 worth of taxes yearly.

In addition to the county, town, city and school governments, they have a State government which levies some $5,000 a year, in taxes.

In addition to the State, county, town, city and school governments they have a National government which has a very ingenious way of levying more taxes than all the rest, but so shrewdly laid on that they do not suspect or feel it.

All these taxes being burdensome, the principal inhabitants, that is, the wealthy men, decline to pay them. They have a way of swearing them off. The poorer men of course come to their relief and pay their taxes with great promptness and regularity. This arrangement seems to give general satisfaction.

---

[3] At the time of this article, the city was in the process of gravelling its roads. For years, the debate over how to improve the roads and sidewalks had been a major source of tension between the city council and local businessmen. The recent improvements were going ahead after several months of heated deliberation.

[4] See chapter 6 footnote 1 on page 97.

POLITICS

To keep people from investigating too closely into these tax matters and making it uneasy for the principal inhabitants, the people are cunningly divided into three parties on other issues. These parties are, 1st the Republicans, who are in favor of a republic. 2nd the Democrats, so called on the principal of contraries, because there is nothing democratic about them; and 3rd the Greenbackers, so called because they are too "green" to come "back" to the parties where they could do some good. The principal business of these parties is to regulate the Southern States and so let the politicians do what they like with our own State.

RELIGION

The people generally profess Christianity and practice deviltry. For greater convenience in this they are divided into 26 sects, viz: High Church, Low Church, Reform Episcopalians, Old School and New School and Cumberland Presbyterians, Closed Communion, Open Communion, Free Will and Seven Day Baptists, Unitarians, Universalists, Congregationalists, Spiritualists, Catholics, Swedish Lutheran, German Lutheran, Methodist Episcopal, Wesleyan Methodist, Free Methodist, Campbellites, Mormons, Free Thinkers, and several other minor divisions of opinions.

Some of these divisions maintain an armed alliance with one another, while most are openly hostile. This excites the admiration of the outsiders who reverence their close following of the teachings of Christ in favor of unity and brotherly love, and it gives general satisfaction.

It should be added that only eight of these sects have churches and worship in them. There are, however, eight liquor saloons, and a large portion of the population get their spiritual consolation in them.

EDUCATION

It is the custom of the people to pay a great deal of attention to training and improving their horses, cattle sheep and swine, but very little to the children.

LAWS

The laws which govern Sycamore are peculiar. They punish certain crimes and leave worse ones to go unpunished.

If a man steals a horse or two, he is sent to hard labor in the penitentiary for 13 years; if he goes gunning for his wife and pops her over dead at the first fire, he is boarded at the expense of the county, carefully, kept out of all harm, made famous by the newspapers, and ultimately—well the law that punishes murder with death was never yet executed in this county.[5] If a poor man steals the necessaries of life to support his family he will be sent to the penitentiary; if a rich man robs the poor of his entire property by mortgages and such contrivances, he is considered smart.

The foregoing is about all that we have yet prepared about Sycamore. Taking it on the whole, it is a first-class place to live in; the people are about as good as the people of other cities, and perhaps a little better. A thousand years hence, when this corner stone is removed and these documents are brought to light, we hope that they may be better yet.

---

[5]This is a reference to the sensational case of George Alexander, a black man from Sycamore who tracked down his white, estranged, 19-year-old wife in DeKalb and murdered her with a single shotgun blast. The story became a great spectacle and filled the newspapers for weeks. Alexander was tried and sentenced to death by hanging, but the day before his execution, the Illinois Supreme Court ordered a retrial. At the time this article was written, Alexander still sat in the Sycamore jail, awaiting his retrial. He was eventually sentenced to 25 years in Joliet prison, where he died one year into his sentence.

The Sycamore & Cortland Railroad Boards of Directors, 1858-1883[1]

1858
Founding Board of Directors –
(founded on June 23, 1858)

Orlando M. Bryan
Henry L. Boies
Enos L. Cheesbro, Jr.
Reuben Ellwood
William J. Hunt
Daniel B. James
Edward L. Mayo
Benjamin Page
Horatio F. Page
Harmon Paine
Morris Walrod
John C. Waterman
Timothy Wells

Officers:
President – John C. Waterman
Treasurer – unknown
Secretary – Henry L. Boies

1859
1st Elected Board of Directors–
(elected April 5, 1859)

James. H. Beveridge
Henry L. Boies
Charles O. Boynton
Moses Dean
Reuben Ellwood
William J. Hunt
Daniel B. James
Charles Kellum
Marshall Stark
Stephen Townsend
Henry Wager
John C. Waterman
Thomas H. Wood

Officers:
President – John C. Waterman
Treasurer – W. H. Douglas
Secretary – William H. Beavers
Executive Committee – Henry L. Boies,
Reuben Ellwood, Charles Kellum[2]

1860[3]
Samuel Alden
James. H. Beveridge
Henry L. Boies
Charles M. Brown
Reuben Ellwood
Edwin T. Hunt
William J. Hunt
Charles Kellum
William Lott
James S. Waterman
John C. Waterman
Thomas H. Wood
Ralph Wyman

Officers:
unknown

---

[1]Results of the annual S&C Board of Directors election were usually printed in the *True Republican* and other Sycamore newspapers. The directors were also listed in the annual reports of the Illinois Railroad and Warehouse Commission. Election results could not be located for the years 1866 and 1868.

[2]This committee was responsible for drafting the company's by-laws.

[3]Beginning in 1860, the S&C held its annual election on the first Monday in January.

1861

James. H. Beveridge
Henry L. Boies
Charles M. Brown
Moses Dean
Reuben Ellwood
John R. Hamlin
William J. Hunt
Charles Kellum
Carlos Lattin
Charles Townsend
John C. Waterman
Thomas H. Wood
Ralph Wyman

Officers:

President - unknown
Treasurer - unknown
Secretary - William H. Beavers

1862

James. H. Beveridge
Henry L. Boies
Moses Dean
Reuben Ellwood
Edwin T. Hunt
William J. Hunt
Charles Kellum
Jacob Siglin
Marshall Stark
James S. Waterman
John C. Waterman
Thomas H. Wood
Ralph Wyman

Officers:

President - William J. Hunt
Treasurer - William J. Hunt
Secretary - William H. Beavers

1863

James. H. Beveridge
Henry L. Boies
Charles M. Brown
Roswell Dow
Reuben Ellwood
Edwin T. Hunt
William J. Hunt
Charles Kellum
Charles Townsend
James S. Waterman
John C. Waterman
Thomas H. Wood
Ralph Wyman

Officers:

President - William J. Hunt
Treasurer - Roswell Dow
Secretary - Henry L. Boies

1864

Samuel Alden
James. H. Beveridge
Henry L. Boies
Charles M. Brown
Roswell Dow
Reuben Ellwood
Edwin T. Hunt
William J. Hunt
Charles Kellum
Charles Townsend
James S. Waterman
John C. Waterman
Thomas H. Wood

Officers:

President - James H. Beveridge
Treasurer - Roswell Dow
Secretary - H. L. Boies

1865

Samuel Alden
James. H. Beveridge
Henry L. Boies
Charles M. Brown
Roswell Dow
Reuben Ellwood
Edwin T. Hunt
William J. Hunt
Charles Kellum
Charles Townsend
James S. Waterman
John C. Waterman
Thomas H. Wood

Officers:

President - Edwin T. Hunt
Treasurer - James S. Waterman
Secretary - Henry L. Boies

1867

James H. Beveridge
Henry L. Boies
Moses Dean
James Ellwood
Reuben Ellwood
Charles Kellum
John H. Rogers
Marshall Stark
J. A. Waterman
James S. Waterman
John C. Waterman
George. P. Wild
Henry Wood

Officers:

President - James S. Waterman
Treasurer - Norman C. Warren
Secretary - Henry L. Boies

1869

Samuel Alden
Henry L. Boies
James Ellwood
Reuben Ellwood
John B. Harkness
Morris Holcomb
Charles Kellum
John H. Rogers
Norman C. Warren
James S. Waterman
John C. Waterman
George P. Wild

Officers:
President - James S. Waterman
Treasurer - Norman C. Warren
Secretary - Henry L. Boies

1870

Samuel Alden
Norman Beckley
Henry L. Boies
Orlando. M. Bryan
Moses Dean
Chauncey Ellwood
Reuben Ellwood
John B. Harkness
Charles Kellum
John N. Maxfield
Calvin Shurtleff
Norman C. Warren
James S. Waterman
John C. Waterman
George P. Wild

Officers:
President - Reuben Ellwood
Vice-President - John C. Waterman
Treasurer - Norman C. Warren
Secretary - Henry L. Boies

1871

Henry L. Boies
Moses Dean
Reuben Ellwood
John B. Harkness
Charles Kellum
John N. Maxfield
Calvin Shurtleff
Frank H. Smith
Norman C. Warren
James S. Waterman
John C. Waterman
George P. Wild

Officers:
unknown

1872

Henry L. Boies
Moses Dean
Chauncey Ellwood
Reuben Ellwood
John B. Harkness
George S. Robinson
Calvin Shurtleff
Frank H. Smith
Norman C. Warren
James S. Waterman
John C. Waterman
George P. Wild
Henry Wood

Officers:
President - James S. Waterman
Vice-President - Chauncey Ellwood
Treasurer - Reuben Ellwood
Secretary - Henry L. Boies

1873

Henry L. Boies
Moses Dean
Chauncey Ellwood
Reuben Ellwood
John B. Harkness
Gilbert A. Maxfield
George S. Robinson
Calvin Shurtleff
Frank H. Smith
Norman C. Warren
James S. Waterman
John C. Waterman
George P. Wild

Officers:
President - James S. Waterman
Vice-President - Chauncey Ellwood
Treasurer - Reuben Ellwood
Secretary - Henry L. Boies

1874

Philander M. Alden
Henry L. Boies
Moses Dean
Richard L. Divine
Chauncey Ellwood
Reuben Ellwood
Charles Kellum
Charles W. Marsh
Gilbert A. Maxfield
George S. Robinson
Calvin Shurtleff
James S. Waterman
John C. Waterman

Officers:
President - James S. Waterman
Vice-President - Chauncey Ellwood
Treasurer - Reuben Ellwood
Secretary - Henry L. Boies

APPENDIX C—LIST OF S&C RAILROAD DIRECTORS, 1858-1883

1875

Philander M. Alden
H. M. Avery
Henry L. Boies
Richard L. Divine
Everell F. Dutton
Alonzo Ellwood
Chauncey Ellwood
Reuben Ellwood
J. S. Reynolds
George S. Robinson
Calvin Shurtleff
James S. Waterman
John C. Waterman

Officers:
President – James S. Waterman
Vice-President – Chauncey Ellwood
Treasurer – Reuben Ellwood
Secretary – Richard L. Divine

1876

Philander M. Alden
H. M. Avery
Henry L. Boies
Richard L. Divine
Everell F. Dutton
Alonzo Ellwood
Chauncey Ellwood
Reuben Ellwood
J. S. Reynolds
George S. Robinson
Calvin Shurtleff
James S. Waterman
John C. Waterman

Officers:
President – James S. Waterman
Vice-President – Chauncey Ellwood
Treasurer – Reuben Ellwood
Secretary – Richard L. Divine

1877

Philander M. Alden
H. M. Avery
Henry L. Boies
Richard L. Divine
Abram Ellwood
Alonzo Ellwood
Chauncey Ellwood
Reuben Ellwood
J. S. Reynolds
George S. Robinson
Horace M. Stevens
James S. Waterman
John C. Waterman

Officers:
unknown

1878

Philander M. Alden
H. M. Avery
Henry L. Boies
Richard L. Divine
Abram Ellwood
Alonzo Ellwood
Chauncey Ellwood
Reuben Ellwood
J. S. Reynolds
George S. Robinson
Horace M. Stevens
James S. Waterman
John C. Waterman

Officers:
unknown

1879[4]

Philander M. Alden
Henry L. Boies
Richard L. Divine
Everell F. Dutton
Abram Ellwood
Alonzo Ellwood
Chauncey Ellwood
Reuben Ellwood
J. S. Reynolds
George S. Robinson
Horace M. Stevens
James S. Waterman
John C. Waterman

Officers:
President – James S. Waterman
Vice-President – Chauncey Ellwood
Treasurer – Reuben Ellwood
Secretary – Richard L. Divine

1880

Philander M. Alden
Henry L. Boies
Richard L. Divine
Everell F. Dutton
Abram Ellwood
Alonzo Ellwood
Chauncey Ellwood
Reuben Ellwood
J. S. Reynolds
George S. Robinson
Horace M. Stevens
James S. Waterman
John C. Waterman

Officers:
President – James S. Waterman
Vice-President – Chauncey Ellwood
Treasurer – Reuben Ellwood
Secretary – Richard L. Divine

[4]In 1879, the directors voted to change the company name to the Sycamore, Cortland & Chicago Railroad (SC&C)

1881

Philander M. Alden
Everell F. Dutton
Abram Ellwood
Alonzo Ellwood
Chauncey Ellwood
John D. Ellwood
Reuben Ellwood
J. S. Reynolds
George S. Robinson
Jefferson Stark
Horace M. Stevens
James S. Waterman
John C. Waterman

Officers:

President - James S. Waterman
Vice-President - Chauncey Ellwood
Treasurer - Reuben Ellwood
Secretary - Philander M. Alden

1882

Philander M. Alden
Everell F. Dutton
Abram Ellwood
Alonzo Ellwood
Chauncey Ellwood
John D. Ellwood
Reuben Ellwood
A. S. Robinson
Jefferson Stark
Frank E. Stevens
Horace M. Stevens
James S. Waterman
John C. Waterman

Officers:

President - James S. Waterman
Vice-President - Chauncey Ellwood
Treasurer - Reuben Ellwood
Secretary - Philander M. Alden

1883[5]

Philander M. Alden
Everell F. Dutton
Abram Ellwood
Alonzo Ellwood
Chauncey Ellwood
John D. Ellwood
Reuben Ellwood
John L. Pratt
A. S. Robinson
Jefferson Stark
Horace M. Stevens
James S. Waterman
John C. Waterman

Officers:

President - James S. Waterman
Vice-President - Chauncey Ellwood
Treasurer - Reuben Ellwood
Secretary - Philander M. Alden

---

[5]The C&NW took control of the SC&C on July 2, 1883, at which time the SC&C directors resigned their positions.

Depot Agents for the S&C (1859-1883) and C&NW (1883-1963):

U. B. Prescott – 1859-1861 (also conductor)
Edward M. Knapp – 1861-1862 (also conductor)
Norman Beckley – 1862-1874
Richard E. Hunt – 1874-1877
Elry Hall – 1877-1900[1]
John O. Owen – 1900-1910
Fred A. Onthank – 1910-1919
William B. Jaycox – 1919-1925[2]
Dave Anderson – 1926-1927
T. Lyle Seaton – 1927-1933
Frank J. Kiely – 1933-1936
Albert A. Smith – 1936-1937
Leonard C. Hoeft – 1937-1941
F. A. Hitchens – 1942-1958
Martin Hampa – 1958-1966[3]

Engineers and Conductors on the S&C Local Train (1859-1937)

Engineers:

George Chilson – 1859-unknown
William Ayre – exact years unknown
George Field – exact years unknown
John Tucker – 1865-1899[4]
James Trotter – 1899-1902
A. A. Dysart – 1903-1923[5]

Conductors:

U. B. Prescott – 1859-1861 (also depot agent)
Edward M. Knapp – 1861-1862 (also depot agent)
Ed Rose – 1862-1872[6]
George M. Sivright – 1872-1880[7]
Ed Rose – 1880-1901[8]
James Masterson – 1901-1937[9]

Depot Agents for the M&NW (1887-1888), CStP&KC (1888-1892), and CGW (1887-1978)

Marcellus C. Shields – June – Oct. 1887
R. A. Scoffern – Oct. – Dec 1887
R. H. Gollay – Dec. 1887 – April 1888[10]
Marcellus C. Shields – 1888-1899
Patrick Curran – 1899-1900
W. U. Howard – 1900-1902
I. E. Palmer – 1902-1903
C. E. Hurd – 1903-1904
I. E. Palmer – 1904-1906
G. H. Martin – 1906-1907
W. E. Brew – 1907-1908[11]
Charles F. Koehn – 1909-1928
Walter C. Hine – 1928-1934
Haydn E. Goodley – 1934-1948
Frank Spoor – 1948-1951
J. Donald Snyder – 1951-1968[12]
Larry Mohr – 1968-1973
Charles "Chuck" W. Finch – 1973-1978

---

[1] After Hall's departure, Fred Peck served two months as a temporary agent.

[2] J. H. Weir took over in January 1926 but quit after only two weeks.

[3] The C&NW sold the depot in 1963, but rented space inside to continue running its freight operations. Hampa was the last depot agent while the C&NW owned and operated the depot. He oversaw the rented office until he retired in 1966.

[4] After the C&NW took over the S&C in 1883, John Tucker and Ed Rose remained on the local train. When the Northern Illinois line came through town in 1885, the local train included runs to DeKalb.

[5] It is unknown who took over the engineer position from the time Dysart retired in 1923 until the C&NW discontinued the Sycamore local in 1937.

[6] Rose left to operate a coal business near the depot. He returned to his old position eight years later.

[7] There are newspaper accounts of John D. Ellwood, son of Chauncey Ellwood and also freight agent at the depot, serving as a substitute conductor in the late 1870s and early 1880s.

[8] See footnote 4.

[9] Masterson was the last regular conductor of the Sycamore Local. The C&NW discontinued service to Cortland in 1930 and to DeKalb within weeks of Masterson's retirement in 1937.

[10] The M&NW got off to a rocky start. A stressful work environment forced them to go through three depot agents in less than a year.

[11] After Brew's departure, J. A. Schmeltzer served as acting agent for six weeks.

[12] Snyder worked his first year as a temporary agent until the CGW hired Hugh Duncan as its permanent agent. Duncan was transferred after only three months and Snyder took over again, this time as permanent agent.

BIBLIOGRAPHY

Newspapers:

DeKalb County:

City Weekly (1872-1902)
DeKalb Chronicle (1879-present)
DeKalb County Republican Sentinel (1854-1861)
DeKalb Review (1883-1921)
Genoa Issue (1884-1904)
Sycamore Tribune (1902-1965)
The True Republican (1857-1968)

Outside of County:

Belvidere Northwestern
Chicago Times
Chicago Tribune
New York Times
Rockford Register Star
St. Charles Valley Chronicle

DeKalb County Histories:

Bigolin, Stephen and Phyllis A. Johnson, et al. *A Journey through DeKalb County*. DeKalb, IL: Daily Chronicle, 2001.

Bigolin, Stephen and Nancy Beasley. *Sycamore: A Walk through History*. Sycamore, IL: Ten-Bit Committee, 1983.

The Biographical Record of DeKalb County, Illinois. Chicago: The S. J. Clarke Publishing Company, 1898.

Boies, Henry L. *History of DeKalb County, Illinois*. Chicago: O. P. Bassett, 1868.

City of Sycamore. Sycamore City Council. *City Council Minutes, 1859-2002*.

Combination Atlas Map of DeKalb County, Illinois. Genoa, IL: Thompson & Everts, 1871.

Davy, Harriet Wilson. *From Oxen to Jets: A History of DeKalb County, 1835-1963*. Dixon, IL: Rogers Printing Company, 1963.

Gross, Lewis M. *Past and Present of DeKalb County, Illinois*, 2 vols. Chicago: The Pioneer Publishing Company, 1907.

Marsh, Charles W. *Recollections, 1837–1910*. Chicago: Farm Implement News Company, 1910.

McLagan, C. R. *Nostalgia & Glee in Sycamore, Illinois*. Sycamore: D.C. Lithographics, 1960.

Military History & Reminiscences of the 13th Regiment of Illinois Volunteer Infantry in the Civil War in the United States, 1861-1865. Chicago: Woman's Temperance Publishing Association, 1892.

Portrait and Biographical Album of DeKalb County, Illinois. Chicago: Chapman Brothers, 1885.

Prospectus: Geneva Lake, Sycamore and Southern Electric Railway Company. Chicago: C. F. Engstrom & Co., 1898.

Robertson, William E. *The Woodstock & Sycamore Traction Company*. Delavan, WI: National Bus Trader, 1985.

Stats, Charles H. "The Railroads of DeKalb, Sycamore, and Cortland, Illinois, Part 1," *North Western Lines*. Vol. 19, no. 1 (Winter 1992): 32-47.

Stats, Charles H. "The Railroads of DeKalb, Sycamore, and Cortland, Illinois, Part 2," *North Western Lines*. Vol. 19, No. 2 (Spring 1992): 32-49.

United States. Cong. Senate. *Memorial Addresses on the Life and Character of Reuben Ellwood*. Washington: Government Printing Office, 1886.

The Voters and Taxpayers of DeKalb County. Chicago: H. F. Kett & Co., 1876.

Other Printed Sources:

Andreas, A. T. *History of Chicago from the Earliest Period to the Present Time, Volume III: From the Fire of 1871 until 1885*. Chicago: A. T. Andreas Company, 1886.

Bach, Ira J. and Susan Wolfson. *A Guide to Chicago's Train Stations: Present and Past*. Athens, OH: Ohio University Press, 1986.

Bye, Ranulph. *The Vanishing Depot*. Wynnewood, PA: Livingston Publishing Company, 1973.

Currey, J. Seymour. *Chicago: Its History and Its Builders: A Century of Marvelous Growth*. Chicago: The S. J. Clarke Publishing Company, 1912.

Fiore Sr., David J. *The Chicago Great Western Railway*. Chicago: Arcadia Publishing, 2006.

Grant, H. Roger. *The Corn Belt Route: A History of the Chicago Great Western Railroad Company*. DeKalb, IL: Northern Illinois University Press, 1984.

Grant, H. Roger. *Living in the Depot: The Two-story Railroad Station*. Iowa City: University Of Iowa Press, 1993.

Grant, H. Roger. *The North Western: A History of the Chicago & North Western Railway System*. DeKalb, IL: Northern Illinois University Press, 1996.

Halberstadt, Hans and April. *Train Depots and Roundhouses*. St. Paul, MN: MBI Pub. Co., 2002.

Knudsen, Charles T. *Chicago and North Western Railway Steam Power, 1848-1956: Classes A-Z*. Chicago: Knudson Publications, 1965.

Laws of the State of Illinois Passed by the Twenty-First General Assembly, Convened January 3, 1859. Springfield: Bailhache & Baker, 1859.

Lee, Judson Fiske. "Transportation: A Factor in the Development of Northern Illinois Previous to 1860," *Journal of the Illinois State Historical Society*. Vol.1, No. 1 (April 1917): 17-85.

Petitti, John A. *The Railway Station: A Study in Cultural-Historical Geography.* Dissertation.Northern Illinois University, 1979.

Railroad and Warehouse Commission of Illinois. *4th Annual Report of the Railroad and Warehouse Commission of Illinois for the Year Ending November 30, 1874.* Springfield: State Journal Steam Print, 1874.

Railroad and Warehouse Commission of Illinois. *5th Annual Report of the Railroad and Warehouse Commission of Illinois for the Year Ending November 30, 1875.* Springfield: State Journal Book & Stereotype Rooms, 1876.

Railroad and Warehouse Commission of Illinois. *6th Annual Report of the Railroad and Warehouse Commission of Illinois for the Year Ending December 1, 1876.* Springfield: D. W. Lusk, 1876.

Railroad and Warehouse Commission of Illinois. *8th Annual Report of the Railroad and Warehouse Commission of Illinois for the Year Ending November 30, 1878.* Springfield: Weber & Co., State Printers, 1879.

Railroad and Warehouse Commission of Illinois. *9th Annual Report of the Railroad and Warehouse Commission of Illinois for the Year Ending November 30, 1879.* Springfield: Weber & Co., State Printers, 1880.

Railroad and Warehouse Commission of Illinois. *10th Annual Report of the Railroad and Warehouse Commission of Illinois for the Year Ending June 30, 1880.* Springfield: H. W. Rokker, State Printer and Binder, 1881.

Railroad and Warehouse Commission of Illinois. *11th Annual Report of the Railroad and Warehouse Commission of Illinois for the Year Ending June 30, 1881.* Springfield: H. W. Rokker, State Printer and Binder, 1882.

Railroad and Warehouse Commission of Illinois. *12th Annual Report of the Railroad and Warehouse Commission of Illinois for the Year Ending June 30, 1882.* Springfield: H. W. Rokker, State Printer and Binder, 1883.

Railroad and Warehouse Commission of Illinois. *13th Annual Report of the Railroad and Warehouse Commission of Illinois for the Year Ending June 30, 1883.* Springfield: H. W. Rokker, State Printer and Binder, 1884.

Reusing Railroad Stations. New York: Educational Facilities Laboratories, 1974.

Richards, Jeffrey and John M. MacKenzie. *The Railway Station: A Social History.* Oxford: Oxford University Press, 1986.

Scott, Frank W. *Newspapers and Periodicals of Illinois, 1814-1879.* Springfield, IL: The Trustees of the Illinois State Historical Library, 1910.

Stennett, W. H. *The North and West Illustrated.* Chicago: Chicago & North-Western Railway Co., 1879.

INDEX

(numbers in *italics* refer to images or image captions)